The ADA Programming Language

A GUIDE FOR PROGRAMMERS

Second Edition

I. C. PYLE

Professor of Computer Service
University of York, England

Prentice-Hall **International**

Englewood Cliffs, New Jersey   London   Mexico   New Delhi
Rio de Janeiro   Singapore   Sydney   Tokyo   Toronto   Wellington

British Library Cataloguing in Publication Data

Pyle, I.C.
    The ADA programming language.—2nd ed.
    1. Ada (Computer program language)
    I . Title
    001.64'24   QA76.73.A15
    ISBN 0–13–003906–3

Library of Congress Cataloging in Publication Data

Pyle, I.C. (Ian C.), 1934—
    The Ada programming language, 2nd edn.

    Includes index.
    1. Ada (Computer program language) I. Title.
QA76.73.A35P94   1984   001.64'24   84–17817
ISBN 0–13–003906–3

ISBN 0-13-003906-3

PRENTICE-HALL INTERNATIONAL (UK) LTD. *London*
PRENTICE-HALL OF AUSTRALIA PTY. LTD., *Sydney*
PRENTICE-HALL CANADA INC., *Toronto*
PRENTICE-HALL OF INDIA PRIVATE LIMITED, *New Delhi*
PRENTICE-HALL OF JAPAN, INC., *Tokyo*
PRENTICE-HALL OF SOUTHEAST ASIA PTE., *Singapore*
PRENTICE-HALL INC., *Englewood Cliffs, New Jersey*
PRENTICE-HALL DO BRASIL LTDA., *Rio de Janeiro*
PRENTICE-HALL HISPANOAMERICANA, S.A., *Mexico*
WHITEHALL BOOKS LIMITED, *Wellington, New Zealand*

10 9 8 7 6 5 4 3 2
Printed in Great Britain by
Whitstable Litho Ltd., Whitstable, Kent

Contents

To Margaret

Preface

The Ada programming language, sponsored by the United States Department of Defense, was designed under the leadership of Jean D. Ichbiah. The language is a major advance in programming technology, bringing together the best ideas on the subject in a coherent way designed to meet the real needs of practical programmers. It is the first result of a substantial effort to identify the requirements for programming and satisfy them effectively.

Ada is a registered trademark of the U.S. Government (Ada Joint Program Office). As most readers will know, the language is named after a real person, Augusta Ada, Countess of Lovelace, who first programmed a computer, before either computers or programming had been recognized as such.

This book is written primarily for practicing programmers of embedded computer systems, giving a full presentation of the power of Ada to those whose working environment will be greatly changed by it during the next few years. Other readers will include programmers of non-embedded systems, for whom most of the facilities will be relevant, and teachers of programming who will benefit from the breadth and coherence of Ada's facilities. In addition, the book should be of value to managers of programming projects, since Ada strongly assists the development of large programs.

In keeping with the primary aim of the book, the style of presentation presumes a knowledge of programming. Topics are introduced in the context of embedded computer systems, in an order which reflects the normal pattern used in programming. This is not necessarily the best order for introductory teaching of the skill of programming itself.

Chapters 1 to 5 cover the basic features of Ada, which any programmer needs to know. The subsequent chapters deal with more advanced features, which should only be studied after the basic features are thoroughly understood. Chapters 6 to 8 deal with particular programming concepts in Ada which will probably be new to most programmers. Chapters 9 and 10 cover the issues of program structure, which take traditional ideas as the start, but make significant extensions. Chapter 11 deals with machine specific issues, and shows how they can be expressed in a machine independent language. Chapters 12 and 13 give an advanced treatment and more details on topics introduced previously. Several chapters finish with some programming exercises, which readers may use to test their understanding of the ideas presented. The solutions to these exercises are given elsewhere in the book, as examples of other aspects of Ada programs. The appendices contain certain notes and definitions of various particular items in Ada.

The official definition of Ada is the Language Reference Manual (ANSI/MIL–STD 1815A 1983). There are various supplementary documents, including a Formal Definition. This book differs from an official definition, in that the official definition of a language must satisfy both programmers and compiler-writers: two very different kinds of reader. Unfortunately, this usually means that the official definition goes barely far enough to satisfy the compiler-writers, and tends to have complications of notation and formality which make it unsatisfactory for programmers. In contrast, this book is intended to explain the language to programmers, who wish to learn Ada without having to become compiler specialists.

The language has been revised since the first edition of this book, as a result of experience and discovered problems; also, it has been accepted as a standard by ANSI and is under consideration for standardization by ISO. The second edition takes account of these changes, and contains a substantially new chapter on input/output (where the language is significantly different), and important changes on tasks and exceptions. Numerous minor alterations have been made, to remove errors or to improve the presentation.

I wish to thank the many people who have helped me during the course of preparing this book, particularly Ian Wand and Brian Wichmann; valuable comments on the first edition came from Nico Habermann. The syntax diagrams are derived from a program written by Colin Runciman and David Keeffe. Most of the typing for the first edition was done by Val Fry.

Most of all, I thank my family for their encouragement and support while Ada has been living with us.

January 1985   I.C.P

CHAPTER 1

Introduction

Ada is for programming embedded computer systems - that is, systems in which a computer is directly connected to some apparatus or plant which it monitors and/or controls. This means that Ada can be used for conventional programming (which actually accounts for the majority of embedded computer system programming) and also for the special technical requirements concerning input/output, timing relationships, contingency programming to cope with errors, and long-term maintenance.

Embedded computer systems range from intelligent terminals and smart instrumentation to air traffic control or factory automation, via laboratory data monitoring, numerically controlled machine tools, navigation and guidance systems, stored program controlled telephone exchanges, batch and continuous production control, environmental monitoring, and future domestic products containing microcomputers. The computer involved may be large or small, single or a collection of many processors, or part of a computer network.

It is expected, however, that the program concerned in each system would have a lifetime of several years, and consequently that people other than the original programmers would be involved in maintaining it. This concern for maintenance underlies much of the style of Ada.

Ada gives special attention to the ease of reading and understanding programs - it is based on the realisation that it is more important to be able to read a program and understand it clearly than to be able to write it quickly or briefly. We therefore tend to use fairly long names and identifiers in an Ada program, and state the assumptions which the design of the program implies. The reason for this is that the writer of the program does his job once, but maintainers of the program may have to read the program many times throughout its life.

1

1.1   An Ada program

Programs in Ada specify not only the actions inside computers, but also
the interactions between the computers and the environment in which they
are embedded. Since the interactions with the environment can be quite
tricky to program, it is usual to design separate pieces of program to
deal with the various kinds of input/output devices, and to keep the
resulting pieces of program in libraries. For a simple Ada program, we
use an existing library package to handle the input/output, and specify
the particular actions we want by calling on facilities made available
by the package.

    In this first example we show a trivial program in Ada. The program
is written as a procedure, which specifies the actions to be carried
out. In an Ada development environment, many procedures will be held in
a library, where they are available for use in other programs. In
practice, all programs are likely to refer to the library for units
defining many commonly required actions such as input/output and
mathematical functions. A package called STANDARD is always available;
it is specified in Appendix A. For this example, we use a library
package called TEXT_IO. (Its definition is also given in Appendix A.
It is significant that the package specification is itself written in
Ada.) A program must begin by listing the units it needs; these will be
extracted from the library by the translator.

```
with TEXT_IO; use TEXT_IO;
procedure MAIN is
begin
   NEW_LINE;
   PUT ("Hello");
   NEW_LINE;
end MAIN;
```

The program is written using special key-words such as **with**,
procedure, **begin** and **end**, together with other words such as TEXT_IO,
PUT. The keywords are fixed for all Ada programs, and show the structure
of the program. The other words are called identifiers, and are invented
by the programmers to denote the particular entities concerned in the
program. Section 1.4 gives further details about the form of an Ada
program.

    This program needs the library unit TEXT_IO (and no other), which
defines the procedures NEW_LINE and PUT (among others), and sets up
input/output files on suitable devices. The program prints the message

Hello

on a new line on the standard output device. Notice that the program
has the name MAIN which is given at the beginning and end, so that the
body of the program is clearly delimited.

1.2   Another program

This is a slightly more complicated program, but still very trivial and
unrealistic. It adds together two simple integers.

```
with TEXT_IO; use TEXT_IO;
with LOCAL_TEXT_IO; use LOCAL_TEXT_IO;
procedure MAIN is
  A, B : INTEGER range 0 .. 999;
  use INT_IO;
begin
  GET (A); GET (B);
  NEW_LINE;
  PUT ("The sum of ");
  PUT (A); PUT (" and "); PUT (B);
  PUT (" is "); PUT (A + B);
  NEW_LINE;
end MAIN;
```

Notice that the names A and B are used to hold internal values; these
are read in by the procedure GET and output by the procedure PUT, both
defined for type INTEGER in a locally-defined library package called
LOCAL_TEXT_IO, using facilities provided in TEXT_IO. In order that the
program can know what to expect for the values before they are used, the
type and range for each must be declared at the head of the program.
The package STANDARD (which includes the definitions of INTEGER and "+")
is automatically available for every program unit.

Ada's security rules ensure that proper values are provided for A and
B: the program will fail if there is bad input, as with most other
languages. However, Ada provides a way for the programmer to determine
what is to be done in such a situation, by the concept of exceptions
(see chapter 6). The program could thus be made more elaborate, with a
loop to repeat the prompt for proper input.

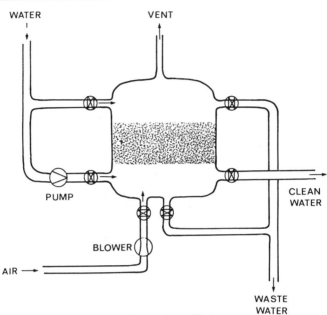

Figure 1a: Filtration Unit

1.3   A real program

Any program for a genuine embedded computer system will be quite large, and should be written as a collection of separate units in order that it can be maintained effectively. Here is one unit of a program to control a filtration plant (see figure 1a). River water is pumped through a filter and clean water is delivered. After a time, the filter gets clogged with debris and has to be cleaned by blowing air through and draining out the sump; filtering can then resume. Occasionally a fault in the valves may make it necessary to close down the whole plant.

```
with MAJOR_PHASES; use MAJOR_PHASES;
procedure SINGLE_FILTER is
begin
  START_UP;
  loop
    DELIVER_WATER;
    CLEAN_FILTER;
  end loop;

exception
  when others =>        -- FAULT or other trouble
    CLOSE_DOWN;
end SINGLE_FILTER;
```

Further details of the filtration unit are given in later examples.

Notice that this program unit shows how the action of SINGLE_FILTER is achieved in terms of application-specific procedures. These would be expressed in a separate unit that contains the specifications of the other procedures etc.:

```
package MAJOR_PHASES is
   procedure START_UP;
   procedure DELIVER_WATER;
   procedure CLEAN_FILTER;
   procedure CLOSE_DOWN;
   FAULT : exception;
end MAJOR_PHASES;
```

The details (bodies) of the procedures such as START_UP are written in a corresponding package body.

1.4   Form of an Ada program

The text of the Ada program consists mainly of two kinds of words and various punctuation marks. Words like **procedure, is, separate, end** (conventionally written in small letters, and printed in bold here) are reserved for special uses in Ada, and determine the main structure of the program. These are known as keywords. The other words, like SINGLE_FILTER, START_UP, FAULT, CLOSE_DOWN (conventionally written in capital letters) are invented by the programmer, to denote the various entities in the program; these words are technically called identifiers. They must always be different from the Ada keywords. It does not affect the meaning of a program whether the letters are large or small: the case is not significant.

As well as the main text of the program, whose structure is prescribed by the Ada language, there may be comments on any line, introduced by a double hyphen. Comments may contain any characters without restriction, for the rest of the line. They are used by the programmer to give additional information to the reader of the program, but this is not checked in any way by the compiler.

Another special construct in an Ada program is called a **pragma**: this is a phrase used to give information to the compiler about translating the program.

```
pragma INLINE ( START_UP );
```

means that the body of the procedure START_UP is to be built in wherever it is called, as an open subroutine, rather than calling it as a closed subroutine.

Pragmas do not affect the meaning of a program, but may affect the way it is implemented (e.g. choice of optimisation). The possible pragmas in Ada are listed Appendix D.

1.5   Identifiers and naming

Identifiers are the fundamental creation of the programmer: they name the entities that occur in the particular program he is designing. An identifier is made up using letters, digits and underline characters (used to link words in an identifier, since it cannot contain a space), and must be different from the Ada keywords, disregarding the case of the letters. Note the implication that identifiers may not contain spaces, and may not spread over from one line to another.

The words used to make an identifier should be carefully chosen to be a suitable name for the entity concerned: for example a verb (or verb clause) for a procedure (which denotes an action), and a noun (or a noun clause) for a data object (variable or constant). A type may be named by a suitable abstract noun. Choosing appropriate names is an important aspect of programming. These suggestions are of course not enforced by Ada, and do not constrain the creativity of the programmer. Examples of names are given throughout the book, as we introduce the various kinds of entity that can occur in an Ada program.

1.6   The environment of Ada programs

Ada programs are intended for execution in embedded computer systems — implying significant differences from the usage of conventional programming languages. The differences concern the way Ada programs are developed, and their operational environment. The main consequence is that Ada programs are usually cross-compiled on a host computer, distinct from the target computer for operational use; another important consequence is that an Ada program is likely to be the only program in a computer, with complete responsibility for its activities, not sharing facilities or implying an "operating system" of the conventional kind. (The Ada program may involve units written in other languages, provided that their interfaces and overall structure are consistent with Ada.) The Ada programmers specify how the various parts of the program interact with one another and with the equipment connected to it.

The translation of an Ada program into its executable form is more than traditional compilation. It includes also the operations of linkage-editing and library module incorporation (which are done separately with other languages), and the provision of run-time facilities to implement the various semantic features of the language such as inter-task communication and dynamic storage allocation. Some specific differences between Ada and other programming languages are noted in Appendices B (Fortran) and C (Pascal).

1.6.1   Ada Programming Support Environment

For the development of Ada programs, an Ada Programming Support Environment (APSE) is planned. At the time of writing (1984), several projects to produce APSEs are under way, and some minimum environments for editing, compiling and loading are now available. The requirements for a full Ada environment have been described in outline, but the actual details vary from one project to another.

Translation of an Ada program involves compilation of the separate units, with cross-checking of interfaces and provision of other required units from a library. The environment includes all the necessary utility programs and the data-base to contain the compiled units. This of course implies backing store equipment and peripherals for programmers to use – completely different from the target environment of the embedded computer system.

In order that Ada programs can be tested, it is expected that the support system would include facilities for simulating features of the target environment. These, and the other programs in the support environment, would also be written in Ada. In this case, Ada programs may share a computer with other programs, under the control of a suitable operating system.

1.6.2   Ada Run-time Environment

Ada programs are executed in one or more computers embedded in a target environment. The run-time environment comprises hardware and software which together implement the semantics of Ada. How the run-time facilities are split between hardware and software is not prescribed by Ada; different computers require different run-time software to implement Ada on them.

An Ada program may be run on a single-computer system; this is the common way to presume its implementation. However, Ada does not require there to be only one computer, and a program with suitable restrictions (corresponding to the lack of direct communication between the processor in one computer and the store in a different computer) may be implemented in a multi-computer system. No details have yet been established for the restrictions necessary for multi-computer implementation of an Ada program.

A computer running an Ada program is likely to be dedicated to a specific task - controlling the system in which it is embedded. Consequently the Ada program in it is probably the only program in the computer, not sharing facilities with others. The definition of Ada does not absolutely require this, but the language provides no way of sharing facilities with another program. Thus Ada implies a single program but not necessarily a single computer.

Exercises

1. By analogy with A and B in section 1.2, declare YEAR to be an integer between 1901 and 2099 inclusive.
   (See Appendix A, package CALENDAR, type TIME.)

2. Invent suitable names for the valves in the filtration unit in figure 1a.
   (See section 2.1)

3. Cleaning the filter requires a blast of air and flushing with water (twice), then draining the sump. Invent names for the actions, presume they are specified as in MAJOR_PHASES, and write the statements for the body of CLEAN_FILTER.
   (See section 5.2)

CHAPTER 2

Types and Values

In any program we are concerned with many different values of different kinds. A fundamental idea in Ada is that every data item has a particular type, which determines the possibilities for the values it may have. For example, an integer has a value such as 1, 23, -54 or 7215802; a character has a value such as 'A', 'x', '5', '%'. In common with other 'strongly-typed' programming languages, Ada requires the programmer to specify the type for every data item concerned in the program, so that its usage can be checked. Most checking is done when the program in Ada is compiled, and does not imply any run-time overhead. Ada includes some predefined types; but most of the types in a program will be invented by the programmer, suitable for the particular application involved.

A type, then, gives the set of possibilities for a data item — specifying not so much what its value currently happens to be, but what it might ever legitimately be. This is of great importance in program checking and maintenance: compilers make sure that the usage of every data item is consistent with its set of possibilities, and when a programmer needs to change a program, the type helps him to understand the purpose of a data item.

2.1 Scalar Types

The simplest types are called scalars, and include numbers (integers and real), characters (ASCII, or any other specified character set), truth values (TRUE and FALSE) and enumeration types (in which the possible values are listed explicitly).

9

An enumeration type is written

type DAY_NAME **is** (MONDAY, TUESDAY, WEDNESDAY,
                        THURSDAY, FRIDAY, SATURDAY, SUNDAY);

This allows data items of type DAY_NAME to have values which are one of the given words. The notation DAY_NAME'FIRST means MONDAY and DAY_NAME'LAST means SUNDAY. Enumeration types are a powerful way of showing a set of possibilities:

type VALVE_STATUS **is** (OPEN, CLOSED);

type VALVE **is** (WATER_INLET,
    AIR_INLET, FLUSH_WATER, AIR_EXHAUST, SUMP_WATER,
    CLEAN_WATER, DIRTY_WATER);

type PRESSURE **is** (THIN, LOW, MEDIUM, HIGH);

type SECURITY_CLASSIFICATION **is** (UNCLASSIFIED, RESTRICTED,

    CONFIDENTIAL, SECRET, TOP_SECRET);

Truth values record whether or not a condition is true. Ada has the predefined type BOOLEAN for this purpose. It is actually an enumeration type, with only two possible values, TRUE and FALSE.

Numbers must always be given with a range, so that the lowest and highest possible values are stated. For integers, this is sufficient to define the type:

type CENTS **is range** 0 .. 99;
type BYTE **is range** 0 .. 255;
type PROC_NO **is range** 0 .. 255;
type BIG **is range** 1 .. 20000;
type CHANNEL **is range** 0 .. 31;

(This means that any attempt in a program to take such a data item outside the range would be detected as an error, usually at run time). The lowest and highest values need not be given directly, but may be written as expressions (see chapter 3). Each implementation of Ada has a predefined type INTEGER which covers the whole range of values that can be expressed in a machine word, also SHORT_INTEGER and LONG_INTEGER for implementation-determined ranges shorter and longer than a machine word. Ada allows the programmer to write machine-independent programs by stating the range explicitly as above, or (when the situation demands it), to go for machine dependence with consequent loss of portability by use of a predefined implementation-dependent type.

For characters, there is a predefined character set CHARACTER (see Appendix A). Other character sets may be introduced as enumeration types; for example

```
type HEX_DIGIT is ('0', '1', '2', '3', '4',
                   '5', '6', '7', '8', '9',
                   'A', 'B', 'C', 'D', 'E',
                   'F');
```

Notice that single characters may be given as possible enumeration values, enclosed in single quotes. An enumeration type containing characters may also contain other literal values given as identifiers, for non-printable characters (e.g. NUL, ENQ, CR, LF in the predefined character set).

All the types introduced above refer to discrete data values. They are collectively called discrete types.

The final group of scalar types refer to continuous quantities, although the values are of course still actually discrete approximations to them. They are for approximate calculations - either floating point with a particular number of significant digits, or fixed point with a particular absolute accuracy (called delta).

```
type ANGLE is digits 4 range 0.0 .. 360.0;
type HEIGHT is digits 10 range 0.0 .. 1.0E5;   -- 1.0E5 = 100000.0
type FLOATING_POINT is digits 10 range -1.0E38 .. 1.0E38;

type FINE is delta 0.1 range 0.0 .. 1.0;
type VERY_FINE is delta 0.001 range 0.0 .. 1.0;
type FRAC is delta 0.001 range 0.0 .. 1.0;
type DURATION is delta 0.00005 range -86400.0 .. 86400.0;
type VOLTS is delta 0.001 range 0.0 .. 5.0;
```

(meaning VOLTS are accurate to one millivolt, up to five volts.) Each implementation of Ada has a predefined type FLOAT, which covers the whole range of values that can be expressed in a machine floating-point word, also SHORT_FLOAT and LONG_FLOAT for implementation determined floating point values shorter and longer than a machine word. Further details on real types are given in chapter 12.

2.1.1   Subtypes

There are many cases where the programmer expects a data value to take a subset of the values possible for a particular type, and it is more convenient to regard this as a constrained form of the base type rather than a completely separate type. If we have

    subtype WEEK_DAY **is** DAY_NAME **range** MONDAY .. FRIDAY;

then any variable declared as a WEEK_DAY is of the type DAY_NAME but its values are constrained to be in the range MONDAY to FRIDAY. Any assignment to such a variable may require a run-time check to ensure that the constraint applies. Similarly,

    subtype LENGTH **is** FLOAT **range** 0.0 .. 200000.0;

allows objects to be declared which are type-compatible with FLOAT, but constrained to the stated range.

Two particularly important subtypes are predefined:

    subtype NATURAL **is** INTEGER **range** 0 .. INTEGER'LAST;
    subtype POSITIVE **is** INTEGER **range** 1 .. INTEGER'LAST;

indicating possibly zero or definitely positive integral values up to the maximum of the implementation. (Note that this is different from the 1980 definition of Ada.)

In this book, we also use

    subtype UP_TO_ONE **is** FLOAT **range** −1.0 .. 1.0;
    subtype POSITIVE_FLOAT **is** FLOAT **range** 0.0 .. FLOAT'LAST;
    subtype LOWER_CASE **is** CHARACTER **range** 'a' .. 'z';

The idea of subtypes and constraints is to allow the programmer to state the intended set of values which might arise, both as an aid to his own thinking when writing the program, and to assist subsequent maintenance programmers who may have to change it. Subtypes are constructed by specifying an existing type by name, and, if required, giving a further constraint. There are several different kinds of constraint, which are explained in chapter 12.

2.2   Records

Almost all useful data values are more complicated than scalars:
typically they include a number of distinct components, each with its
own type.

```
type SECTOR is
  record
    RADIUS : LENGTH;
    WIDTH  : ANGLE;
  end record;
```

This defines a compound data type SECTOR consisting of two components –
one called RADIUS which is of type LENGTH, the second called WIDTH, of
type ANGLE. If there is a variable S of type SECTOR, its components are
selected by writing S.RADIUS and S.WIDTH respectively.

A value of type SECTOR with RADIUS value 1.0 and WIDTH value 90.0
could be written

   (RADIUS => 1.0, WIDTH => 90.0)

or with expressions (of the right kind) where we show numbers. These
compound values (called aggregates) may also be written with just the
composed values in the correct order, thus

   (1.0, 90.0)

A record can have any number of components, of the same or different
types:

```
type CABLE is
  record
    REDWIRE : BOOLEAN;
    BLUEWIRE : BOOLEAN;
  end record;

type VALVE_PARAMETERS is
  record
    TRANSITION : DURATION;
    CONDITION : VALVE_STATUS;
    CONTROL : CHANNEL;
  end record;
```

and adjacent components of the same type may be written together:

```
type SECTOR_3D is
  record
    R: LENGTH;
    THETA, PHI: ANGLE;
  end record;

type WIND_LAYER is
  record
    SPEED, HEIGHT : NATURAL;
    AIR     : PRESSURE;
  end record;

type POSITION is
  record
    EAST, NORTH : LENGTH;
    HEADING : ANGLE;
  end record;
```

A POSITION consists of three components of which EAST and NORTH are both of (sub)type LENGTH, and HEADING is of type ANGLE. A possible data value for a variable of type POSITION is

```
(EAST => 23.7, NORTH => 62.0, HEADING => 180.0)
```

The components in a record may be of any named type or subtype (but not the outer record type, or any type containing it). A constraint on the type or subtype may be given explicitly:

```
type TIME_OF_DAY is
  record
    HR  : INTEGER range 0 .. 24;
    MIN, SEC : INTEGER range 0 .. 59;
  end record;
```

The components of a record may themselves be records (with the obvious restriction that they can not contain themselves):

```
type TRACK is
  record
    HERE : POSITION;
    NOW  : TIME_OF_DAY;
  end record;
```

The components of a variable of type TRACK themselves have components: with the variable T, of type TRACK, we have components

```
    T.HERE   -- of type POSITION
    T.NOW    -- of type TIME_OF_DAY
```

and also subsidiary components such as

```
    T.HERE.EAST   -- of type LENGTH
    T.NOW.HR      -- of type INTEGER, constrained to range 0..24
```

Records may have variants (see section 12.3)

2.3   Arrays

Frequently data values include a number of distinct components all of
the same type; the individual components are distinguished by an index
which is a discrete type (i.e. an integer or an enumeration type, which
includes Boolean and character).

```
    type COL_VEC is array (1 .. 4) of FLOAT;
    type SECTOR_LIST is array (1 .. 5) of SECTOR;
```

Any data value of type SECTOR_LIST consists of five components all of
type SECTOR.   Thus, if SL is of type SECTOR_LIST, it has components
SL(1), SL(2), SL(3), SL(4), and SL(5), all of type SECTOR; consequently

```
    SL(3).WIDTH
```

is the WIDTH of the third component of SL, and is of type ANGLE.

A possible value of SL is

```
    (1 => (RADIUS => 10.0, WIDTH  => 360.0),
     2 => (RADIUS => 20.0, WIDTH  => 180.0),
     3 => (RADIUS => 40.0, WIDTH  =>  90.0),
     4 => (RADIUS => 80.0, WIDTH  =>  45.0),
     5 => (RADIUS => 160.0, WIDTH =>  22.5))
```

If several components have the same value, they may be written together
as

```
    (1   => (RADIUS => 50.0,  WIDTH => 360.0),
     2|3 => (RADIUS => 150.0, WIDTH => 120.0),
     4|5 => (RADIUS => 0.7,   WIDTH => 5.0))
```

or

```
(1    => (RADIUS => 50.0,   WIDTH => 360.0),
 2..4 => (RADIUS => 0.5,    WIDTH => 7.0),
 5    => (RADIUS => 0.7,    WIDTH => 5.0))
```

or

```
(1|3    => (RADIUS => 0.5, WIDTH => 7.0),
 others => (RADIUS => 0.7, WIDTH => 5.0))
```

The keyword **others** stands for all index values not previously mentioned.

The index of an array may be of an enumeration type:

type LED_CODE **is array** (HEX_DIGIT) **of** BYTE;

for which a possible data value is

```
('0' => 16#5F#, '1' => 16#18#, '2' => 16#6D#,
 '3' => 16#79#, '4' => 16#3A#, '5' => 16#73#,
 '6' => 16#76#, '7' => 16#19#, '8' => 16#7F#,
 '9' => 16#3B#,
 'A' => 16#1F#, 'B' => 16#7D#, 'C' => 16#43#,
 'D' => 16#5D#, 'E' => 16#67#, 'F' => 16#27#)
```

corresponding to use of a seven-segment LED display as shown in figures 2a and 2b. (Notice that hexadecimal numbers are introduced by 16; similarly octal numbers are written 8#...#.)

The elements of an array may be of any named type. If the elements are required to be records, the element-type must be first declared and given a name. (It is not allowed to give the element-type-definition within the array definition.) The element-type may be constrained either by an intermediate subtype declaration or by attaching a constraint to the element type in the array definition. Thus we may write

```
type VALVE_CONTROL is
  record
    OPERATE : CHANNEL;
    CHECK   : CHANNEL;
  end record;

type CONTROL_CHANNELS is array (VALVE_STATUS ) of VALVE_CONTROL;

type VALVE_CHANNELS is
  record
    CONTROL : CONTROL_CHANNELS;
```

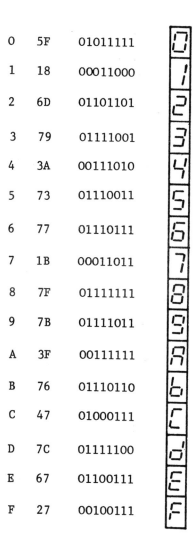

0	5F	01011111
1	18	00011000
2	6D	01101101
3	79	01111001
4	3A	00111010
5	73	01110011
6	77	01110111
7	1B	00011011
8	7F	01111111
9	7B	01111011
A	3F	00111111
B	76	01110110
C	47	01000111
D	7C	01111100
E	67	01100111
F	27	00100111

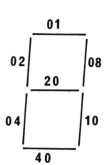

Figure 2a: Seven-segment LED   Figure 2b: LED characters

```
    LAMP    : CHANNEL;
end record;
```

The components of an array may be records or other arrays (but of course not themselves), and the components of a record may be arrays. For any kind of component (enumeration, constituent array, inner record, derived type), the type must be declared explicitly in a type or subtype declaration, and the type or subtype name used in the outer declaration.

An array whose index is an enumeration type, and whose components are BOOLEAN, represents a set (in the mathematical sense) of the elements of the enumeration type. Thus

type DAY_SET **is array** (DAY_NAME) **of** BOOLEAN;

gives us a set of possible days - for example

(SATURDAY| SUNDAY => FALSE, **others** => TRUE)

Similarly

type VALVE_SET **is array** (VALVE) **of** BOOLEAN;

introduces a type with data values such as

(FLUSH_WATER | SUMP_WATER .. DIRTY_WATER => TRUE,
   others => FALSE)

Note that all the components of the array must have their values specified (TRUE or FALSE).

Arrays may have multiple indices, each a discrete type with a particular range:

type MATRIX **is array** (1 .. 4, 1 .. 4) **of** FLOAT;
type GRID **is array** (1 .. 100, 1 .. 100) **of** BOOLEAN;

so that a data item of type GRID, say G, has components (all of type BOOLEAN) such as

G(1,1), G(15,25), G(99,1), G(100,100)

and the whole array G has a possible value

(**others** => FALSE)

The indices may have different types:

type RATE **is array** (DAY_NAME, 0 .. 23) **of** FLOAT;

A data item of type RATE would have a component for each possible day name with each integer from 0 to 23. All the components are floating point.

The component-type of an array must always be named. Frequently it is a record, in which case the record definition must be made in a distinct type declaration.

2.3.1   Strings

A particularly useful kind of array is one where components are characters (and with one index, of type integer, subtype POSITIVE). This is called a string. The number of characters in the string must be fixed for an individual data item (in other words, the number of components in the array must be static).

Formally, STRING is defined (see Appendix A) as a type in which the string length is not specified, but only its subtype (POSITIVE). When the programmer introduces any data item as a string, he must specify the number of characters it is to contain, either by giving the initial value or the particular range for the index, thus:

MESSAGE : STRING (1 .. 5);

This introduces MESSAGE as a string of exactly five characters, so its possible values include "HELP!", "ENTER", "*****", "12345" and "   " (five spaces). String values are given by enclosing the appropriate sequence of characters in double quotes; if the double quote character itself is required, it must be written twice. To avoid mistakes, the string may not spread over more than one line.

Control characters such as carriage return, line feed, form-feed and bell are written using the appropriate identifiers: CR, LF, FF, BEL (see Appendix A). The same method is used for denoting characters available on the target system which may not be available for use in the source program – for example if the target can output lower case letters but the program has to be written all in capitals, the identifier LC_C denotes the lower case letter C.

Strings (both literals and values of variables or constants of type STRING) can be concatenated by using the operator &, so that the value of "ABC" & "DE" is the same as "ABCDE", and other values for MESSAGE include "?" & CR & LF & BEL & "?".

2.4   Data items

Every data item (variable or constant) in a program has a particular
type, which is specified when it is introduced. A data item for a
particular part of the program (block or unit body) is introduced by a
declaration which gives its name, type or subtype, and optionally an
expression for its initial value. Such an object is taken as a variable
unless it is explicitly stated to be a constant.

```
MAX_SIZE    : constant INTEGER := 132;
PI          : constant FLOAT := 3.14159;
REVOLUTION  : constant ANGLE := 360.0;
D           : LENGTH;
CLEARANCE   : SECURITY_CLASSIFICATION;
THETA       : ANGLE;
LED_3       : HEX_DIGIT;
WD          : WEEK_DAY;
H           : HEIGHT;
S           : SECTOR;
T           : TRACK;
FRED        : FINE;
NOW         : TIME_OF_DAY;
ORIGIN      : POSITION;
C           : CHARACTER := '?'; -- initial value
IS_CLEARED  : BOOLEAN := FALSE;
```

Several similar variables may be introduced together;

```
X, Y, Z : FLOAT;
I, J, K : INTEGER;
U, V, W : FLOAT := 0.0;   -- all initialised
A_COUNT, B_COUNT : NATURAL;
TODAY, TOMORROW : DAY_NAME;
P,Q  : PRESSURE := LOW;   -- both initialised
L,M,N  : FRAC;
RADIUS, R1, R2 : FLOAT;
HERE, THERE : POSITION;
HARD, SHINY, WET : BOOLEAN := ASK("Initial value ");
```

An initialisation expression is evaluated for each variable, so migh
give them different values.   For arrays, the type definition may b
stated directly in the object declaration (avoiding the need to declar
and name the array type separately); objects introduced in this way al
have different types.   Constraints may also be stated   directly
corresponding to a subtype declaration.

```
VALVE_DATA   : array (VALVE) of VALVE_CHANNELS;
ALTIMETER    : array (1 .. 5) of CABLE;
IMAGE, LINE  : array (1 .. MAX_SIZE) of CHARACTER;
C1, C2       : INTEGER range 0 .. 99;
R, RR        : FLOAT range 0.0 .. 3.0E8;
NAME         : STRING (1 .. 30);
```

Other types (enumeration, record or derived types) must be declared in a
type declaration, and the type name used in the object declaration.

To refer to a particular element, we use indexing for an array and
component selection for a record:

```
VALVE_DATA (WATER_INLET)              -- of type VALVE_CHANNELS
VALVE_DATA(DIRTY_WATER) . CONTROL     -- an array
VALVE_DATA(FLUSH_WATER).CONTROL (OPEN) -- of type VALVE_CONTROL
VALVE_DATA(SUMP_WATER).CONTROL(CLOSED) . OPERATE -- of type CHANNEL
VALVE_DATA(AIR_INLET).LAMP            -- also of type CHANNEL
```

.5   Names and Objects

n a simple program each object has a single name and each name denotes
 single object. In a more complicated program, names and objects may be
elated in other ways. The same object may have several names (known as
liases) or no name at all. Each name is valid in a particular part of
he program (over which it is said to be visible), and in distinct parts
f the program it is possible for the same name to be used without
onfusion for completely different purposes.

Names are used to denote many kinds of entity in Ada: not only data
bjects (variables and constants) but also types, modules, subprograms,
ntries and exceptions. When the entity is introduced in the program, it
s given an identifier (or possibly a character string in the case of a
unction subprogram, to overload an operator). This identifier is the
ocal name for the entity, which can be used wherever the declaration is
irectly visible: principally the statements which follow the
eclaration. In other parts of the program, it is still possible that
he entity can be referred to, but in this case a fuller name would have
o be used, to establish which part of the program contains the required
eclaration.

Names (other than simple identifiers) are formed by using currently
isible names or function calls as prefixes, followed by various kinds
f suffix. The way in which a name is so used as a prefix does of

course depend on the kind of entity it denotes. Similarly, function calls as prefixes depend on the kind of object they return. A name that denotes an array, for instance, or a function call that returns a whole array, may take an index, and the compound name then forms the name of a component of the array. A name that denotes a record (or a function call that returns a record) may take a selector, and the compound forms the name of a component of the record. Names and function calls of all kinds may take attribute qualifiers, which denote predefined attributes of the entity concerned. (The particular attribute qualifiers available depend on the kind of entity denoted: see Appendix E.) For example, IMAGE'BASE and LINE'BASE are the (different) types of the objects introduced in section 2.4.

Thus in the context of the declarations

type SYMBOL_SET **is** (COMMON, EQUIVALENCE, DIMENSION, FORMAT, LOGICAL,
                    SUBROUTINE);
type L_V **is**
        record
           LINE_NO : POSITIVE;
           VALUE : INTEGER;
        end record;

KEY_TABLE : **array** (SYMBOL_SET) **of** L_V;

SYMBOL : SYMBOL_SET;

the identifier KEY_TABLE is the name of the whole array, and accordingl may be indexed. We can therefore construct names such as

KEY_TABLE(SYMBOL);

to denote a component of the array. Because this component is itself record, we can attach a selector to it to choose a particular field fro the record. Thus

KEY_TABLE(SYMBOL).LINE_NO

is the name of a component of the record, which is a scalar of typ POSITIVE. We can have qualified names related to all of these, fo example

SYMBOL_SET'FIRST

(the first value of the enumeration type: COMMON);

KEY_TABLE'LENGTH

(the number of elementary records in the array: 6), or

    KEY_TABLE (SYMBOL)'SIZE

(the number of bits used to represent this elementary record in the array). Similarly

    SYMBOL_SET'SUCC

is the name of a function (see section 5.1) with formal part

    (X : in SYMBOL_SET) return SYMBOL_SET;

When this function is applied to an actual argument (which must be a value of type SYMBOL_SET), it returns another value in SYMBOL_SET: the value which succeeds X, if any; it raises the exception RANGE_ERROR if X has the value SYMBOL_SET'LAST.

Names may be formed by attaching indexes, selectors or attribute designators like this without limit, depending only on the nature of the entity (not on the name itself). If an array is multidimensional, then the appropriate number of index values must be given.

A local name may be introduced for an existing object by renaming it, thus:

    L : POSITIVE renames KEY_TABLE (SYMBOL).LINE_NO;

The object which this declaration refers to is fixed when the declaration is met in the program. Thus the particular value of any index (SYMBOL here) at that time determines which object is to be known as L, even though SYMBOL might be subsequently changed.

2.6   Numbers

It is good programming practice to distinguish numerical values that occur naturally, and to declare them explicitly. This both reduces the likelihood of accidental error (since transposition of digits cannot be automatically checked) and helps program maintenance (anticipating the change in circumstances that will require the value to be changed).

A number is declared like a constant but without a type, thus:

    K: constant := 1024;
    PROC_MAX : constant := 5;

```
HALF : constant := 0.5;
E : constant := 2.71828;
HIGHEST : constant := 64 * K - 1;
```

The expression on the right may involve previously declared numbers, combined by arithmetic operators (but not functions).

2.7   Strong Typing

Ada is a strongly typed language, which means that the types of all data values used in the program are checked for consistency with their usage. Keeping types distinct has been found to be a very powerful means of detecting logical mistakes when a program is written and to give valuable assistance whenever the program is being subsequently maintained. In Ada, every type definition introduces a new type (even with derived types, explained in section 12.1, where one looks the same as another). Checks for type consistency are strictly applied. Thus

```
type OUNCE is range 0 .. 15;
type HEX   is range 0 .. 15;
```

allow values of both types to cover the same numbers, yet to be guaranteed distinct in use: any data value of type OUNCE is always distinguished from data values of type HEX.

The type consistency rule means that in any assignment

```
X := EXPRESSION;
```

the types of X and the expression must be the same: if they are different, the programmer gets a diagnostic message from the compiler. This has some surprising consequences: if X is of type FLOAT, then you cannot write X := 0; because 0 is a literal denoting an integer value. Instead you must write a literal denoting a real value, such as

```
X := 0.0;
```


Similarly, if I is of type INTEGER, you cannot write X := I; because the types of X and I are different. You must write

```
X := FLOAT(I);
```

where the expression on the right is called a type conversion: it converts the value given to the stated type (see chapter 3)

In general in Ada, it is good practice to have many different types, because the compiler can then ensure they are kept separate. You should only use the same types for values which can in principle be equally meaningful in the sense that the same operations can be applied to them.

Another way of interpreting the "strong typing" rule is in terms of the abstract values which can occur. Each type defines a set of abstract values, and any object of that type can only take values from that set. Strong typing means that the abstract values for any type are absolutely distinct from those of any other type (even though their representations may be handled by the computer similarly). This means that any overlap between one type and another is logically impossible.

Exercises
(Possible answers to these will be found in other examples in the book).

1. Messages are sent with precedence ROUTINE, PRIORITY or FLASH. Define the appropriate type.

2. Measurements are in feet and inches (with no fractions). Define the type for such measurements (not to exceed one mile).

3. Dates are given by year (from 1900 to 2099), month (using three letter abbreviation for the name) and day in month. Neglecting the fact that some months are actually shorter than 31 days, define a suitable type. Write down some values of this type, including some which are formally legal although not sensible dates because of the simplifying assumption.

4. To check that dates are sensible, we need to know the number of days in each month. Declare an object of a suitable type to express this, and state its value for a leap year.

5. Define a type suitable for PDP-11 output devices, in which there is a control and status register (one word) and a buffer register (one character).

6. Define a type suitable for holding an operation code, for which the possibilities are: modify, open, close, reset link, reset initial call, restart.

7. Define a type suitable for associating a key with an item, having a status indication to show whether the association is valid, deleted or empty.

CHAPTER 3

Expressions

An expression is a formula for calculating a value. The type of the
value calculated, and the types of all constituents in the expression,
are determined at compile time to give strong checking for
inconsistencies. In this chapter we explain the rules for writing
expressions in Ada, first for particular types of data then in general.

Expressions are mainly used for numeric types (section 3.1) but are
also used to calculate truth values from logical expressions (section
3.2). Other types which may arise in expressions are discussed in
section 3.3.

The general rules concerning expressions (section 3.4) distinguish
operators and operands. The various operators are explained in section
3.5, and operands in section 3.6.

3.1 Numeric Expressions

Ada includes standard facilities for dealing with data values of the
numeric types explained in section 2.1, so that expressions of integer
or approximate quantities can be written in the normal way. The strict
type matching rules are applied in expressions, so a 'mixed' expression
containing quantities of different types (e.g. an integer and a floating
value) must usually be written with explicit type conversions.

3.1.1   Integer Expressions

The operators + - * / have their usual meanings (division giving an
integer, formed by truncating the real result towards zero). The
operands must have the same integer type. The operators **rem** and **mod**
give the remainder on integer division, differing in the sign and
truncation conventions:

    I **rem** J   -- has the sign of I, hence truncation towards zero;
    I **mod** J   -- has the sign of J, hence truncation opposite J.

The exponentiation operator ** raises an integer to a power. To ensure
that the result is also an integer, the power must be non negative
(otherwise the exception CONSTRAINT_ERROR is raised).   The operator **abs**
gives the absolute value.

In the following expressions, we assume that the variables I and J
have values 13 and 5 respectively.

    I / 2   -- 6
    I / J   -- 2, since 13 = 2 * 5 + 3
    I **rem** J   -- 3, since 13 = 2 * 5 + 3
    I **rem** (-J)   -- 3, since 13 = (-2) * (-5) + 3
    I **mod** (-J)   -- -2, since 13 = (-3) * (-5) + (-2)
    (-I) **mod** J   -- 2, since (-13) = (-3) * 5 + 2
    J ** 3   -- 125
    abs (J - I)   -- 6
    2 * J + 4   -- 14 = (2 * J) + 4
    2 * (J + 4)   -- 18

An integer expression whose mathematical value is outside the
implemented   range causes the NUMERIC_ERROR exception to be raised; this
includes the case of division by zero.

3.1.2   Floating Point Expressions

The operators + - * / have their usual meanings. The operands must have
the same floating point type. The exponentiation operator ** raises a
floating point value to an integer power, so that the result is still a
real value.   The operator **abs** gives the absolute value.

In the following expressions, we assume that the variables X and Y
have values 25.2 and 3.0E8 respectively.

```
   - X                --   -25.2
   X + 5.2            --    30.4
   0.25 * X           --     6.3
   X / Y              --     8.4E-8
   Y ** 2             --     9.0E16
   X / 10.0 + 0.06    --     2.58
```

A floating point expression is evaluated approximately, depending on the
precision of the constituents: the number of digits specified. (There
is a full mathematical model of the approximate numbers and operators on
them, which gives the error bounds on the result.)   If the mathematical
value of an expression is outside the   implemented   range,   the
NUMERIC_ERROR exception is raised; this includes the case of division by
zero.

3.1.3   Fixed Point Expressions

The operators + and - have their usual meanings. For multiplication and
division, fixed point values may be combined with integers. A fixed
point value multiplied by an integer (or vice versa) produces a value of
the same fixed point type.   A fixed point value divided by an integer
also produces a value of the same fixed point type.   (Note that this
does not apply to an integer divided by a fixed point value.)

   Two fixed point values (not necessarily of the same type) may be
multiplied or divided together, but in this case the required type for
the result must be stated explicitly: it must be a fixed point type, but
need not be the same as the types of the constituents. The operator **abs**
gives the absolute value in the same type as its argument.
Exponentiation is not defined for fixed point types.

   In the following expressions, we assume that the variables E and F
have the same fixed point type and values 0.1 and 0.6 respectively

```
   F - E              --    0.5 approximately
   4 * E              --    0.4
   F / 2              --    0.3
   FRAC (0.5 * F)     --    0.3 (type FRAC is defined in section 2.1)
   abs (E - F / 2)    --    0.2
```


   If the mathematical value of the expression is   outside   the
implemented range, the NUMERIC_ERROR exception is raised.

3.2   Logical Expressions

Expressions in Ada may deal with truth values (of type BOOLEAN), testing
the truth of relations or conformance with constraints. (The types of
the values in the expression are checked at compile time, depending on
the operators used, but constraints may need run-time checking.) Logical
expressions are used in situations where a truth value is required (such
as in if statements) as well as in expressions generally.

3.2.1   Relations

Any two values of the same scalar type may be compared, and the results
taken as a truth value.   The comparison is written using one of the six
relational operators. Certain non-scalar values may also be compared.

    The following examples assume the same values for variables as the
section above, and variables P, C with values LOW, '?' respectively:

    J /= 0   --   TRUE because 5 /= 0
    I < J   --   FALSE
    I - 3 = 2 * J   --   TRUE, since both sides equal 10.
    X > Y   --   FALSE
    abs (X + 5.2) > 40.0   --   TRUE
    E <= F/2   --   TRUE
    P = LOW   --   TRUE
    C /= '?'   --   FALSE

(Note that /= means not equal, <= means less than or equal to, and >=
means greater than or equal to.) Any two values of the same type (not
necessarily scalar) may be tested for equality unless they have been
declared to be **limited** (see section 12.2).

    SL(1) /= SL(2)   --   comparing sectors in list (see 2.4)

For arrays or records this means testing whether all components are
equal. (Any different components make the compound values unequal.)

    Two one-dimensional arrays may be compared if the elements are of a
discrete type, to determine their relative position in dictionary order.

    "Ada"   <   "Adam"   --   TRUE
    "Augusta"   <   "Byron"   --   TRUE

Note that the array lengths need not be the same.

3.2.2   Conformance

We can test whether a value of a scalar type satisfies a range
constraint. The constraint may be stated explicitly or as a subtype.

```
I in range 1 .. 10        -- FALSE, since I = 13
J in NATURAL              -- TRUE, since 5 is in 0 .. INTEGER'LAST
C not in LOWER_CASE       -- TRUE
1.0 / X in UP_TO_ONE      -- TRUE
Y not in POSITIVE_FLOAT   -- FALSE
```

(The same notation may be used with other constraints and corresponding
values.   Accuracy constraints are always taken to be satisfied.)

3.2.3   Boolean Expressions

Truth values may be combined using the operators **not, and, or, xor** with
their usual meanings.   (**xor** means exclusive or, which is the same as
not-equivalence.)   In addition, there are 'short circuit' operators:
and then and **or else**. These avoid the evaluation of the operand on the
right when that is unnecessary.

```
not J = 0                       -- TRUE
I > 10 and J < 10               -- TRUE
I > 20  or J < 20               -- TRUE because J < 20
X < Y xor Y > 1000.0            -- FALSE because both hold.
C in LOWER_CASE and then J /= 0 --  FALSE, without testing J
```

The logical operators **and, or, xor** may not be mixed (to avoid possible
confusion over precedence; use brackets for combinations of them,
showing clearly the order of evaluation wanted. The short circuit forms
are useful for checking conformance to a constraint before using the
value:

```
J /= 0 or else I rem J /= 0      -- TRUE, and safe if J = 0.
C in HEX_DIGIT and then LED(C) /= 0  -- FALSE.
```

Note in the last example that the short circuiting skips evaluation of
the second term, so does not use an illegal index.

3.3   Other kinds of expression

There are some standard facilities for working with enumeration types
and one-dimensional arrays.   Other types (including array and record
types) are permissible components in expressions, and may be combined
using functions or programmer-defined operators.

3.3.1   Enumeration Expressions

The values in an enumeration type are written in order when the type is
declared, and for any given value the previous or following value may be
determined, using the qualifier PRED or SUCC with the type name.

    CHARACTER'SUCC(C)   -- ' ' as the value after '?'
    PRESSURE'PRED(P)   -- THIN, the value before LOW

If the expression tries to calculate the successor of the last value in
the type, or the predecessor of the first value, the exception
CONSTRAINT_ERROR is raised.

3.3.2   Array Expressions

The Boolean operators may be applied to arrays of the same type, if the
element type is BOOLEAN; the result is another array of the same type,
whose value is formed by applying the operator to the constituents
element by element.

    The operator & concatenates two one-dimensional arrays whose element
types are the same; it produces a longer array containing the same
element values.   Concatenation also joins a single element to an array
of elements of the same type

    G or GG   -- assuming both of type GRID (see 2.3)
    "AB" & "CD"   --   "ABCD"
    SL(1) & SL(2)   -- of type array(1 .. 10) of SECTOR

3.3.3   Expressions of programmer-defined types

A type which is declared as a derived type (see section 12.1)
automatically has all the properties of the base type, including
whatever operators are appropriate. A type that is declared as a
private type (see section 7.5) automatically has the equality comparison
operators (= and /=) unless it is limited.

In addition to the operators automatically available (or instead of
them if necessary), explicit operator declarations may be given to allow
operators to apply to other types. Operator declarations are explained
later (section 5.1).

The types of the values in an expression must match the types
expected and produced by the operators. Any inconsistency is detected
at compile time.

3.4   Expressions in general

Expressions are formed from operands and operators. An expression can
consist of a literal value or the name of a variable or constant as
special cases; in general it is one or more operands connected by
operators. There is no limit in Ada to the size of an expression, but
most programmers find that expressions longer than one line are hard to
read and understand.

An expression is evaluated by evaluating the operands and combining
them according to the operators, in an order defined by certain rules of
precedence. The rules have been chosen to reflect common practice in
mathematics and the conventions that have been established in other
programming languages.

3.5   Operands

The operands within an expression can be of the following kinds:

a. Literals, giving values of scalar objects; these may be numbers

```
    12              -- integer (decimal value)
    273.0           -- real number (with decimal point)
    9.81E2          -- real number (with exponent)
    1E5             -- integer (with exponent)
```

```
16#F000#          -- based integer (base 16)
16#F#E3           -- same as 16#F000#
8#0.37777#        -- real number (base 8)
```

or enumeration literals

```
MONDAY            -- of type DAY_NAME
EXPRESS           -- of type PRI_CODE
THIN              -- of type PRESSURE
'?'               -- of type CHARACTER
```

b. Aggregates, giving values of compound objects (records or arrays).
The   values   of   the   components   are   given   by   inner   expressions,
distinguished from one another either by the names of the record
components   or   values of the array indices (thus associating the values
of the components by name), or by their order (corresponding to the
order of the constituents in the type definition, associating the values
of the components by position). The two styles of association may be
combined for different elements within the same aggregate, provided that
positional associations are given first. Named association must be used
if there is only one element, unless the aggregate is qualified as shown
in subsection g below.

```
(RADIUS => 1.0E1, WIDTH => 360.0)  -- SECTOR
(1.0E1, 360.0)          --   same value, if SECTOR
(1.0, 2.0, 3.0, 4.0)  --   possible value for COL_VEC
```

Where the array elements are characters, the aggregate may be written as
a sequence of characters in double quotes:

```
"A string"        --  all on one line
""                --  null string
```

To get a value containing a double quote character, write it twice.   To
get   a value longer than one line, or containing control characters, use
concatenation (see below: the & operator).

c. Names of objects (variables or constants).   An object may be scalar
or compound.

```
REVOLUTION            --  constant ANGLE
FRED                  --  of type FINE
S                     --  of type SECTOR
IMAGE                 --  array of CHARACTER
ALTIMETER(4)      --  of type CABLE
KEY_TABLE(SYMBOL).LENGTH --  of type POSITIVE
```

The name may involve indexes, selectors or qualifiers as explained in
section 2.8. An index value is given by an inner expression, whose
value must be of the right type and range.

d. Allocators, in which a value of an access type is obtained, denoting
a newly created base object with a given value or constraint:

   new MESSAGE_ITEM (5, IMAGE, **null**)

Further details are given in chapter 12; see particularly section
12.5.5.

e. Function calls, in which a value is calculated in a subprogram (see
chapter 5). The value may be scalar or compound, and the function may
have parameters which are given as variables or inner expressions.

```
SIN (PI * X)          -- of type FLOAT
ASK ("Need help?")    -- of type BOOLEAN
ATAN2 (X, Y)          -- of type ANGLE
STRAIGHT (HERE)       -- of type POSITION
```

f. Type conversions, whereby a value in one type is converted to the
appropriate value in a closely related type. This is the way Ada
combines the advantages of strong type checking with the flexibility of
mixed expressions: the programmer has to state the type conversions
explicitly.

```
FLOAT (I + 4)         -- numeric type conversion
CENTS (X / 3.0)       -- rounds and checks range
FINE (PI)             -- conversion to fixed point
WEIGHT (19.32 * FLOAT (L1*L2*L3) )
```

The last example above shows conversion to and from derived types: L1
L2, L3 are assumed to be of a type derived from FLOAT, and WEIGHT is
also derived from FLOAT. An array value can be type converted to
another array of the same size and shape, if the component types are the
same.

g. Qualified expressions, for resolving possible ambiguities and
ensuring that constraints are met. If it is required to specify the
type of a literal (or aggregate), this notation is used.

```
LENGTH'(3.4)          -- of type LENGTH
HEIGHT'(3.4)          -- of type HEIGHT
MONTH_NAME'(OCT)      -- resolves ambiguity
NUMBER_BASE'(OCT)     -- resolves ambiguity
WEEKDATE'(TODAY)      -- checks range
```

SECTOR'(1.0,360.0)   --   same aggregate value as in b above

h. Subexpressions, that is inner expressions   enclosed   in   parentheses
(round brackets)

    (X + 1.0)
    (2.0 * PI * (R + RR))

The second example shows a nested   inner   subexpression.   There   is   no
limit   to   the   number   of   levels   of   nesting   that   can be used in an
expression, but for ease of   comprehension   it   is   preferable   to   keep
within   five   levels.   The compiler checks that the parentheses are in
nested pairs.

3.6   Operators

The operators which can be used to compose expressions are as follows:

    **   --   exponentiation

    abs   --   absolute value
    not   --   logical negation

    * / **mod rem**   --   multiplying and dividing

    + -   --   unary (monadic) number operations

    + -   --   adding and subtracting
    &   --   concatenation

    = /= <= < > >=   --   relational
    in   **not in**   --   membership

    and   **or**   **xor**   --   logical
    and then   --   short circuit
    or else   --   short circuit

Note that there are four unary (monadic) operators; the rest are   binary
(dyadic).   The   operators   **abs**   and   **not**   are   always unary; the number
operators + and - may be unary or binary, depending on their position in
an expression.

    J ** 2
    abs R1
    not WET

```
0.5 * PI
K rem B_COUNT
- 5                         -- unary -
MAXSIZE - 1                 -- binary -
MESSAGE & NAME              -- concatenation
THETA <= REVOLUTION
Q in LOW_PRESSURE           -- special operand on right
HARD or SHINY
```

The membership operators **in** and **not in** take a special kind of right operand: a type or a subtype name (or a range), rather than a data value. Otherwise all the operands are data values, and the result of every operator is a data value.

In conformity with the 'strong typing' rule, the operators refer to particular types of operand, and combine them to form results of known types. These operators are defined in Ada for particular predefined types (see Appendix A: the definition of package STANDARD), and may be extended by explicit programming if required for other types (see section 5.1 on overloading operators).

Note that the subtypes of operands in an expression ensure that the values of the elementary operands are within known bounds; combinations of such operands may however take values outside the bounds. For example,

    CENTS (**abs** (C1 + C2 - 99))

(following the declarations in sections 2.1 and 2.6) is legitimate, even though the inner expression on the right may go outside the range 0 .. 99.

3.7   Evaluating Expressions

An expression comprises one or more operands (as in section 3.5) linked by operators (as in section 3.6), possibly preceded by a unary operator.

The table of operators in section 3.6 shows the order of precedence, highest at the top. The adding and concatenating operators have the same precedence; the relational and membership operators have the same precedence; the logical and short circuit operators have the same precedence.

The rules for evaluation are as follows:

a. Where an operand has operators on both sides of it, and the operators are of different precedence, the operator of the higher precedence is applied first.
b. A binary operator has operands on both sides. Unless the operator is a short circuit operator, both operands are evaluated (in either order) before the operator is applied. When the operator is a short circuit operator, the operand on the left is evaluated before the operator is applied; if necessary, the operand on the right is then evaluated.
c. A unary operator is applied to the resulting operand on its right, taking account of rule a.

The expression may be evaluated in any order consistent with these rules (to allow compilers to optimise the order, which may be different on different computers). Note that many of the forms of an operand may include inner expressions, so finding an operand may involve evaluating the inner expression first.

The rules of precedence can be visualised by using parentheses to show the subexpressions:

   - Y ** Z < 4.0 + 0.5 * X **and** WET

has its constituents evaluated as though it had been written

   ((- (Y**Z)) < (4.0 + (0.5 * X))) **and** WET

Note that the unary operators have lower precedence than multiplying and exponentiating operators, so are applied after them. It is wise to play for safety in cases like this, and use parentheses explicitly in the program to make the intended order of evaluation absolutely clear.

Exercises

1. Given

      INX : INTEGER **range** 1 .. SIZE;

   write an expression which increments INX by 1 if it is in the range, but wraps around from SIZE to 1.

2. Write an expression to calculate one plus alpha squared minus sigma squared, all over two sigma, where the variables are both floating point and non-zero.

3. Given

    subtype INDEX **is** INTEGER **range** 1 .. 10;
    A : **array** (INDEX) **of** FLOAT;
    I : INTEGER;

    write a logical expression to check that two consecutive elements of
    the array (at index values I and I+1) exist and are definitely
    positive.

4. Given the values of HERE and D declared in section 2.4, and

    function SIN (X : ANGLE) **return** UP_TO_ONE;
    function COS (X : ANGLE) **return** UP_TO_ONE;

    write an expression to calculate the value of type POSITION a total
    distance D in a straight course from HERE.

CHAPTER 4

Statements

The actions to be carried out in the program are specified by writing a
series of statements, in the order they are to be executed.

Ada prescribes the basic form of statements, and how they can be
combined to form more complicated actions. At any position in the
program, it is likely that the programmer will need to use some of these
basic statements but also (as shown in section 1.3) some application-
specific statements that call for the performance of actions whose
details are stated elsewhere. Such statements are procedure calls;
they are introduced here, but the details are given in chapter 5.

The basic statements include assignments of values to variables,
selection of actions according to particular criteria, and repetition of
actions. There are also statements for more advanced facilities,
explained in chapters 6 and 7.

4.1   Sequences of statements

Each statement specifies an action to be carried out; a sequence of
statements specifies a series of actions to be carried out, one after
the other, in the order written. Statements are classified as either
simple or compound : compound statements contain internal sequences of
statements (which may in turn be simple or compound).

Any statement, whether simple or compound, may be labelled, to give
it a name. The label is put in front of the statement, enclosed in
double angle brackets:

<<LABEL>> STATEMENT;

39

Some compound statements (loop and declare) may be given a local name using a colon:

    OUTER : **loop**
    -- sequence of statements
    end loop OUTER;

This name is available only in the internal sequence of statements. Every statement is written with a final semicolon.

A simple statement is either sequential or branching. Sequential statements are executed in their order of occurrence; after a sequential statement has been executed, the statement which follows it in the sequence (if any) is executed. A branching statement is normally the last of a sequence of statements: when it has been completely executed, the statement executed next is determined not by its position, but by some other rule, dependent on the particular statement kind. A compound statement may have either characteristic, depending on the simple statements of which it is composed.

If a compound statement contains another compound statement, they are said to be nested. Ada does not limit the depth of nesting, but it can be difficult for the human reader to be sure of his context in a deeply nested structure. It is good practice therefore to write programs using the layout to show the nesting : within each sequence, write the statements (whether simple or compound) underneath one another, starting each at the same left margin. Where there is a compound statement write the statements which form each internal sequence similarly, but with an indented left margin. (There are Ada support tools which lay out programs automatically.)

Using this indented style of writing, the left margin of the program text shows the structure of the program, and there is a natural limit to the depth of nesting - do not let the indented left margins creep right across the page! If your program seems to be developing in this direction, give a particular compound statement a name and make it into a procedure (as explained in chapter 5).

The compound statements in Ada are bracketed by keywords, giving a clear indication of the start and finish of each sequence of statements. They include statements in which the actions to be carried out are selected according to particular criteria (**if** and **case** statements), or are repeated as required (**loop** statements), or have local declarations (**declare** statements); these are all described here. In addition, there are **accept** statements and **select** statements which are described in chapter 7.

4.2   Assignment

A variable is a data item whose value may be changed. A new value is
given to a variable by an assignment statement. The previous value of
the variable (which might be involved in calculating the new value) is
then completely lost. The variable may be of any type (including a
record or an array as a complete entity); the new value given to it must
of course be of the right type, and consistent with any constraints.
(The following examples use data items introduced in chapter 2).

```
I := 0;
X := Y * Z;
S := (RADIUS => 1.0, WIDTH => 90.0);
P.HEADING := P.HEADING + 60.0;
SL(2) := S;
```

Note that the assignment gives the variable a complete new value. If it
is of a compound type, all the components get new values. If the
programmer wants to change some of the components of a record or array
and leave others unchanged, he must write the series of assignments for
the components to be changed in the order required.

4.3   Alternatives

Different actions may be required in different circumstances.   Each of
the different actions is written as a separate sequence of statements,
introduced by the appropriate clause which shows when those statements
are required to be executed.

    There are two basic methods of choosing from the possible actions:
either by testing conditions, or according to the value of a suitable
variable. Different kinds of statements are used for these: **if** to test
conditions, **case** to select by data value.

4.3.1   Selection by condition

In an **if** statement, the programmer states the condition to be tested,
then the sequence of statements to be executed if the condition is true.
If the condition is false, there may be other actions to be carried out,
which may include testing further conditions. Thus the basic idea is to
have a series of conditions to be tested in order, with corresponding
actions to be taken on finding the first condition which is true, and

finally actions to be carried out if none of the conditions are true.

```
if I < 0 then
  I := 0;
end if;

if COUNT < 100 then
  COUNT := COUNT + 1;
else
  XS_COUNT := XS_COUNT + 1;
  COUNT:=0;
end if;

if C /= ASCII("$") then
  D := A_TO_E(C);
else
  D := EBCDIC(" ");
end if;

if TODAY in MONDAY .. FRIDAY then
  WEEKDAY_PROC;
elsif TODAY = SATURDAY then
  SAT_PROC;
elsif TODAY = SUNDAY then
  SUN_PROC;
end if;
```

(Note the redundant test in this example, anticipating possible changes in the future life of the program).

An **if** statement in general consists of a number of conditions to be investigated in the given order; the first which is found to be true determines which sequence of statements is executed. If none of the conditions are true, a further sequence of statements may be executed. The keywords used to identify these parts of the statement are **if** at the beginning, before the first condition, **elsif** before each subsequent condition (zero or more times); each condition is followed by **then** and a sequence of statements; if actions are needed when no condition is true, write **else** and the sequence of statements. The whole of the statement is always terminated by **end if**;

4.3.2   Selection by discriminant value

In a **case** statement, the program gives an expression, whose value (which must be of a discrete type, i.e. integer or enumeration) determines

which actions are required. The programmer states the possible expected
value (or values) as choices for the discriminating expression, then the
series of statements to be executed if the expression has that value.
Several values may be given for each choice, but the values given for
the different choices must of course be distinct, and must cover all the
possible values in the (sub)type.

```
case TODAY is
  when MONDAY|WEDNESDAY|FRIDAY =>
    I:=9; J:=17;
  when TUESDAY|THURSDAY =>
    I:=8; J:=15;
  when SATURDAY|SUNDAY =>
    I:=10; J:=16;
end case;

case CMND is
  when CLOSE_DOWN =>
    STOP;
  when START_UP =>
    SET_GOING;
    PRINT_MESSAGE ("STARTED");
  when others =>
    PRINT_MESSAGE("DONT " &
      "UNDERSTAND");
end case;
```

The choice others means any possible values of the discriminant which
are not given previously. It may only be given as the last choice.

The basic difference between if and case is that in an if statement
the conditions are tested one after the other, whereas in a case
statement the expression's value determines one of the various
possibilities directly.

4.4   Repetition

An action may need to be repeated, for example to carry out some
operations regularly to a series of items, or to iterate some improving
operation. The unit of repetition is written as a sequence of
statements, forming the body of the loop, introduced by a suitable
phrase which may show a condition for stopping the repetitions.

The basic loop simply groups the statements to be repeated, without
implying any termination; this is frequently needed in large program

structures, for example where the computer is continuously monitoring or
controlling something:

```
loop
  DELIVER_WATER;
  CLEAN_WATER;
end loop;
```

The repetitions of a loop may be controlled either by testing a
condition or by counting; these are expressed by the iteration
specification at the start of the basic loop. Independently, during the
course of execution of the loop, a condition might arise requiring exit
from the loop.

Control by a condition is expressed by a **while** clause:

```
I := 0;
while A(I) >= 0 loop
  I := I + 1;
end loop;  -- may get index error
          -- (when no elements of A are negative)
```

The condition is tested before starting each repetition: it may indicate
that the body of the loop is not to be executed at all.

Control by counting is expressed by a **for** clause:

```
for DAY in DAY_NAME loop
  ADJUST_RATE (DAY);
end loop;

for LETTER in HEX_DIGIT range 'A' .. 'F' loop
  MY_LED (LETTER) := 0;
end loop;

for M in 1 .. MAX_SIZE loop
  if MORE_CHARS then
    IMAGE (M) := NEXT_CHAR;
  else
    IMAGE (M) := " ";
  end if;
end loop;
```

The loop parameter M is automatically declared by the **for** clause, with
the appropriate type and range. It applies to all of the loop body. The

limits of the range need not be constants: any expression may be given
for each limit. Unless otherwise specified the loop parameter counts
forwards through the range. However, if the keyword **reverse** is put in,
the loop parameter counts backwards through the range.

```
for M in reverse 1 .. MAX SIZE loop
   exit when IMAGE(M) /= "⌐";
end loop;
```

The **exit** statement is explained in section 4.7.1.

4.5   Call Statement

Higher order actions are constructed out of more elementary ones, and
made available as procedures (or entries) either from libraries which
have already been written, or by the programmers writing the current
program. In this section we describe the simple features of call
statements to execute these higher order actions, which serve most
ordinary purposes. The full details covering the less usual features are
explained in chapter 5 (for procedure calls) and chapter 8 (for entry
calls).

Procedures and entries can have parameters, and each time one is
called to carry out its action, appropriate values and variables must be
specified for its parameters. Every procedure and every entry has a
specification that states exactly what kinds of parameters it needs, if
any.

The call statement gives the name of the procedure or entry to be
executed, followed by the actual parameter values and/or variables to be
used. To call a procedure or entry with no parameters, just write its
name:

```
PRINT_HELP_FILE;
INITIALIZE;
```

To call a procedure or entry which requires parameters, put the required
values or variables in parentheses after the name:

```
DRAW2(X1, Y1 + 1.0E0);
   -- parameters are two values of type FLOAT

CLOSE(MY_FILE);
   -- parameter is a variable of type IN_FILE
```

SIMPLE_BUFFER.READ (IMAGE(M));
-- entry : see 8.1.2.

Note that a value can be given as a suitable expression. The rules for parameters are quite complicated (to allow for the variety of usage in actual programs), but they follow a logical pattern.

The same notation is used to call procedures and entries, because from the point of view of the caller they both carry out some action and then return. The difference is in the way they may interact with the rest of the program: a procedure in Ada is reentrable, so may be also executed in parallel by several tasks concurrently; an entry is not reentrable, and may only be accepted by one task at a time to carry out its action. These details are explained in chapters 5 and 8.

4.6   Block statement

A block statement is a compound statement containing a sequence of statements, optionally preceded by local declarations and optionally followed by local exception handlers (see chapter 6). The local declarations apply within the block but not outside it in the rest of the program.

A block statement may be given a local name, in which case the same identifier must also be given at the end of the statement:

LOCAL_BLOCK: **declare**
-- local declarations
begin
-- internal statements
end LOCAL_BLOCK;

The block statement is introduced by the keyword **declare** if there are any local declarations, which would be the most general case. (If there are no declarations, omit the word **declare**.) After any local declarations, the start of the sequence of statements is marked by the keyword **begin**. If any exception handlers are required they are written after the main statements, introduced by the keyword **exception** (see chapter 6).

4.7   Branching Statements

These are statements whose successor in execution is not necessarily
that which follows it in sequence, but some other, determined by the
particular statement kind. The statements concerned are exit, return,
raise and goto. Some purists regard these as 'unstructured' statements,
since they establish alternative ways of leaving a sequence of
statements. Ada allows them in safe situations.

4.7.1   Exit statement

An exit statement specifies explicit termination of a loop. Within a
loop, whether or not there is an iteration specification given by a **for**
or **while** clause, the repetitions may be stopped by execution of an exit
statement; the whole of the loop statement is then deemed complete.

```
for J in 0 .. 100 loop
  if A(J) < 0 then
    I := J;
    exit;
  end if;
end loop;  -- value of I is unchanged
           -- if no element of A
           -- is negative

for MTH in MONTH_NAME loop
  if MTH = TODAY.MONTH then
    exit;
  end if;
  D := D + DAYS(MTH);
end loop;
```


Note that **exit** usually occurs in an **if** statement; a special short
notation is available for this common and simple case:

```
exit when MTH = TODAY.MONTH;
```

A loop statement may of course be one of the statements in the body of
another loop, and so on. The loops are said to be nested. If an exit
statement is written simply (as shown above), then it terminates
repetition of the smallest loop enclosing it; however, any required loop
of the nest may be terminated by giving the loop a local name and
writing that name in the exit statement:

```
OUTER: loop
  -- outer body
  loop
    -- inner body
    exit OUTER when REQUIRED;
  end loop;
  -- more outer statements
end loop OUTER;
```

4.7.2   Return statement

A return statement specifies the end of execution of a subprogram body,
and indicates completion of the corresponding subprogram call.

If the subprogram is a function, then the return statement must
specify the value to be delivered by the subprogram; it must be of the
right type as determined by the subprogram specification (see section
5.1). Thus a subprogram which returns an integer can contain the
statement

    return COUNT;

where COUNT may be any integer expression. The statement may be in the
body of an inner condition, loop or declare statement - if so it
automatically terminates the inner statements by terminating the
subprogram body.

A procedure which does not return a value may contain a return
statement with no value attached - just

    return;

but in this case the return statement is not essential: reaching the
normal end of the sequence of statements in the body equally indicates
completion of the corresponding procedure call statement.

4.7.3   Raise statement

A raise statement specifies that an exception situation has been
detected, so that normal sequential execution of statements cannot
continue. The full details of exceptions are explained in chapter 6,
including the description of how an exception handler is executed

instead of the rest of the sequence of statements in which the raise statement occurs. The exceptional situations which might arise within a piece of program are given names in the usual way, introduced like this:

MUST_CLOSE_NOW, OPERATOR_ERROR : **exception**;

(Note that this declaration, although it looks like an object declaration, merely states that the identifiers denote exceptional situations; no objects are associated with exceptions.)

A raise statement usually occurs with an exception name, indicating which particular exception has been detected:

raise MUST_CLOSE_NOW;

raise OPERATOR_ERROR;

In the special context of an exception handler, it is permissible to give a raise statement with no name, to indicate that the present handler is incomplete. An example is given in section 6.4 when describing exception handlers.

4.7.4   Goto statement

A goto statement specifies its successor statement explicitly, by giving a statement label:

goto TAIL;

It is particularly difficult to debug programs containing goto statements, and they should be avoided if possible. If you cannot find a way of using the other kinds of statement to achieve the sequence of execution necessary, the potential future problems may be alleviated by giving the **goto** statement itself a label, and putting a "come from" comment with the destination statement, thus:

<<HEAD>> **goto** TAIL;
-- intermediate statements
<<TAIL>> -- come from HEAD
-- statement

The pair of statements connected by a goto and a label must be fairly close together in an Ada program. Specifically, they must both be in the same unit body, that is the same subprogram, package body (initialisation) or task body.

Within that body, if one is in an accept statement the other must also be in the same accept statement; if one is an exception handler the other must also be in the same exception handler.

The goto statement must be in a sequence of statements (usually at the end of the sequence), and this sequence will usually be in a compound statement which is part of an enclosing sequence of statements. The corresponding labelled statement must be one of the statements in a sequence containing or enclosing the goto statement.

4.8   Other normal statements

The normal rules of sequencing apply to delay and null statements which are described in the following sections. They also apply to abort statements, which are described in chapter 13, and to code statements which are described in chapter 11.

4.8.1   Delay statement

The statements in a sequence are normally executed as rapidly as possible: as soon as each statement has been completed, the next statement in the sequence may be started. If you want to insert a timed delay in the sequence, use a delay statement:

delay 5.0 ;

The amount of the delay required must be given in seconds; it can be a constant, a variable or an expression, of type DURATION (defined in package STANDARD: see Appendix A). (A negative value is treated as zero.) The effect of such a statement is to delay starting execution of the next statement in the sequence for at least the specified duration (Other parts of the program may be executed during that period corresponding to other tasks – see chapter 8). Note that a delay statement gives a minimum time: it does not imply any upper limit to the interval before the next statement is started. (A different technique, timeout, explained in chapters 8 and 13 is used for this. Note also that a delay is for a particular period of time (which may of course have been calculated in advance). A different method, rendezvous explained in chapter 8, is used to cause a delay until a particular event happens or some other part of the program is ready.

The delay statement is the ordinary method of achieving timed sequential control, for example opening and closing a set of valves in the proper order.

```
with TIME_SCALES; use TIME_SCALES;
procedure AIR_FLUSH is
  begin
    FAN(ON); delay FAN_RESPONSE;
    AIR_VALVE(OPEN); delay BLOW_TIME;
    AIR_VALVE(CLOSED); delay AIR_CLOSE;
    FAN(OFF);
  end AIR_FLUSH;
```

4.8.2   Null Statement

Sometimes the program structure requires you to write a sequence of statements even if nothing has to be done – for example in an arm of a case statement. The null statement is a positive indication that no action is required. It is used to avoid the error of accidentally omitting a sequence of statements that should be there.

```
case DAY of
  when MONDAY| WEDNESDAY| FRIDAY  =>
    FULL_DAY;
  when TUESDAY| THURSDAY  =>
    PART_DAY;
  when others =>
    null;
end case;
```

Exercises

1. Write assignment statements to double the radius and halve the width of sector S.

2. Write statements to increase a variable of type TIME_OF_DAY by one second on a 24-hour clock, in particular advancing from (23, 59, 59) to (24, 0, 0) and from (24, 59, 59) to (1, 0, 0).

3. Write statements to increase a variable of type DATE by one day, taking account of the different number of days in each month as

given in **array** (MONTH_NAME) **of** NATURAL; when advancing from December 31 to January 1, call procedure NEW_YEAR;

4. With an **array** (1 .. 100) **of** TRACK, write statements to call

   procedure OBSERVATION (T: **in out** TRACK);

on the I-th element of the array, and then use

   function SPEED (T1, T2: TRACK) **return** FLOAT;

on the old and new values. Test whether the resulting value is less than 3.0E8. If it is larger, call

   procedure IMPOSSIBLE (T: **in out** TRACK);

(Note that it will be necessary to save a copy of the old value of the track before calling OBSERVATION in order to have it available for SPEED.)

CHAPTER 5

Subprograms

subprogram is a program unit for describing an action. There are
hree important aspects of subprograms: how to specify their interfaces
section 5.1); how to describe in detail the action concerned (section
.2); and how to call for that action to be carried out (section 5.3,
ollowing from 4.5).

Subprograms include procedures and functions; in many ways they are
lso similar to entries (which are explained in chapter 8). Procedures
re actions to achieve a particular effect; functions are actions to
alculate a value (usually with no other effect on their environment).
function may be called either as a named function or by an operator in
n expression.

Each subprogram has a specification (which gives its signature, see
ubsection h below) and a body (which also includes the specification,
nd gives details of how the action of the subprogram is to be
chieved). In most cases it is not necessary to give the specification
part from the body (section 5.2 below explains).

.1   Subprogram specification

n important feature in Ada is the emphasis given to the specifications.
n the case of a subprogram, the specification tells you exactly what
inds of parameters the subprogram needs, and what kind of effect it
as.

The specification gives the name of the subprogram and all the
ecessary information about its parameters. It is written like this:

53

procedure CLOSE(FILE : **in out** IN_FILE);

This procedure has a single parameter (FILE) which is of type IN_FILE;
value is brought **in** at the beginning of the procedure from the actua
parameter, given when the procedure is called, and a possibly differen
value is sent **out** to that parameter at the end of the procedure. W
might call this procedure by a statement such as

CLOSE (MY_FILE);

where MY_FILE is a variable of type IN_FILE.

Here is another subprogram specification:

procedure ADVANCE (C: INTEGER **range** 1 .. 99;
                     D: INTEGER :=0);

There are two parameters here, both of type integer.   On any call o
this procedure, the first parameter (corresponding to C) must have
value in the range 1 to 99.   The second parameter (corresponding to D
is optional - this is shown by the value given in the specification
which provides a default value for the parameter.

The specification

function ATAN2 (X,Y:FLOAT) **return** ANGLE;

indicates a function of two parameters of type FLOAT returning a resul
of type ANGLE.   It can be called (as explained in section 3.5e) in a
expression such as

ATAN2(T.HERE.EAST, T.HERE.NORTH)

giving the angle from the origin to the current position of track T
Functions need not always produce the same value when called with th
same parameters:

function ASK (QUESTION : STRING) **return** BOOLEAN;

specifies a function called ASK which has a single parameter name
QUESTION, of type STRING. It returns a value of type BOOLEAN each tim
it is called, not necessarily always the same even with the sam
parameter.   Because it is a function, it may be called in an expressic
or where a BOOLEAN value is appropriate.

The various properties of the interface given in a subprogra
specification are as follows.

a. Nature of subprogram

   A subprogram may be specified as a function or a procedure;
this indicates the intention of the subprogram: a procedure is
intended to achieve an effect, a function is intended to calculate
a value. There are special rules concerning a subprogram
specified to be a function – any parameters it has must all be of
mode **in,** and it must deliver a result; that is, it must contain at
least one **return** statement.

b. Name of subprogram

   In most cases the name of a subprogram is an identifier.
However, it is possible to introduce an additional meaning for an
operator by defining a function with the operator symbol (as a
character string) given as its name. This is called overloading
the operator. Subprograms named by an identifier may have any
number of parameters (including zero). Subprograms named by an
operator symbol must be functions and must have the number of
parameters appropriate for that operator symbol (one or two).

c. Parameters

   A subprogram may have parameters, each of which is specified
with an identifier, mode, type and possibly a default value. For
example the specification

   procedure PRINT_HELP_FILE;

tells us that PRINT_HELP_FILE is a procedure which has no
parameters. If there are any parameters, each has a particular
identifier: the formal parameter name. The specification

   procedure DRAW2(X, Y : FLOAT);

tells us that DRAW2 is a procedure which takes in two parameters,
named X and Y. On each occasion this procedure is called, two
values must be given for these parameters.

d. Mode

   In most cases, a parameter stands for a value which the calling
program provides to the subprogram. The direction in which the
value is passed is called the mode of the parameter, and is
written **in, out,** or **in out.** Mode **in** is implied if none is stated
explicitly: the calling program passes a value **in** to the procedure
parameter. For a parameter of mode **in,** the corresponding call

must provide a value (of the correct type) which is given as an expression, including a variable or a constant. For a parameter of mode in out, the value is passed in at the beginning, and out at the end of the subprogram. The mode out means that the procedure passes a value out to the parameter (but does not use its previous value).

For a parameter of mode out or in out, the corresponding call must provide a variable (of the correct type) which may be a simple variable or a component of a record or array.

In the specification:

procedure CHECK_VAL (READING : **in** INTEGER;
                        OK : **out** BOOLEAN);

there are two (formal) parameters: READING bringing a value in to the procedure, of type INTEGER and no default value; and OK taking a value out of the procedure, of type BOOLEAN. Note that the parameters are preferably written on separate lines; this makes no difference to the meaning, but is easier to read.

e. Parameter association

The values and variables given as actual parameters when a subprogram is called must match those specified. The correspondence between the actual parameters given and the formal parameters required may be established either by the order in which they are written or by using the formal parameter names. For association by position, the first actual parameter given corresponds to the first formal parameter required and so on. For association by name, the actual parameter is given with the name of the formal parameter it matches, with different parameters given in any order. See section 5.3 for examples.

f. Default parameters

A subprogram can be specified with defaultable parameters. A subprogram call need not then give the corresponding actual parameter, and the default from the specification will be used. Thus the specification

procedure PRINT_LINES(FILE : IN_FILE ;
                        START_LINE : NATURAL :=1);

has a default value of 1 for the START_LINE parameter. It may be called with or without that parameter:

```
PRINT_LINES(MY_FILE, 100);
PRINT_LINES(HELP_FILE);        -- default value 1 for START_LINE
```

The latter is exactly equivalent to

```
PRINT_LINES(HELP_FILE, 1);
```

The default value may be an expression, which is evaluated when the subprogram specification is met in the program. Defaults may only be used with **in** mode parameters.

g. Result

A subprogram can calculate a value for use in an expression. Such a subprogram is a function. The specification

function SIN(X : ANGLE) **return** FLOAT;

shows that the subprogram produces a result of type FLOAT.

function GRID_COUNT (RADIUS : FLOAT) **return** NATURAL;

returns a count (subtype NATURAL), which might be the number of grid points within a given radius of the origin.

A function may be called during evaluation of an expression, where a value of the appropriate type is required.

```
ACROSS := R * SIN(PHI);
```

and

```
if ASK("NEED HELP?") then
   PRINT_HELP_FILE;
end if;
```

h. Overloading

In Ada, there can be several subprograms with the same name which are distinguished by the properties of their parameters. Using the same name for distinct meanings in the same context is called overloading. This is useful when substantially the same action can be applied to objects of different types. Thus it is necessary to be able to output data of different types using the same output procedure name. The types may be CHARACTER, STRING, BOOLEAN, INTEGER etc, but the output procedure is always PUT.

While the detail of what must be done (e.g. conversion from
internal representation) may be different, the user writes PUT (X)
whichever the type of X (after a suitable package declaration –
see section 11.5). Actually however, there are several distinct
procedure declarations to cover the different cases, such as

```
procedure PUT ( ITEM : in CHARACTER );
procedure PUT ( ITEM : in STRING );
procedure PUT ( ITEM : in NUM );
procedure PUT ( ITEM : in ENUM );
```

(The last two have further parameters in their full forms, but
that is not relevant here.) The choice of the procedure called is
made by the compiler, based on type matching. There is no
overhead at run-time to select the correct procedure.

The properties of the parameters which distinguish different
subprograms with the same name are their order and (base) types,
together with the (base) type of the result, if any. (The base
type here means that any constraints in the stated type or subtype
are disregarded.) All of this information, together with the
subprogram name, is known as its parameter type profile, or
signature. Note that parameters with default values are included
in the profile, but not the values themselves. This makes it
difficult to use overloaded subprograms that are resolved by
default parameters.

The same principles apply to procedures, entries, enumeration
literals, functions and operators. In the case of operators, the
existing operator symbols (+, *, <=, not etc.) can be overloaded
to apply to other types, for example:

```
function "*" (X : MATRIX; Y : COL_VEC) return COL_VEC is
  C : COL_VEC;
  XY : FLOAT;
begin
  for I in COL_VEC'FIRST .. COL_VEC'LAST loop
    XY := 0.0;
    for J in COL_VEC'FIRST .. COL_VEC'LAST loop
      XY := XY + X(I, J) * Y(J);
    end loop;
    C(I) := XY;
  end loop;
  return C;
end "*";
```

The action of an overloaded operator should be of the same kind as the ordinary meaning of the operator. It is the programmer's responsibility to ensure this: remember that the subsequent reader of the program will assume ordinary properties (associativity, commutativity) when he sees an operator.

.2   Subprogram bodies

he body of a subprogram gives the details of what is to be done henever the subprogram is called. The body begins with the pecification of the subprogram; it may then have local declarations introducing entities which are valid for the subprogram body but owhere else in the program). The main part consists of a **begin** block hich gives the sequence of statements to be executed, and optionally an xception handler.

Here is a subprogram body (with a prefix that gives its context for eparate compilation):

```
with FILTER_OPERATIONS; use FILTER_OPERATIONS;
procedure CLEAN_FILTER is

begin
   CHANGE_TO_CLEANING;
   WATER_FLUSH(1);
   AIR_FLUSH;
   WATER_FLUSH(2);
   DRAIN_SUMP;
   CHANGE_TO_NORMAL;
end CLEAN_FILTER;
```

ere is another subprogram body:

```
function ASK(QUESTION : STRING) return BOOLEAN is
    -- output message QUESTION and check for Y/N reply
  REPLY : CHARACTER;
begin
  loop
    PUT(QUESTION);
    GET(REPLY);
    SKIP_LINE;
    if REPLY = 'Y' then
      return TRUE;
    else if REPLY = 'N' then
      return FALSE;
    else
      PUT("Please reply Y or N");
    end if;
  end loop;
end ASK;
```

This has a local variable REPLY which is used in the body, and a series
of statements to be executed according to the normal rules until a
return statement is reached; **return** marks the logical end of execution
of the subprogram (see section 4.7.2). When the specification includes
a **return** part, the statement gives the particular value to be delivered
as the result of the function. In the above example the values returned
are constants but in general they could be any expressions of the
specified type. For example

```
function STRAIGHT (HERE : POSITION;
                   D : LENGTH)
                 return POSITION is
begin
  return POSITION'
    (NORTH => HERE.NORTH + D * COS (HERE.HEADING),
     EAST => HERE.EAST + D * SIN (HERE.HEADING),
     HEADING => HERE.HEADING);
end STRAIGHT;
```

This calculates a new position on a straight course.

A subprogram body is very similar to a block (see section 4.6),
except that it starts with the specification instead of the word
declare. After the specification there may be local declarations, and
there always is an executable part introduced by the word **begin** which
may be defended by exception handlers.

The declarations may be of any kind, including subprograms and other
program units. However, since the program tends to be difficult to see

clearly if too much text is included here, it is preferable to declare
bodies of inner units as **separate** (see chapter 10), unless they are very
small.

The formal parameters in the specification, together with the local
declarations, establish entities for the subprogram body. Formal
parameters have the force of object declarations with the specified type
or subtype; those with mode in or in out are effectively initialised to
the value of the corresponding actual parameter or default value (and
those with mode out have no significant value initially). Parameters
with mode in out or out have significant final values - the value of the
parameter at the end of the subprogram is assigned to the variable in
the caller stated as the corresponding actual parameter.

Within the executable part of the subprogram body, the main sequence
of statements expresses how the action of the subprogram is to be
carried out.

For a function, the specification contains a **return** part, and the
statements in the body must include a **return** statement with an
expression of the type specified, to define the result of the
subprogram. For a procedure, the specification does not contain a
return part, but a **return** statement may be used (without an expression)
to mark the end of execution of the body.

A subprogram body occurs either in the declarative part of some
larger program unit or on its own as a separate compilation unit (see
chapter 10). If it is in a declarative part of a subprogram or block,
the specification given with the body is usually sufficient and does not
have to be repeated. However, there are two cases where a specification
must be given by itself early in the declarative part, and also again
with the body late in the declarative part. The cases are

    a.   When two or more subprograms include calls of one another: a
         specification must be given before any call of the subprogram.

    b.   When a subprogram is defined as part of a package (see section
         7.3): the specification must be given in the visible part of the
         package.

Other than these two case, it is sufficient to give the specification
at the beginning of the body of a subprogram.

5.3   Subprogram calls

The action that a subprogram carries out may depend on parameters which
are provided for each call : thus at different places in the program the
action may be carried out using different values or variables. On each
call of a subprogram, the right kinds of parameters must be used – for
example, if the procedure expects to receive a value of a particular
type, then the call must provide a value of that type.

Essentially the subprogram call must specify information to match the
parameters in the specification. Every parameter has a name, mode, type,
and possible default value.

The actual parameters to be used in a subprogram call are given
either in the proper order, or with the proper names, as stated in the
subprogram specification, or in a mixed form (starting in order, then
using names).

In the context of the specifications in section 5.1, a procedure call

CHECK_VAL (5, IS_CLEARED);

would be executed with the value 5 matching the first parameter
(READING), and the variable IS_CLEARED matching the second parameter
(OK). The actual parameters are in the same order as in the
specification, so names are not necessary. If a procedure has many
parameters, it is clearer to use the names for the parameters
(particularly if there is a sequence of parameters of the same type). We
could express the same call as

CHECK_VAL (READING => 5, OK => IS_CLEARED);

or

CHECK_VAL (OK => IS_CLEARED, READING => 5);

Notice that the linking symbol => is used to associate the formal
parameter name with the required value or variable, like the notation
for an aggregate. The mode indicates the direction the data value
passes between the procedure call statement and the corresponding
procedure body: in, out or both.

If the mode is in, the parameters in the procedure call statement
must give a value of the right type. If the mode is out, the parameter

must be a variable capable of receiving a value of the stated type.   If
the mode is **in out**, the parameter must be a variable and its existing
value may be used by the procedure.

If the procedure specification includes a default value for an **in**
parameter,   then   there   is   no   need for the procedure call to give any
corresponding actual parameter. Consequently the number of actual
parameters may be less than the number of formal parameters, and if any
subsequent parameters are needed they must be identified by their names.
For example,

   procedure ADVANCE (C: **in** INTEGER **range** 1 .. 99;
                       D: **in** INTEGER := 0);

can be called with one or two parameters:

   ADVANCE (5);

calls the procedure with value 5 for C and the default value 0 for D.

   ADVANCE (7,2);

calls it with 7 for C and 2 for D, as also does

   ADVANCE (D => 2, C => 7);

The values for an **in** parameter may of course be given as an expression
of any complexity, and an **out** or **in out** parameter may similarly be a
variable of any complexity (such as a record or array).

   ADVANCE (MAX_SIZE - L1);
   CHECK_VAL (J - K, GRID (J,K));

Since a variable is a particular case of an expression, it may be used
for any mode of parameter - but the difference in context is important,
and the mode determines whether the original value of the variable may
be used in the procedure body, a new value may be assigned to it, or
both. The following table shows the relationship:

   mode   -- effect with variable

   in   -- used
   out   -- assigned
   in out   -- used and assigned

There is no difference in meaning between giving the parameters by position or by name: it is simply a matter of convenience in writing and reading. If there are many parameters, say more than five, it would probably be preferable to use names, to emphasise their distinctiveness, particularly if many of them could take the same value. It is permitted to use name parameters with functions but not with operators; however, this is not likely to be common or as useful.

Exercises

1. Write the specification for a procedure called SA, with two parameters, of types CAMAC_ADDRESS and F_OP1 respectively.

2. Write the body for a procedure READLN which inputs characters up to the next LF character.

3. Write a sequence of statements to operate the valves AIR_INLET and DIRTY_WATER, with an interval of at least 5 seconds between them, then after a further 2 seconds check both values, using the procedure MOVE_VALVE (V : VALVE); and procedure CHECK_VALVE (V : VALVE);

4. Write the specification for a procedure to carry out the processing in section 4.3.1. example 4, using TODAY as a parameter.

5. Write a call of procedure TEXT_IO.SET_LINE_LENGTH with the FILE parameter being the variable F1 and the N parameter having the value 80.

CHAPTER 6

Exceptions

Ada is designed to permit defensive, or fault-tolerant programming. This is in contrast with traditional styles of programming, in which there is an implicit assumption that everything is correct - the program, the translator, and the computer hardware (with only some concessionary provision for faults in peripherals or operator behaviour).

Notwithstanding the emphasis on verification and testing of Ada programs, it must be acknowledged that there will be occasions when unexpected situations arise and the system must be programmed to deal with them in whatever way is best in order to allow normal operation to continue. Such situations are called exceptions; in general they indicate conditions not intended to arise, which make further normal processing impossible.

Any action might fail. To keep a real-time system in continuous operation, the designer must be able to specify a recovery action to be taken as the effective replacement for the remainder of the action which was not successfully completed. This is a form of software redundancy.

There are a number of exceptions predefined in Ada, for situations which are logically possible in the language. For example, with an array, the expression given for an index may have a value out of bounds: IMAGE (I + J) might have I + J not in range 1 .. MAX_SIZE, in which case there is no such component of the array. The language-defined exceptions are explained in section 6.6 below. In addition to the predefined exceptions, any number of further exceptions may be declared, for particular exceptional situations relevant to the program. Programmer-declared exceptions are explained in section 6.1.

The action of indicating that there is an exceptional situation is called raising the exception. Some constructs in a program may

65

implicitly raise an exception (IMAGE (I + J) is an example); the program may also contain explicit statements to raise exceptions.

For each exception, whether predefined or explicitly declared in the program, the programmer may declare handlers to carry out whatever recovery action is necessary and then to resume the normal sequence of execution of the program. The place in the program where normal execution is resumed depends on the position of the corresponding exception handler - the handler always comes at the end of a block and completion of the handler has the same effect as normal completion of the block.

Exceptions are dealt with according to the dynamic block structure of a program. As each statement is executed, it may involve the execution of statements elsewhere in the program (by subprogram calls); in this sense all the blocks of a program are dynamically nested during execution. When an exception arises, the dynamic block structure is "unwound" in the course of recovery and resumption of normal processing, from the smallest block enclosing the offending statement to the first dynamically enclosing block containing a handler for the relevant exception.

In this chapter we explain exceptions in sequential programs. (There are some special properties of exceptions in the context of tasks, which are discussed in chapter 13).

6.1   Declaring exceptions

Each exception is denoted by an identifier, which must be introduced by a suitable declaration:

    STICKY_VALVE : **exception**;
    BAD_PARAMETER : **exception**;
    TAPE_DRIVE_FAULTY, BAD_TAPE_BLOCK : **exception**;

A number of identifiers may be introduced in the one declaration; this has no special significance - they are all introduced as exception names. As with all declarations, the identifiers so introduced apply throughout the current context: they may be used in the subsequent declarations and executable statements. Exception declarations may occur in the visible part of a package specification (where most kinds of declaration are allowed), but since they are not data objects they may not occur as procedure parameters.

A local name may be introduced for an existing exception, thus

TRANSFORM_ERROR : **exception renames**
         TRANSFORM_PACKAGE.MATRIX_SINGULAR;

This presumes that there is a package called TRANSFORM_PACKAGE which contains the declaration of MATRIX_SINGULAR, and introduces the name TRANSFORM_ERROR locally for it. Renaming does not hide the old name for an exception, but can be used to introduce a suitable local name.

The predefined exceptions of Ada are listed in section 6.6. The situations they refer to are programming faults that cannot generally be detected at compile-time. The identifiers introduced there are automatically available in any compilation unit. In contrast, any identifiers introduced by the programmer are available in other compilation units only if they have a suitable **with** clause (see chapter 9). Apart from this difference relating to visibility, there is no difference between the predefined and user-defined exceptions.

6.2   Raising exceptions

An exception, whether predefined or user-defined, may be raised anywhere in the scope of its declaration by a **raise** statement (see section 4.7.3). For example, in the procedure which changes a valve setting and checks that it has moved, if the program detects that the value has not reached the proper position in a reasonable time it could execute

   raise STICKY_VALVE;

which would indicate the failure to the rest of the program. This would normally occur in some conditional part of the program, for the case when the exceptional condition has been detected. There may of course be any number of **raise** statements for any exception. Within an exception handler, the raise statement can be given without an exception name, thus

   raise;

The effect of this statement is to reraise the exception which caused the handler to be entered (even if that exception cannot be named). It implies a further raise of the exception which is currently being handled. This technique allows a particular part of the program to give a specified partial handler for an exception, which is executed first, before passing on to a general handler for it.

A predefined exception is raised implicitly if the corresponding fault is detected in the program. An exception, whether predefined or user-defined, may also be raised implicitly by a call of a subprogram (procedure, function or operation). This happens if an exception arises during execution of the subprogram body and there is no handler for it within the subprogram. (The exception is then said to be propagated: see section 6.4).

Although exceptions can only be explicitly raised in the scope of their declarations, the implicit raising of exceptions can occur in situations outside that scope, as a result of propagation.

Whenever an exception is raised, the current block is executed no further, and a handler is executed instead.

6.3   Handling exceptions

A handler for an exception, to carry out the specific recovery action after it has arisen and before normal processing can continue, may be written in any block in the scope of the declaration for the exception. Exception handlers are always written at the end of a block: the word **exception** is put after the last normally executable statement, and introduces the exception part of the block. This consists of a series of handlers, written like alternatives in a **case** statement, with exception names as the selectors. There can be several handlers for one exception, in different blocks.

Each particular handler is introduced by a **when** clause giving the relevant exception name (possibly several exception names if the same recovery action is to serve for more than one exception), then after the => sign, a sequence of statements forming the body of the handler.

Elsewhere in the program containing STICKY_VALVE, where it calculates the required valve setting and calls the procedure to make the change, there could be

```
exception
when STICKY_VALVE =>
    -- statements to warn operator
    -- log fault
    -- and change parameters
    -- for related valves
end;
```

The last handler in a block may be introduced by **when others**, in which case it applies to any exception detected in the block which is not named in the previous handlers - including any exception which cannot be named in the current context.

For example, suppose we had an undefended **declare** statement,

```
declare
  A : FLOAT;
begin
  A := X * X;
  Y := A * EXP(A);
end;
```

and we wish to defend it against the possible exception NUMERIC_ERROR (which could occur implicitly during either * operation or the EXP function). We can add an exception part in which Y is given the largest floating-point value if this situation is detected:

```
declare
  A : FLOAT;
begin
  A := X * X;
  Y := A * EXP(A);
exception
  when NUMERIC_ERROR =>
    Y := FLOAT'LAST;
end;
```

The sequence of statements in a handler may be any statements allowed in the current block. In particular, if the block forms the body of a subprogram, the statements may refer to the parameters of the subprogram, and would normally contain a **return** statement. Further, if the subprogram returns a value (as in a function or operator) then each handler should finish with a **return** statement giving a value of the correct type. If an exception arises during execution of an exception handler, the action is as though the exception had arisen in the associated main block without the current handler.

While the several handlers in the exception part of a single block must of course refer to distinct exceptions, it is possible for there to be different handlers for the same exception in different blocks (whether disjoint or nested). This allows the programmer to adapt the recovery action to the broad context in which each exception may arise. In this case, the handler which is used on each occasion is that of the smallest block which dynamically encloses the statement being executed

when the exception is raised. Depending on the position at which the
programmer puts the handler, the recovery action would be small-scale or
large-scale: on completion of the statements in the handler, the whole
of that program unit is deemed to be complete, and normal processing
continues.

Thus a handler may contain statements for dealing locally with an
exception, and either permit normal processing to continue from the end
of the current block, or call for further handling in the dynamically
enclosing block, for the same exception name by

raise;

or a named exception BAD_PARAMETER by

raise BAD_PARAMETER;

6.4   Propagating exceptions

Whenever an exception arises, whether it is a user-defined exception,
the subject of a **raise** statement, or one of the predefined exceptions,
the normal course of execution of the program ceases and a handler is
sought for the exception: one with the exception name in its **when**
clause, or one introduced by **when others.** As soon as a matching handler
is found, its sequence of statements is executed instead of the
remainder of the block containing it.

In the first instance a matching handler is sought in the block
currently being executed. If there is none (particularly if the block
has no exception part), or if the handler itself detects an exception,
then the exception is raised implicitly in the dynamically enclosing
block. This is called propagating the exception. If the handler raises
another exception (by an explicit raise statement or any statement which
implicitly raises an exception) then this exception is propagated to the
dynamically enclosing block.

Propagation is automatic through a compound statement to the
enclosing sequence of statements (i.e. from part of an **if, case, loop,
accept, select** statement or block to the sequence of which that
statement is part). In the case of propagation through an **accept**
statement, an exception is also raised in the associated task (see
chapter 10). This continues through nested statements until a matching
handler is found or the sequence of statements is that of a main program
or task.

The application of the general rule on propagation leads to the ollowing cases, where the effect may not be immediately obvious. If he exception arises (directly or by propagation) in the sequence of tatements which form a subprogram body, then the dynamically enclosing lock is that containing the current call of that subprogram – either a rocedure call statement or a function call or operator call in an xpression. Note that the possibility of exceptions in the evaluation of n expression means that the exception could arise when dealing with the eclarations of a block (from the calculation of a default value or an nitial value which turns out to be impossible for the declared object).

If an exception arises in a declaration, it is propagated back from he block containing the declaration to the statement or declaration hat called it, until a statement is reached; a handler is then sought n the block containing that statement.

If the exception arises in the initialisation part of a package (and here is no local handler), then the unhandled exception is considered o have arisen in the package declaration, so is propagated to the nclosing block. If the package is a separately compiled library unit, his prevents execution of the whole program: the initialisation cannot e carried out. If the package is a subunit, then the exception is ropagated to the unit containing the corresponding stub

package body P **is separate;**

rom which it is propagated as from a declaration.

If the exception arises (directly or by propagation) in the sequence f statements which are the substance of an **accept** statement, then in ddition to propagating the exception to the block of which the **accept** tatement is part, an exception is also raised in the task which is urrently in rendezvous through the corresponding **entry** declaration. his is at the point of the statement in the task which calls the entry.

If the exception arises in the body of a task, then an unhandled xception is not propagated: it is deemed to be **null.** The task is erminated and no further action taken.

There is inevitably a certain amount of overhead associated with xception handling, particularly to propagate an exception. The aim in da is to have no overhead in normal execution (in particular no verhead on entering a program unit containing exception handlers) but o tolerate some overhead after an exception has arisen. This ensures hat performance is only lost when it is necessary to achieve safety.

6.5   How to use exceptions

A simple use of exceptions is to check for consistency as the progra
runs, by the use of assertions.

   As the actions of a program are carried out, the state of the syste
changes; however relationships between variables in the system may hav
to remain true while their individual values change. A useful way o
checking that the program is running correctly is to test suc
relationships at appropriate stages. This can be done by declaring:

```
   ASSERT_ERROR : exception;
   procedure ASSERT (CONDITION: BOOLEAN) is
   begin
      if not CONDITION then
        raise ASSERT_ERROR;
      end if;
   end ASSERT;
```

An assertion gives a condition which is supposed to apply at that poin
in execution.

   ASSERT (AREA > 0);

   ASSERT (X * Y < Z);

The decision on placing assertions in a program is an essential part o
the program design, as it involves consideration of the trade-of
between the risk and the time taken to carry out the run-time check.

   The most common places for assertions are on entry to subprograms, t
check that the values provided for in parameters are suitable, o
completion of loops, and after a set of alternatives (to stat
properties which should now hold). If the assertion is found durin
execution to be false, the sequence of statements containing it is no
executed further, and the exception ASSERT_ERROR is raised. Assertion
may also be useful on exit from a procedure, to confirm that the result
satisfy required relationships.

   Exceptions allow you to program for survival after a catastrophe
The general technique for making programs fault-tolerant (with respec
to faults in both the control software itself and the devices which i
controls) can be summarised thus:

   a. At each stage in the design process, consider that any action
       might fail; assess the seriousness of such a failure. Identify

the conditions which could prevent completion of a significant action.

b. Review methods of protective redundancy which would allow the system to recover to a normal condition after a fault. Choose alternative actions within appropriate cost and performance constraints.

c. Identify what tests are needed to detect the fault. Write **raise** statements within the chosen tests.

s with assertions, the difficult balance is that between the cost of requent testing for faults, and the risk of damage because of onsequences from a fault before it is detected. One way is to work ackwards from each output action, and put a positive check as early as ossible before it. A recovery action may be to retry the action during hich the fault was detected (hoping it was transient), to carry out a ess satisfactory but nevertheless acceptable substitute, or to report he trouble and call for outside help.

This approach leads to a program in which there can be recoverable rocedure bodies, such that alongside the ordinary procedure body there s a recovery section, activated on detection of an appropriate fault uring execution of the ordinary body. The recovery section might be ntered at any stage while executing the body (not necessarily between ctions), and must bring the whole action to a well defined finish.

It is a good practice to plan a program so that the exception andlers can cope with a situation which might have been detected at any ime within the defended block. Remember that the raising of the xception indicates only the symptom, not the cause, of the trouble.

Remember also that the exception handler for **others** will catch any xception not explicitly mentioned in the current exception part; as a onsequence it can be entered in obscure circumstances. It should only e used for the most extreme cases, and make minimal assumptions about he state of the system on entry.

.6   Predefined exceptions

ertain exceptional situations can arise during the execution of the Ada rimitives in a program. These are treated as though an exception defined in the language) occurred in a lower level, which is propagated o the surrounding program unit. The situations and corresponding anguage-defined exceptions are as follows (see Appendix A).

CONSTRAINT_ERROR -- The current value is inconsistent with th current requirement. This exception is raised whenever an expression i evaluated with a value out of range for its context (RANGE_CHECK), a array component is referenced with an index value out of rang (INDEX_CHECK), an array operation is attempted with incompatible array (LENGTH_CHECK), a record component is referenced with a field selecto for the wrong variant (DISCRIMINANT_CHECK), an access type object i referenced with an access value of **null** (ACCESS_CHECK), or simila situations (for example when matching subprogram parameters).

NUMERIC_ERROR -- The mathematical result of a predefined numeri operation is not within the implemented range. This exception is raise if the result of a calculation is too large (OVERFLOW_CHECK) o mathematically infinite (DIVISION_CHECK). The actual limits fo detecting this situation depend on the implementation, and there is n guarantee that the exception will be raised anyway. (The attribut MACHINE_OVERFLOWS indicates whether it will.)

PROGRAM_ERROR -- Execution is blocked. This exception is raised i the program tries to execute something not yet in existenc (ELABORATION_CHECK) perhaps because of the wrong ordering o declarations, or meets a select statement (see section 13.3.4) with al its arms inhibited, and no **else** part. Such a statement can neve complete its execution.

STORAGE_ERROR -- Storage is needed which cannot be provided. Thi exception is raised if the program requires more storage space than i available (STORAGE_CHECK) when elaborating the declarations in subprogram, or by execution of an allocator or use of dynamic storage i a task.

TASKING_ERROR -- Communication with the required task cannot occur This exception is raised if an entry call is being executed, and th task containing the corresponding accept statement is terminated befor it can accept the entry.

Some of these exceptions require run-time checks to detect th situation, which the programmer may wish to suppress. The pragr SUPPRESS is provided for this purpose, identifying one of the abov checks and a list of names of entities for which the check is not to b made. (This is not to imply that the corresponding condition will n arise; but if it does, the effect is unpredictable.)

Exercises

. Given

```
subtype SHORT is range 1..5;
function PEX(I : NATURAL) return SHORT is
  S : SHORT := I;
begin
  return 6 - S;
end;
```

check that PEX(4) returns the value 2 and PEX(7) raises an
exception. (Note that the exception would have been raised slightly
differently if S had been declared of type NATURAL). Modify the
body of PEX to defend it against the possibility of a parameter
value outside the range for which 6 - I is of subtype SHORT, so that
it raises the exception BAD_PARAMETER in that case.

. Write a procedure to read an item from a table, given a key, using
an inner call (EXAMINE) that provides an **out** parameter to indicate
whether the keyed item is present; make the procedure raise an
exception if the requested item does not exist in the table.

CHAPTER 7

Packages

The facilities described in the previous chapters allow you to write a
simple program in Ada, relying on a previously written library to
provide all the further information needed. For a program of any
complexity (more than 50 statements, say) you need to be able to split
it into manageable units which can be individually designed and checked.
Most programming languages allow you to write subprograms, which have
been described for Ada in chapter 5, as program units for describing
actions.   This chapter deals with packages, which are the second of the
three kinds of program unit in Ada. (The third kind of program unit, a
task, is explained in chapter 8).

    A program in Ada is written as a number of logical pieces, each of
which covers one aspect of the problem. A package is the general form of
one such logical piece; it defines a set of facilities which the rest of
the program may use. These might either be specially designed for the
program currently being written, or already in existence because a
similar problem has arisen previously. The fundamental idea is to
separate the use of a facility from its provision.   In this way a
program can be arranged to show what is meant to happen without a
clutter of detailed implementation.

7.1   Packages of data

Several parts of the program may need to refer to the same common data.
The declarations for these variables and constants logically belong
together, and such a collection is one form of a package. Any part of
the program that needs to refer to this data can then do so, without
having to repeat all the declarations.

76

Thus we may have a collection of objects associated with a graphical
splay:

```
package VIEW_POINT is
    XP, YP, ZP: FLOAT;  -- viewer position
    XC, YC, ZC: FLOAT;  -- centre of view
    FIELD : FLOAT;      -- field of vision
    AXES : BOOLEAN;     -- whether axes wanted
end VIEW_POINT;
```

id this specifies a package. The objects may be constants or variables,
id they can be given initial values if needed. Elsewhere in the
`ogram (wherever the declaration of this package is visible), the
>jects in the package may be referred to, by names such as

VIEW_POINT.XP
VIEW_POINT.AXES

>r in a shorter notation explained below). The entities in the
ickage may be used in any way consistent with their declaration: in
iis case, as variables, either to be assigned new values or to have
ieir current values used. Here are some more package declarations
ictually derived from a program in another language : see appendix C).

```
package STORE is
    SCALE  : FLOAT;
    K      : INTEGER;
    JUMP   : INTEGER := 11;
    A      : FLOAT;
    SM     : FLOAT;
    INPUT  : INTEGER;
    IFM    : INTEGER;
    ALAT   : FLOAT;
    ALONG  : FLOAT;
    EORW   : CHARACTER;  -- not INTEGER
    NORS   : CHARACTER;  -- not INTEGER
    CHANGE : BOOLEAN := FALSE;
    FRACT  : BOOLEAN := FALSE;
    SIG    : BOOLEAN := FALSE;
    VAL    : BOOLEAN;
    LEG    : BOOLEAN;
end STORE;

package NSEW is
    N      : CHARACTER := 'N';
    S      : CHARACTER := 'S';
    E      : CHARACTER := 'E';
```

```
    W       : CHARACTER := 'W';
  end NSEW;

  package UNHIO is
    KIN    : constant INTEGER := 1;
    KOUT   : constant INTEGER := 3;
    K7     : constant INTEGER := 7;
    K8     : constant INTEGER := 8;
    ISCR1  : constant INTEGER := 21;
    ISCR2  : constant INTEGER := 22;
    ISCR3  : constant INTEGER := 23;
    ISCR4  : constant INTEGER := 24;
  end UNHIO;

  package BTP is
    BIGTHT : FLOAT;
    BIGPHI : FLOAT;
  end BTP;

  package RFUNC is
    CSP    : FLOAT;
    TSP    : FLOAT;
    SP     : FLOAT;
  end RFUNC;

  package FORMAT
    FMT    : STRING := "(2(F9.0,A1),T1,F5.0)";
  end FORMAT;
```

A package may be given among the declarations within the program (where
it applies like other declarations), or compiled separately as a library
unit (see chapter 10). In the latter case, any other compilation unit
may refer to the library unit by giving its name in a context clause
written:

    with STORE;

prefixed to the heading of the unit using STORE, within which the
entities may be named as

    STORE.SCALE
    STORE.LEG

Note that it is not necessary to repeat the contents of the package.

    A shorthand notation is available for referring to entities in
package without prefixing the package name, if no confusion can arise

he declaration

   use STORE;

ay be used wherever the package STORE is visible, and allows the names
ithin STORE to be used directly unless an identical name is already
isible or is made visible similarly from another package.   (Remember
hat the names in one package need not be all different from those in
nother: they might have been written by different people.) Thus by
riting

   with STORE; **use** STORE;

he objects in the package may be referred to by their simple names

   SCALE
   LEG

provided that the names are not otherwise used in this context.) If it
appens that these names are in use already, or are repeated in
ifferent packages, the **use** declaration is ineffective and the longhand
ame must be written.

.2   Packages with defined types

   A package is also a good way to connect the definition of an
pplication-dependent type with the objects of that type which the
rogram can use, for example

   package VALVE_DETAILS **is**
      type VALVE **is** (WATER_INLET,
         AIR_INLET, FLUSH_WATER, AIR_EXHAUST, SUMP_WATER,
         CLEAN_WATER, DIRTY_WATER);
      type VALVE_STATUS **is** (OPEN, CLOSED);
      type VALVE_PARAMETERS **is record**
           TRANSITION : DURATION;
           CONDITION : VALVE_STATUS;
           CONTROL : NATURAL;
         end record;
      CONTROL_VALVE : **array** (VALVE)
         of VALVE_PARAMETERS;
   end VALVE_DETAILS;

The rules for using this package are exactly as described in section
7.1. We can use the types and objects declared here in ordinary
declarations and statements, with names formed as explained above. For
example we can if necessary declare as working variables other objects
of type VALVE_DETAILS.VALVE or VALVE_DETAILS.VALVE_STATUS . In another
program unit starting

with VALVE_DETAILS;

we could refer to these either using their full names or by putting

use VALVE_DETAILS;

and the simple identifiers. Thus we could declare

SUSPECT_VALVE : VALVE;

and have statements like

SUSPECT_VALVE := AIR_INLET;

CONTROL_VALVE(FLUSH_WATER).CONDITION := OPEN;

to manipulate and use the packaged objects.

7.3   Packages with subprograms

We frequently have a set of subprograms which are closely associated
there might also be some data or special types which they use. In this
case the package is written in two pieces - a specification and a body
The purpose of this is to show clearly what information the user of the
package needs to know, without burdening him with implementation detail
that may be irrelevant. The specifications of the subprograms give all
the information needed to call them (explained in sections 5.1 and 5.3)
The package body contains all the corresponding subprogram bodies. We
could for example declare another package :

```
with VALVE_DETAILS;  use VALVE_DETAILS;
package VALVE_MOVEMENT is
   procedure MOVE_VALVE(V : VALVE);
   procedure CHECK_VALVE (V : VALVE);
   procedure MOVE_AND_CHECK_VALVE (V : VALVE);
end VALVE_MOVEMENT;
```

. programmer can then write another part of the program, headed by

with VALVE_DETAILS, VALVE_MOVEMENT ;

o refer to the types and objects in package VALVE_DETAILS and the
rocedures in VALVE_MOVEMENT. Using full names we might have

VALVE_MOVEMENT.MOVE_VALVE (SUSPECT_VALVE);
    -- call with full procedure name

r in the shorthand notation,

use VALVE_DETAILS, VALVE_MOVEMENT;

ollowed by statements such as

MOVE_VALVE(SUSPECT_VALVE);

y defining the procedures with parameters of the type VALVE, the
rogrammer has arranged that they can only be used with properly
eclared objects. For any package containing subprograms, there must be
 package body (see section 7.6).

.4   Packages with private types

here are some circumstances when we have a special type for the
roblem, and subprograms to work with values of that type, and we want a
eans of ensuring that no other operations can be applied to the
orresponding objects. This might be for example with control blocks
ere some internal checks or private details are stored on behalf of
he user. Such types are called private data types, and are discussed
irther in section 12.4.

In this case we have the package specification and package body as in
ection 7.3, but the package specification is itself split, into a
isible part and a private part. The purpose is again to show clearly
he information needed by the user of the package; the visible part
ontains the declaration of the special type and the subprogram
pecifications, while the private part gives details of the type and
lues for any constants needed, together with any representation
pecifications (see section 11.6). Several private types may be
eclared in the same package.

package PDP_11_INTERRUPT_CONTROL **is**
   type CSR **is private**;

```
    procedure ENABLE(DEVICE : CSR);
    procedure DISABLE (DEVICE : CSR);
private
    type CSR is array(0..15) of BOOLEAN;
    pragma PACK (CSR);
end PDP_11_INTERRUPT_CONTROL;
```

This introduces a special type, so that in another part of the program suitable objects can be declared. For example, after with and use clauses for PDP_11_INTERRUPT_CONTROL,

    LA36 : CSR;

introduces an object of this private type, for which the possible operations are

    ENABLE(LA36);

and

    DISABLE(LA36);

Values of a private type can be assigned and compared with one another but none of their internal details can be used outside the package body unless the package provides subprograms to do so.

Sometimes the values of the special type must be kept unique, so that at most one object has any given value (such as a file control block). We can prevent assignments between objects of the type by declaring

    type FILE_CONTROL_BLOCK **is limited private;**

The word **limited** in this declaration makes any objects of the given type eligible only for use as parameters to subprograms which work with that type.

7.5   Reference to packaged entities

The entities declared in any package can be used elsewhere in the program after they have been declared, as determined by the following rules:

    a. If the package specification is in the declarative part of some
        program unit, then its scope extends throughout that program

unit, after the specification.   (If the package needs   a   body,
then   that   or   the   stub   must   also be in the same declarative
part.)

b. If the package specification is separately compiled   as   a   main
unit,   then   its   scope extends over all other compilation units
that specify the package name   in   their   context   clause   (i.e.
state that they must be compiled **with** the given package): e.g.

with VIEW_POINT;

The entities declared in the package can be used in ordinary   statements
and declarations, with names like components of a record:

```
VIEW_POINT.XP := 100.0;
if VIEW_POINT.AXES then
    DRAW_AXES;
end if;
```

This notation is used for packaged objects and anything else declared
in   a   package.   There   is   a short-hand notation to allow the names of
packaged entities to be given more briefly.   You may put

use STORE, UNHIO;

before a series of declarations, to open the   context   to   that   of   the
specified   unit   or   units.   Having done so, you may use just the entity
name without the package name as a prefix. You can put   several   package
names   in   a   use-list;   the   corresponding   entity   names   are then all
available.   This short-hand applies only to names that are not   declared
in   more   than   one place among the specified units or local context, in
order to prevent ambiguity.   Further details are given in section 9.4.

.6   Package specification in general

A package specification can occur either among   the   declarations   in   a
program   unit   or   as   a   separate compilation unit (see chapter 10).   It
makes a collection of entities available for other parts of the   program
to use.

The main part of a package specification is its visible   part,   which
gives   the   public information about the entities it contains. A package
specification may also contain   a   private   part,   which   gives   further
details about types and constants. (The private information is needed by

the translator, but not by any programmer using the package).

All kinds of program entity can be declared in a package: constants
variables, types, subprograms, exceptions, tasks and inner packages (fo
more closely associated entities).

If a subprogram in a package may detect an exception which should   b
handled by its caller, the package specification should say so:

package TIMED_VALVE_MOVEMENT **is**
  procedure MOVE_VALVE(V : VALVE);
  VALVE_TIME_OUT : **exception**;
end TIMED_VALVE_MOVEMENT;

As a package is a program unit, it may contain smaller program   unit
and   be   itself contained in a larger program unit, corresponding to th
logical structure of the problem. This can be   seen   in   the   predefine
package definition TEXT_IO (see Appendix A).

7.7   Package bodies in general

A package body is distinct from a package specification;   every   packag
needs   a   specification,   but sometimes a body is not necessary.   If t
package   provides   any   subprogram,   task,   or   inner   package,   the
specifications must be collected in the package specification, and the
corresponding bodies written   in   the   package   body.   If   the   packag
contains   any   variables   whose   initial   values   must   be calculated
executing statements, the initialisation must be written in the   packag
body.

A package body need not occur immediately after its   specification
it   may   even be written as a separate compilation unit (see chapter 10
If several packages are declared in the same declarative part,   all   t
specifications   must   come   first.   Any necessary bodies must be provid
later in the same sequence of declarations,   either   directly   as   sho
below,   or   by providing a "stub" indicating a separate compilation un
(see section 10.4).   This allows each body to refer to entities declar
in   the   other   packages,   without   forward   references.   The body of
package consists of a declarative part and an optional executable par
The   declarative   part contains the bodies of all subprograms specifie
and   also   any   other   declarations   they   need   :   local   variables
procedures,   etc.   Anything   declared   in the body which was not in t
specification part is entirely restricted to the body: it cannot be us
in any other part of the program.

```
package body VALVE_MOVEMENT is

    function SENSE_VALVE(C : NATURAL) return VALVE_STATUS is
    begin
        -- discover status by I/O on channel C
    end SENSE_VALVE;

    procedure EFFECT_VALVE(C : NATURAL, S : VALVE_STATUS) is
    begin
        -- set status by I/O on channel C
    end EFFECT_VALVE;

    procedure MOVE_VALVE(V : VALVE) is
      VP : VALVE_PARAMETERS renames CONTROL_VALVE(V);
      S : VALVE_STATUS;
    begin
      S := SENSE_VALVE(VP.CONTROL);
      if S /= VP.CONDITION then
        EFFECT_VALVE(VP.CONTROL, VP.CONDITION);
      end if;
    end MOVE_VALVE;

    procedure MOVE_AND_CHECK_VALVE(V : VALVE) is
      VP : VALVE_PARAMETERS renames CONTROL_VALVE(V);
    begin
      while SENSE_VALVE(VP.CONTROL) /= VP.CONDITION loop
        EFFECT_VALVE(VP.CONTROL, VP.CONDITION);
        delay VP.TRANSITION;  -- see section 4.9.3.
      end loop;
    end MOVE_AND_CHECK_VALVE;
end VALVE_MOVEMENT;
```

Subprograms in the body may be used to implement tricky aspects of
 te package — without risk of misuse or interference by other parts of
te program.   In the above package body (corresponding to the
ecification in section 7.3), the subprograms SENSE_VALVE and
FECT_VALVE may be used in the rest of the package body but not outside
.   In this way, special or privileged actions may be confined to
stricted sections of the program.   This feature of Ada makes it
ssible to ensure safe use of potentially dangerous facilities, for
ample in library packages.

Variables declared in a package specification or body retain their
lues throughout the lifetime of the package — their values are not
st between calls of subprograms in the package. These are sometimes
lled "own" variables (of the package).   Those in the body are

available for communication between one of the subprograms and another.

The executable part of the package body is executed when the package declaration is elaborated, and is used to initialise objects in the package (whether declared in the specification or the body). The body may also contain exception handlers, in case an exception arises during initialisation; such a handler does not apply after initialisation of the package.

Exercises

1. In the same compilation unit as the packages specified in section 7.1, there is a subsequent program unit which uses ALAT, ALONG, KIN and KOUT. What must be written at head of this unit?

2. Write the package specification for the objects and types concerned with time, tracks and sectors in chapter 2.

3. Specify a package for a collection of procedures SA operating on CAMAC address (consisting of a crate number up to 63, a static number up to 31, and a subaddress up to 15) and a function code (0 to 31); if the function code is less than 8, the procedure produces a data word; if the function code is between 16 and 23 the procedure absorbs a data word.

CHAPTER 8

Parallel Programming

A program for an embedded computer system is usually dealing with many activities that are happening at the same time. An effective way of designing such a program is to identify the several strands of activity, each sequential, that have to be running together. Ada recognises this style of programming, and permits a program to be written as a number of quasi-independent sequences of statements, arranged so that each sequence is executed in its own order, without any prescribed ordering between one sequence and another. These are called tasks.

The several tasks may run on separate processors in a multi-computer system, or in a single processor by sharing its computing time among them, resulting in interleaved execution. Of course, if the program can be run on a single processor then the several tasks could, in principle, be merged into a single sequence of statements, fixing the way the tasks interleave. This does not allow for the variety of timing that may arise in practice, and the resulting program would be obscure, convoluted, and hard to maintain. Writing the program in distinct tasks for the parallel strands is usually more convenient and shows a clearer solution to the problem.

The idea of multi-tasking is of course not unique to Ada, although there are not many high-level languages with multi-tasking facilities. In other languages the parallel strands of activity may be called processes or activities.

It is inherent to Ada that the tasks are expected to cooperate, being aware of one another's existence, and being designed to work with one another to solve an overall problem. If several tasks have to share a resource, they are expected to be programmed to use the resource responsibly; in particular, if any task acquires a resource that other tasks would need, it should release it in a reasonable time. Failure

to do this would be a fault in the program, to be detected and put right
before operational use.

This chapter deals with the basic properties of tasks - how they are
declared, and how they are executed (section 8.1); it also covers the
basic facilities for communication between one task and another, called
a rendezvous (section 8.2). The concept of a rendezvous in Ada is new;
its implication on task structure is discussed in section 8.3, giving
rise to a distinction between active and passive tasks. The few
special facilities for active tasks are described in section 8.4
(leaving passive tasks to Chapter 13). In the final section, we
describe how tasks are used in Ada for dealing with input/output and
interrupt handling (section 8.5).

There are a number of more advanced features of tasks which are
explained in chapter 13.

8.1   Tasks and their relationships

Every task in Ada is written in the declarative part of some enclosing
program unit, which is called its parent. The execution of the parent
determines the overall start and finish of execution of the task. If
several tasks are written in the same declarative part, they are
executed in parallel with one another (and in parallel with the body of
the parent unit). We call these sibling tasks. The parent unit may be
a subprogram, a declare block, a package or another task.

Whenever the parent unit comes to be executed, all the tasks in its
declarative part are started, and each is executed in its own sequential
order, independent of the order of the others (unless there are explicit
statements to relate them). Each task may come to the end of its
statements and thus finish its execution, or it may be brought to an end
by the influence of other tasks. Only when all the tasks declared in
the parent unit have finished (and the parent itself has reached its
end) is the parent deemed to have finished its execution. Thus the
execution of tasks in Ada is fully nested.

The normal structure of a multi-task program is to write the several
tasks that do the actions required, and declare them as siblings in the
same parent; the body of the parent is responsible for overall control,
in particular to ensure that the tasks are running properly, and to
close them down when necessary.

It is useful to distinguish two kinds of tasks among the siblings
which we call active and passive. Passive tasks provide some service

o the others, such as buffering messages between two active tasks.
ach passive task may provide a set of services (with appropriate
ames), and the active tasks call for these services as they need to use
hem.

.1.1   Declaring a task

task is written with a specification and a distinct body (like a
ackage),

```
    PARENT:
    declare      -- parent unit
      P: constant PRESSURE := CURRENT_PRESSURE;

      task ALERT;     -- specification

      task body ALERT is    -- body
      begin
       if P = LOW then
          NEW_LINE;
          PUT (ASCII.BEL);
       end if;
      end ALERT;

    begin      -- execution of parent
    --    statements for parent
    end PARENT;
```

his simple task ALERT would begin execution within its parent (which
as an initialised constant P, of type PRESSURE). The body of the task
ests the value of P and gives the warning if it is LOW, in parallel
1th the execution of the parent and any other sibling tasks.

   A simple task is declared in this way; another way of declaring a
ask (as one of several similar tasks) is explained in chapter 13.

   The specification gives the task name and lists any services it
rovides. Services are specified like procedures, but introduced by the
ord **entry**. Sibling tasks (or the parent body) may call for these
ervices. The body gives local declarations and the sequence of
tatements to implement the services provided by the task, when it
ccepts a call to one of its entries.

8.1.2   Interaction between tasks

To be effective, tasks must be able to communicate with one another. I
accordance with the normal visibility rules of Ada, the statements (an
declarations) inside a task body may refer to entities declared outsid
it, for example other declarations in the parent unit.   Thus one tas
may refer to entities declared in the specification of a sibling task
as well as other declarations of its parent.

Any task specification may declare entries, which   provide   service
for use elsewhere in the parent unit (normally in its sibling tasks).

```
task ONE_MINUTE is
  entry GO;
  entry CHECK;
end ONE_MINUTE;

task body ONE_MINUTE is
begin
  loop
    accept GO;
    delay 60.0;
    accept CHECK;
  end loop;
end ONE_MINUTE;
```

Another task may call these entries:

```
ONE_MINUTE.GO;  -- starts the delay
-- other statements taking less than one minute
ONE_MINUTE.CHECK;
```

The CHECK entry waits until one minute after the GO entry. (This is a
artificial example which is used only to introduce the interaction.
serious timer would have more facilities and checks built in.)

An entry may have parameters, for communicating data values betwe
tasks.   Here is a (passive) task to act as a simple communicati
channel, into which characters may be written and read by differe
tasks.   The two services, WRITE and READ, must be used alternatel
(It buffers one character at a time.   A more complicated example whi
buffers several characters is given later.)

```
task SIMPLE_BUFFER is
  entry WRITE (CH : in CHARACTER);
```

```
      entry READ   (CH : out CHARACTER);
    end SIMPLE_BUFFER;

    task body SIMPLE_BUFFER is
      CHAR : CHARACTER;
    begin
      loop
        accept WRITE (CH : in CHARACTER) do
          CHAR := CH;
        end WRITE;
        accept READ (CH : out CHARACTER) do
          CH := CHAR;
        end READ;
        exit when CHAR = ASCII.EOT;
      end loop;
    end SIMPLE_BUFFER;
```

e might have two active tasks PRODUCER and CONSUMER, where the first
roduces characters to be dealt with in the second; we want to link
hem by the simple buffer.

```
    task PRODUCER;
    task CONSUMER;

    task body PRODUCER is
      C1: CHARACTER;
    begin
      -- loop
      -- produce C1
      SIMPLE_BUFFER.WRITE (C1);
      -- end loop
    end PRODUCER;

    task body CONSUMER is
      C2: CHARACTER
    begin
      -- loop
      SIMPLE_BUFFER.READ (C2);
      -- use C2
      -- end loop
    end CONSUMER;
```

e discuss the properties of entries and accept statements in section
.2.

8.1.3   Controlling a task

Each task begins execution when its parent starts executing its body, i
parallel with it. The parent can monitor the execution of the task (a
can any other task to which it is visible, but the parent is the natura
one to do this), and take steps if the task does not operate properl
(stopping it if necessary). The task itself controls its own norma
completion and proper termination points; it may also state it
priority, indicating its relative degree of urgency in comparison wit
other tasks.

Faults in a task can be detected by other tasks or the parent. The
can determine whether a task is currently alive (and thus capable o
accepting calls to any entries it may have) by using the attribut
designators CALLABLE and TERMINATED. The statements in the body o
PARENT in section 8.1.1 could include

```
if ALERT'CALLABLE then
   -- the task has not yet reached its end, and
   -- there is no abnormality in its execution
elsif ALERT'TERMINATED then
   -- the task has been terminated
end if;
```

Strictly, there is no way that ALERT'TERMINATED could be true in thi
case, because the task does not have any terminate statements showin
possible termination points (see section 13.3.3).

The priority of a task may be set by a pragma in its specificatio
part, for example

```
pragma PRIORITY (5);
```

among the entry declarations of ONE_MINUTE. This means the ONE_MINUT
must never be held up by tasks with lower or unspecified priority
whether this is done by hardware or software depends on th
implementation. The range of possible priority values is als
determined by the implementation (see SYSTEM.PRIORITY in Appendix A).

8.2   Communication between tasks

The normal method of communication between tasks in Ada is called
rendezvous. This means that two tasks coincide for a period of time
after which they resume their parallel execution. A rendezvous join

ogether a task calling for a service and the task providing that
ervice; the caller is normally an active task and the provider a
assive task.

The task calling for the service does so by executing an entry call
tatement (which is written like a procedure call statement, but with
he entry name instead of a procedure name); this says it wishes to
ave the rendezvous. The task providing the service expresses its
eadiness to carry out the service by reaching an accept statement; this
ays it is ready for the rendezvous.

Whichever of the tasks is first at the rendezvous, it waits for the
ther to arrive.

When both calling and accepting tasks have arrived, the rendezvous
ction takes place (as specified in the accept statement). At the end
f the rendezvous, the calling task continues after the entry call
tatement and in parallel the accepting task continues execution after
he accept statement.

If several tasks call the same entry, the accepting task carries out
he rendezvous with the first to arrive. The accepting task usually
ontains a loop so that the accept statement is repeated. This has the
ffect of dealing with the entry calls one at a time, in their order of
rrival.

The action to be taken at the rendezvous is specified in an accept
tatement (in the accepting task), and the specification for that task
akes the rendezvous visible by declaring it as an entry. Every entry
n the specification must have a corresponding accept statement (perhaps
ore than one) in the body:

```
entry WRITE (CH : in CHARACTER);   -- in specification
---
accept WRITE (CH : in CHARACTER) do   -- in body
   CHAR := CH;
end WRITE;
```

he rendezvous action for WRITE is to copy the value of the parameter
iven at the entry call into the local variable CHAR. Note that the
alling task cannot be doing anything else during the rendezvous, so any
ctions involving variables of the calling task (through parameters) are
roperly synchronised.

There need not be any action at the rendezvous:

```
task CONTROL_LIFT is
```

```
    entry GO;        -- in specification
  end CONTROL_LIFT;

  task body CONTROL_LIFT is
  begin
    loop
      accept GO;   -- in body
      -- normal execution
    end loop;
  end CONTROL_LIFT;
```

As soon as both tasks have reached the rendezvous (in either order), both may continue. This is purely a synchronising device.

The parameters of the accept statement allow data values to be communicated between two tasks, in both directions: **in**, (default) at the beginning of the rendezvous, and **out** at its end (possibly both).

As well as the rendezvous method, tasks may communicate by sharing variables. By virtue of the visibility rules, an object declared in the parent task may be used in the children, and this can lead to trouble. Distinct sibling tasks may refer to the same variable while they are executing in parallel, so that one task may be accessing it while another is changing it.

In order to ensure that a shared variable is updated with its proper value in one task, so that another may use it, the pragma SHARED (see appendix D) may be used:

```
  S : ITS_TYPE;  -- to be shared
  pragma SHARED(S);
  task T1;
  task T2;
  task body T1 is
  begin
    -- may use S
  end T1;
  task body T2 is
    -- may also use S
  end T2;
```

Without the pragma SHARED, there is no guarantee that the values of S in the two tasks will be the same. The points where the variable is read or updated are known as synchronization points.

.3   Asymmetry of rendezvous

The junction of a calling task and an accepting task to form a
rendezvous is not symmetrical, and it is useful to appreciate the
implications of the difference.

a. The calling task must know the name of the accepting task (and its
   entry point), but not vice versa. Thus a task with entries offers
   a service to other tasks, limited only by the visibility rules.
b. An accepting task may wait for the first of several entries to be
   called, whereas a calling task must state one specific entry it
   wishes to call. Thus there is greater non-determinism in the
   accepting task.
c. Failure of a task in rendezvous is not passed from the calling to
   the accepting task, but is passed from the accepting to the calling
   task.

The naming difference is perhaps the most fundamental.   To
understand it better, consider the alternatives: either the two
communicating tasks could each name the other, or they could both name
some common entity through which they communicate.

If communicating tasks were required to name each other, the
redundancy would introduce further opportunities for checking, but it
would be impossible to write a general-purpose task that could be used
with arbitrary other tasks at run-time.

If communicating tasks were required to name a common medium of
communication (such as a pipe or file), the kinds of communication which
could be expressed would be inherently bound to the facilities offered
by that medium;   and there would still be the asymmetry between each
task concerned and the common medium.

Ada is designed with the latter scheme in mind, but the means of
communication are not built into the language – they are indeed
programmed. Although the language does not insist on a distinction
being made between different kinds of task, which we call passive tasks
and active tasks, it is probably helpful to design multi-task
communication on this basis. The passive tasks should be written to
provide desired means of communication, and the active tasks can then
communicate through them.

8.4   Active tasks

The normal pattern for Ada tasks then is for the declarative part of
some program unit (the parent) to contain passive and active tasks, with
the body of the parent controlling them. The passive tasks provide the
facilities needed for communication between the active tasks.

   It can be expected that a few kinds of communication will be commonly
used (e.g. bounded buffers), and appropriate library units will be
written to provide them. The programmer using tasks will mainly write
active tasks, taking advantage of previously written passive tasks. We
defer to Chapter 13 the further discussion of passive tasks, and
concentrate here on writing active tasks.

   Writing an active task is almost indistinguishable from writing an
ordinary sequential program. As well as the sequential features, it
may call entries in its passive siblings, but these are very similar to
procedure calls.

   The name in an entry call consists of the task name with its entry
name; there is no way of automatically eliding the task name as there is
for package names after a **use** clause. However, any individual entry may
be renamed as a procedure, for example in an active task

>   **procedure** BUFFERED_WRITE (C : CHARACTER := ASCII.EOT)
>   **renames** SIMPLE_BUFFER.WRITE;
>   **procedure** BUFFERED_READ (C : **out** CHARACTER)
>   **renames** SIMPLE_BUFFER.READ;

Note that the renaming can change the parameter names and defaults. I
have here given a default to BUFFERED_WRITE so that when called with no
parameter it marks the end of the sequence of characters.

   From the point of view of the active task, an entry call is just like
a procedure call apart from timing: a procedure is started immediately
(perhaps in parallel with other executions of the same procedure, called
from other tasks) but an entry may have to wait for the passive task to
be prepared to accept it. There are two programming features that may
be used to deal with this, both varieties of **select** statement (covered
further in chapter 13).

3.4.1   Entry time-out

f a task makes an entry call as an ordinary statement, it waits
perhaps indefinitely) until the called task is prepared to accept that
ntry. We can use a select statement to limit the period of time it is
repared to wait.

```
select
   CONTROL_LIFT.GO;
   OK := TRUE;
or
   delay 0.5;
   OK := FALSE;
end select;
```

he call of CONTROL_LIFT.GO (which must be an entry) will be taken if
he called task accepts it within 0.5 seconds, otherwise the other arm
ill be executed.

Notice that it is the start of execution of the entry which is
hecked, not its finish. The time-out is cancelled as soon as the entry
s accepted.

3.4.2   Conditional entry call

onditionally calling a rendezvous allows a task that calls an entry to
ave an alternative action if the called task is not prepared to accept
he call immediately.

```
select
   SIMPLE_BUFFER.READ ( C2 );    -- entry call
   -- statements using C2
else    -- nothing is immediately available
   -- alternative actions
end select;
```

Note that in both these forms of select statement there are only two
rms: the arm trying to call the entry, and the alternative.

8.5   Input/Output tasks

It is a common feature of embedded computer systems that they include
application specific input/output devices that must be programmed as
part of the project. We can do this in Ada using tasks to carry out the
input/output operations, including device handlers and interrupt
handlers.

8.5.1   Interrupt handling

An interrupt is considered in Ada to be a hardware-generated entry call.
The programmer writes the necessary interrupt handler as an accept
statement in a handling task. The Ada entry is linked with the
appropriate interrupt entry address by giving its representation
specification (see chapter 11).

In the PDP-11, character input from a keyboard generates an interrupt
at location 8#100# (say), with the relevant character in the data buffer
register. We write the handler for this, copying the character read
into a local variable, from which another task can take it:

```
task KB_HANDLER is
  entry TAKE (CH : out CHARACTER);
  entry KB_DONE;
  for KB_DONE use at 8#100#;
end KB_HANDLER;

task body KB_HANDLER is
  CHAR : CHARACTER;  -- local variable
  DBR : CHARACTER;  -- hardware register
  for DBR use at 8#177462#;
begin
  loop
    accept KB_DONE do
      CHAR := DBR;
    end KB_DONE;
    accept TAKE (CH : out CHARACTER) do
      CH := CHAR;
    end TAKE;
  end loop;
end KB_HANDLER;
```

On reaching accept KB_DONE, the task enables the corresponding interrupt
(indicating its readiness for the rendezvous); it sets the interrupt

vector address to refer to the body of the accept statement. The interrupt is disabled for the rest of the task. Note that this task never ends.

The priority of a task may be given by a pragma; the possible values for priorities depend on the target computer used.

8.5.2   Input/Output Control

Between the interrupt handlers and the higher levels of a program, it is often useful to have distinct tasks to deal with particular aspects of the low-level device control. For example, the valves in the filtration unit are opened and closed in some particular way which is of no concern to the rest of the program.

```
task VALVE_ACTION is
  entry MOVE_VALVE (V : VALVE);
  entry VALVE_DONE;
end VALVE_ACTION;

task body VALVE_ACTION is
  C : NATURAL;
  S : VALVE_STATUS;
begin
  loop
    accept MOVE_VALVE (V : VALVE) do
      C := CONTROL_VALVE (V).CONTROL;
      S := CONTROL_VALVE (V).CONDITION;
    end MOVE_VALVE;
    --  statements to establish status S on channel C
    accept VALVE_DONE;
  end loop;
end VALVE_ACTION;
```

Sibling tasks may call

    VALVE_ACTION.MOVE_VALVE (AIR_VENT);

to get the valve into the position previously assigned to the appropriate valve parameter.

The entry VALVE_DONE must be called (for example by an interrupt) before another attempt to move a valve will be accepted.

The following program is for a small PDP-11, to make it ring a bell
every second. The output is done by a simple task which puts a
character in the printer buffer then waits for the 'i/o done' interrupt.
The delay is designed to use the line clock (which interrupts 50 times a
second).

```
procedure BLEEP is

  task XMIT is
    entry PUT(C:CHARACTER);
    entry DOIO;
    for DOIO use at 8#64#;
  end XMIT;

  task body XMIT is
    package PDP_11 is

      type BIT is (OFF,ON);
      type BITS is array (0..15) of BIT;

      procedure ENABLE(CSR: out BITS) ;

      procedure DISABLE(CSR: out BITS) ;

      for BIT use (OFF=>0, ON=>1);
      pragma PACK(BITS);
    end PDP_11;

    use PDP_11;
    XBR:CHARACTER;
    XSR:BITS;
    for XBR use at 8#177566#;
    for XSR use at 8#177564#;

    package body PDP_11 is

      procedure ENABLE(CSR: out BITS) is
      begin
        CSR(6):=ON;
      end ENABLE;
      pragma INLINE(ENABLE);

      procedure DISABLE(CSR: out BITS) is
      begin
        CSR(6):=OFF;
      end DISABLE;
      pragma INLINE(DISABLE);
```

```
        end PDP_11;
      begin
        loop
          accept PUT(C:CHARACTER) do
            XBR := C;
          end PUT;
          ENABLE(XSR);
          accept DOIO;
          DISABLE(XSR);
        end loop;
      end XMIT;

      package TIMING is
        procedure DELAY_TICKS(N:NATURAL);
      end TIMING;

      package body TIMING is
        TICK:constant DURATION:=0.02;
        procedure DELAY_TICKS(N:NATURAL) is
        begin
          delay N*TICK;
        end DELAY_TICKS;
      end TIMING;

      use TIMING;
    begin
      loop
        DELAY_TICKS(50);
        XMIT.PUT(ASCII.BEL);
      end loop;

    end BLEEP;
```

This program is written with nested units. The inner modules XMIT and
TIMING deal with application-specific input/output.

Exercises

1. Write a piece of program to discover whether a pool of values
    contains an item with a particular key, giving the value if it is
    present.   The items in the pool are being inserted, changed, and
    deleted by several concurrent tasks at a lower hardware priority.

2. Write an interrupt handler for a character printer.   The character
    to be printed must be put in a hardware register; the interrupt
    indicates that it has been accepted.

CHAPTER 9

Program Structure

The principles of structured programming and the concept of abstract data types (in which details of the implementation are hidden), are essential for the reliable construction of large programs by many programmers. In this chapter we turn to the program text itself and the manner of its development and modification.

The general relationships among the entities in a program concern the identifiers in the program, and the meanings they have. We discuss the rules for visibility of declarations, which lead us to describe the structure of a program in terms of blocks and modules.

There can be many identifiers in an Ada program, denoting variables, constants, types, procedures, exceptions, tasks, etc., and each applies throughout a particular part of the program. This is true both for the predefined identifiers such as INTEGER and CONSTRAINT_ERROR as well as for identifiers defined by the programmer such as X, I, OBJECT, ASSOCIATED_TRACK. The meaning of an identifier is determined by the way it is introduced - usually in a declaration at the head of a block or module. The positions in the program where it may be used depend on the position of the declaration, taking account of overloading (see section 5.1h) and renaming (explained below). The same applies also to the operator symbols such as + * and to enumeration literals (which may be characters). In this chapter we explain the structure of an Ada program, and consequently where in a program any particular declaration is "visible", so that the identifier it declares can be used.

A program in Ada has a logical and a physical structure. These are closely related but not identical. The logical structure consists of "program units", which may be nested inside one another. The physical structure consists of "compilation units" which are always separate from one another.

A program unit can be a subprogram, package or task. For each kind
f program unit there may be a specification and a body. Any kind of
rogram unit may contain units of the same or different kinds inside it.
ach compilation unit is a distinct program unit, with an appropriate
ontext clause at its head.

The program as a whole consists of a collection of compilation units,
ll separate, and each compilation unit consists of a program unit that
ay contain other program units inside it, nested to any depth.   It is
ossible for the text inside one compilation unit to refer to other
ompilation units, provided that the other compilation units are
entioned in the introductory context clause.

In this chapter we concentrate on the program units, which show the
ogical structure; compilation units, which show the physical structure,
re explained in chapter 10.

.1   Visibility of Declarations

ecause it may happen that the same identifier is used for different
urposes in different parts of the program (for example when different
eople are writing separate parts and decide independently to choose a
articular name), we need to be able to associate any identifier used in
he program with the proper meaning. We say that a declaration is
"visible" in those parts of the program where its identifier can be
sed. The visibility rules ensure that there is no confusion: each use
f   the   identifier   has   the   meaning given by the corresponding
eclaration.

Each identifier (other than a statement label, block or loop
dentifier, or a loop parameter) which is used in a program must be
eclared somewhere in the program, or in the library packages it uses or
he standard environment. Statement labels, block identifiers and loop
dentifiers must be unique within their program unit (including those
ested in inner contexts). The statement labels, block and loop
dentifiers and loop parameters are implicitly declared by their
ccurrence, as explained now.

.1.1   Statement labels

statement may be labelled, so that it may be referred to in a goto
tatement. The labelled statement is of course one of a sequence of
tatements, which may be part of a compound statement, and may contain

other compound statements.

The first occurrence of the label identifier in the program may be a
the head of the labelled statement (for a backward - directed **got**
statement) or in a **goto** statement (for a forward jump). This firs
occurrence acts as a declaration for the identifier as a label, an
applies from that point until the end of the innermost enclosing progra
unit. This may be a subprogram body or a package body or a task body
whichever is the smallest.

A **goto** statement can specify the label of any statement which is i
the same sequence of statements, or in an enclosing sequence o
statements (if the **goto** statement is in a compound statement), subjec
to the rules given in section 4.7.4.

9.1.2   Block and loop identifiers

A block (declare statement) may be named, with a block identifier at th
beginning and end of the block. Entities declared inside the block ma
be distinguished using this name. Similarly, a loop may be named
giving the loop identifier at the beginning and end of the loop. A loo
identifier may be used in an exit statement.

```
OUTER: declare
  I,J : INTEGER;  -- these are OUTER.I, OUTER.J
begin
  -- see also section 9.3.1
end OUTER;

L1: loop
  -- any inner loop may contain
    exit L1 when REQUIRED;
  -- rest of loop(s)
end loop L1;
```

The occurrence of the identifier naming the block or loop acts as
declaration.

9.1.3   Loop parameters

A loop introduced by a **for** clause, such as

```
for I in 1 .. 200 loop
```

```
    VECTOR(I) := 0.0;
  end loop;
```

stablishes a new scope consisting of the sequence of statements which
orm the body of the loop. In the loop body, the loop parameter (I in
his case) is available as though it had been declared as a **constant** of
he type defined by the range part of the **for** clause, thus:

```
  I : constant INTEGER range 1 .. 200;
```

The range in a **for** clause need not be of integers: it may be any
iscrete type, such as an enumeration type).

    The fact that the loop parameter is effectively declared as a
onstant means that it is illegal to make any assignment to it inside
he body, or to use it as an **out** or **in out** parameter of a procedure.

    The fact that the loop parameter has a scope extending over the
tatements forming the body of the loop means that it has no
ignificance in statements outside the loop, so there is no way by which
tatements outside the loop can refer to the loop parameter (for
xample, after an **exit** statement).

```
  for I in 0 .. 100 loop
    -- manipulate members of array A while positive
    exit when A(I) < 0.0;
  end loop;   -- value of I is now inaccessible
```

    If there had been another declaration of the same identifier I in the
rogram unit containing this loop, the outer declaration would be
idden. If it is necessary to know the value of the loop parameter
utside, then its value must be assigned to another variable before
eaving the loop.

.2   Declared identifiers

or each declaration, there is a defined region of the program over
hich the declared identifier has the meaning given in the declaration;
his is called the scope of the declaration. Within this scope, there
s a particular region where the identifier may be immediately used,
ithout any additional information. In this region, the declaration is
aid to be "directly visible".

Within the scope but not in the region of direct visibility, th
declaration is said to be hidden; it is possible by appropriat
additional information (of various kinds) to arrange for one or mo
hidden declarations to be made visible. The identifiers they decla
can then be used with the declared meanings.

The regions of the program over which a declaration is relevant, bo
for scope and for direct visibility, are related to the progr
structure. We first explain the structures relevant to certain kinds c
entities in the program, then proceed to the general position on scope
in an Ada program.

Scopes are mainly determined by the block and module structure of
program. The block structure relates to subprogram bodies and decla
statements; module structure relates to packages and tasks. Within th
major units determined by the program structure, certain construc
introduce special regions relevant to enumeration types, records a
procedure parameters.

9.3   Block Structure

The classical form of block structure, which is available in Ad
provides for declarations to be valid within the part of the progr
immediately following them. We have declare statements, which a
blocks in the executable part of the program, and subprograms, which a
blocks in the declarative part of a program.

9.3.1   Block structure with declare statements

The declare statement is the simplest form of block structure in Ad
The word **declare** introduces one or more declarations, which are follow
by **begin** then a sequence of statements, possibly with some excepti
handlers, and finally the word **end**. Each of the declared identifie
may be used in any subsequent declaration in the block, and througho
the sequence of statements and exception handlers. Thus any identifi
introduced in the declarative part of the block has that meaning for a
the rest of the block. Its scope is all the block after th
declaration.

There is no theoretical limit to the size of the block or the size
the declarations or statements inside it, but for practical purposes
is wise to keep declare blocks smaller than one page of text: f
anything larger, a module structure will be easier to handl

articularly for program maintenance.

The identifiers that are introduced in the declarative part of any lock must all be distinct (with the exception of overloaded enumeration iterals and procedures: see section 9.7). However, since the declare tatement occurs in a position where many identifiers may already be isible, there is the possibility that an identifier declared inside the lock is the same as an identifier visible in the context of the declare tatement. In this case, the declaration at the head of the block takes recedence for the statements in the block, hiding the outer eclarations for the same identifier. So in general, if the program has . nested block structure with declare statements in the executable part f larger declare statements, an identifier used in the program is nterpreted according to the smallest enclosing block in which it is eclared. (It is possible to have a block without any declarations, in hich the statement starts with the word **begin** rather than **declare**; such . construct allows a particular set of statements to be guarded by pecific exception handlers.)

An outer declaration that is hidden by a declaration for the same dentifier in an inner block is still in scope, but not directly isible: its full name must be used to identify it. In the following lock,

```
OUTER: declare
   I, J : INTEGER;   -- outer declarations
begin
   -- statements may use outer declarations
   INNER: declare
      J, K : INTEGER;   -- inner declarations
   begin
      -- J, K mean INNER.J, INNER.K
      -- I means OUTER.I
      -- OUTER.J needs full name
   end INNER;
   -- I, J mean OUTER.I, OUTER.J
end OUTER;
```

.he identifier J is declared as a variable in the outer declarations and .gain in the inner declarations. Within the statements of the inner lock, the inner declaration for J hides the outer declaration for J, so :he simple name J in the inner block relates to the inner declaration 'ather than the outer one.

Although we illustrate this rule using identifiers for variables, the .ame principles apply to all declarations: types, procedures, packages :tc. Furthermore, the kind of entity which an identifier denotes in an

outer block need have no relationship at all with a declaration in an
inner block.

There is a complicating possibility that an identifier declared in an
outer block may be used (as opposed to declared) in the declarative part
of an inner block - perhaps as an initialisation value for a variable,
or as a type name. In this case it is dangerous to try to redeclare that
identifier in the same inner block. So in the following block, the
declarative part of the inner block should not redeclare the identifiers
ITEM or P.

```
declare
  type ITEM is new INTEGER;
  P, Q : ITEM;
begin
  -- statements may use P and Q
  declare
    R : ITEM;
      -- subsequent declarations should not redeclare ITEM
    S : ITEM := P;
      -- subsequent declarations should not redeclare P
  begin
    -- statements may use P, Q, R, and S.
  end;
end;
```

9.3.2   Block structure with subprograms

A procedure or a function declaration is another form of block
structure, which is basically similar to a declare statement but has the
added feature of formal parameters.

The formal parameters of the procedure or function are introduced in
the subprogram heading, and have the same effect on the subprogram body
as declarations that may occur between the heading and the word **begin** at
the start of the executable part of the subprogram. Thus the identifiers
introduced as formal parameters may be used in any subsequent
declaration and throughout the sequence of statements forming the
executable part. The formal parameters are allowed only to be data
objects, that is constants or variables. (They may not be types or other
program entities such as procedures, exceptions, packages or tasks.) The
identifiers which are introduced as the formal parameters must be all
distinct, from one another and from any local declarations. All these
identifiers are visible in the subprogram body.

```
function PEX (I : NATURAL) return SHORT is
  S : SHORT := I;
begin
  return 6 - S;
exception
  when CONSTRAINT_ERROR =>
    raise BAD_PARAMETER;
end PEX;
```

Within this subprogram, we have the formal parameter I and the local variable S. The body also refers to two types (NATURAL and SHORT) and two exceptions (CONSTRAINT_ERROR and BAD_PARAMETER) which must have been declared outside the subprogram.

The subprogram declaration is itself in some context where many identifiers are visible, and the same rules apply as for a declare statement. Thus any identifier visible at the position of the subprogram declaration is also visible from inside the subprogram declaration unless that identifier is hidden by giving it a local meaning for the subprogram, either as a formal parameter or by a local declaration.

9.4   Module structure

Whereas blocks in a program serve the primary purpose of limiting the visibility of identifiers declared in them, modules (whether packages or tasks) serve the complementary purpose of expanding the visibility of identifiers declared in them. Certain of the declarations in a module have a scope which is greater than the module containing them. Identifiers which may have such an expanded visibility must be declared in the visible part of the module - the specification part. We call these the public declarations. All other identifiers declared in the module, namely those declared in the implementation part or the private part of the specification, can never be visible outside the module, and are treated in the same way as identifiers in a block structure. (Note however that there may be separately compiled subunits of the module body, which although physically separate are logically inside the module.)

A package or a task (module) specification introduces the identifier for that module; as with other declarations, this identifier is directly visible in the context of the module declaration.

Throughout the scope of the package declaration, its public declarations are also in scope but they are hidden. They may be made visible throughout any specified program unit (provided that there is no ambiguity) by a use clause. Making the public identifiers visible throughout a unit is called exposing them. Because the current unit may happen to contain a declaration for the same identifier as is made public by the package, or several packages which are exposed in the same unit may happen to contain public declarations for the same identifier, the exposure of public identifiers applies only to those for which there is no such possible ambiguity.

Whether or not there is a use clause, any public identifier in scope may be accessed throughout the scope of the module by component selection, since there is then no possible ambiguity. In a context where the module name is visible, a component selection (consisting of the module name, a period, then the public identifier) constitutes the name of the entity which was declared in the visible part of the module. Thus with the module specified

```
package GINO_F is
  procedure DRAW2(X,Y : FLOAT);
  procedure MOVTO2(X,Y : FLOAT);
end GINO_F;
```

in a context where GINO_F is visible, the procedures can be called by statements such as

```
GINO_F.MOVTO2(X1, Y1);
GINO_F.DRAW2(X1 + 1.0E0, Y1);
```

The name so formed has all the properties of the declared entity: for example, if it is a record, its components may be selected, and if it is an inner module then the public identifiers of that may be accessed by further component selection. Using this technique, each time the public identifier is to be referred to, its full name must be given, starting with the visible module name.

The alternative technique, by which all the public identifiers of a module or set of modules are made visible together (apart from potential ambiguities), is to write a use clause. This is written as though it were a declaration; it gives one or more module names, and exposes their public identifiers in the current block or module. So where GINO_F is visible, the following construction allows the unambiguous public identifiers of that package to be used without needing their full names:

```
declare
  use GINO_F;
```

```
   procedure DRAW2 (LENGTH, BREADTH : FLOAT) is
   begin
   -- local declaration
   end DRAW2;
begin
   MOVTO2(X1, Y1); -- from GINO_F because no ambiguity
   GINO_F.DRAW2(X1+1.0, Y1);  --explicitly from GINO_F
   DRAW2(3.0, 4.0);  -- implies local declaration
   end;
```

f the exposure of a particular identifier is inhibited by a local
eclaration, or by duplication of public identifiers in different
odules exposed together, then any desired public declaration may be
ccessed by using the full name of the declared entity.

.5   Renaming

ames of entities can get quite complicated, as we have seen in section
.5.   There are ways of introducing simple names for the most common
inds of entity, to refer to them easily in a particular context.

.5.1   Renaming objects

ny object may be renamed to provide a simple way of referring to it.
he new name acts as a synonym for the old name, which remains valid.
his has been mentioned in section 2.5, and used in section 7.7. Within
he procedures MOVE_VALVE and MOVE_AND_CHECK_VALVE, the declaration

     VP : VALVE_PARAMETERS renames CONTROL_VALVE(V);

ives the simple name VP to the element of array CONTROL_VALVE with
ndex V, using the current value of V. The renamed object may be a
omponent of a record or a member of an array; in the latter case, the
alue of the index (or indices) is determined at the point of the
enaming declaration. The new name VP refers to the same object
hroughout its scope (i.e. one call of the procedure), regardless of
hanges to any variables involved in indices (such as V in this case).
he renamed object may be a constant or a variable; renaming does not
ffect that, or any constraints that apply to it.

9.5.2   Renaming subprograms

Any function or operation may be renamed, without affecting it
parameter and result type profile. An operator may be renamed as
function, and a function with one or two parameters may be renamed as a
operator (as appropriate for the parameters). The formal paramete
names, and any default parameter values, may be changed on renaming
Renaming does not hide the original name.

Any procedure or entry may be similarly renamed as a procedure
without affecting its parameter type profile. This allows an entr
(non-reentrable) to be presented in the same way as a procedure.

9.5.3   Renaming exceptions or packages

Any exception and any package may be renamed; both names are then vali
and equivalent.

9.5.4   Other entities

It is not possible to rename other kinds of entity, such as tasks
types, generic units or labels in programs. In the case of types, it i
possible to get the same effect as renaming by introducing a subtyp
with no further constraints than the base type.

9.6   Uniqueness of identifiers

In all the various places where identifiers may be introduced, there ar
rules to ensure that the identifiers are distinguishable from on
another. For most declared entities (including variables, constants
types, exceptions, modules) where the identifier stands alone, thi
requires that distinct identifiers must be used for the differen
entities declared together. This rule is relaxed for the values of a
enumeration type: each individual enumeration type must have a distinc
set of values, but the identifiers introduced as the values of one typ
do not have to be distinct from the identifiers introduced as the value
of another type; such identifiers are said to be overloaded. The rul
is also partially relaxed for subprograms, which can have parameter
(and each subprogram has a specific number of parameters, which may b
zero). Since their identifiers are always used with a list o

parameters of specified types, it is possible for several subprograms to have the same identifier, provided that their parameters are sufficiently different. This is called overloading the subprogram, and is explained fully in section 9.7.

In each of the following, where several identifiers are introduced together, they must all be different:

    a. Values of an enumeration type.
    b. Components of a record type.
    c. Entities introduced in a block or module (taking both specification and body together), apart from overloaded subprograms. These entities include formal parameters, local declarations, block and loop identifiers and statement labels.

Between any one set of declarations and another, an identifier may be repeated, and the rules of visibility determine which meaning is implied by any use of the identifier. It is illegal to use an identifier where no declaration for it is visible – it then has no meaning.

9.7   Local contexts

In some special constructions, identifiers from another part of the program may be used, even though they are not normally visible. This might arise because of potential ambiguity or to establish associations. These special cases concern overloaded enumeration values, record components, and name associations for aggregates or subprogram parameters. This is called visibility by selection.

9.7.1   Values of enumeration types

Each enumeration type declaration gives the set of identifiers (or characters) that are the possible values in the enumeration type. These identifiers or characters are known as enumeration literals; any such identifier is normally available for use in expressions of the appropriate enumeration type, provided that no other declaration is given for it. For any individual enumeration type, the possible values must of course all be distinct, but different enumeration types need not have disjoint possible values. Thus:

type NUM_BASE is
    (BIN, OCT, DEC, HEX);

```
type MON_NAME is
    (JAN, FEB, MAR, APR,
     MAY, JUN, JUL, AUG,
     SEP, OCT, NOV, DEC);
```

can exist in the same context even though they both have possible values
OCT and DEC.

An identifier which is a possible enumeration value for more than one
enumeration type (or also of a function without parameters) in the same
context is said to be overloaded. In this case, the identifier may only
be used in an expression where the context determines the type: it is
not directly visible in the context in which it is overloaded. However
the enumeration type name (which can not be overloaded) is available for
use, to introduce a qualified expression.

Within this qualified expression the enumeration value may be given
as any possible ambiguity has been eliminated. Thus the qualified
expression constitutes a local context, in which the identifier gives
the value in the specified enumeration type.

In the context of MON_NAME and NUM_BASE, the identifiers BIN and JAN
may be used directly, but for the overloaded enumeration values one must
write NUM_BASE'(OCT) or MON_NAME'(DEC) if the context does not resolve
the ambiguity.

An array which is indexed by an enumeration type implies
qualification for its index values. Consequently, an element of such a
array may be specified by using the enumeration value as the index
without needing explicit qualification. For example, with

```
DAYS_IN_MONTH : array (MON_NAME) of NATURAL
    := (31, 29, 31, 30, 31, 30,
        31, 31, 30, 31, 30, 31);
        -- value for a leap year
```

any use of

```
DAYS_IN_MONTH(OCT)
```

implies

```
DAYS_IN_MONTH(MON_NAME'(OCT))
```

so automatically resolves the potential ambiguity.

9.7.2   Record component identifiers

The identifiers of record components are not directly visible in the context of the declaration of either the record type or any of the record objects; however, they become visible in the local contexts of component selections and record aggregates. The type of the record must be in scope for any possibility of access to components of an object of that type.

```
type DATE is
   record
      YEAR : INTEGER range 1901 .. 2099;
      MONTH : MON_NAME;
      DAY : INTEGER range 1 .. 31;
   end record;
```

A record type declaration introduces the identifiers and types for its components. These identifiers (YEAR, MONTH, DAY in the above example) are <u>not</u> directly visible in the context of the type declaration. An object of that record type may be declared wherever the type declaration is visible, and in that context the type identifier may not be redeclared (as with ITEM in section 9.3.1). There may be an inner context in which the record type declaration is redeclared but the record object is still visible: in this context, all the constituents of the data object are hidden (as though it were of a private type: see section 7.4).

In a context where the type identifier is visible, a record aggregate may be specified, of the form shown in section 2.3.

```
(1900, JAN, 1)
(1999, NOV, 31)  -- legal but not sensible
(2000, FEB, 29)  -- component values given by position
(MONTH => FEB, DAY => 29, YEAR => 2000)
         -- components given by name
DATE'(1979, OCT, 13)  -- qualified expression
```

If there is no ambiguity over the aggregate, its type need not be stated explicitly. However, in general, the aggregate is given as a qualified expression, in which the record type is stated.

The association of a component with a value may be by position or by name, using the same notation as for record aggregates and subprogram parameters. Zero or more component values may be given, in the same order as in the declaration, followed by the rest in any order, prefaced by their component identifiers. (An aggregate containing only one element must be written using the component name, to show that it is an aggregate.) This is a special context where the component identifiers are visible on the left hand sides of name-associated components, but not on right hand sides or in position-associated components, for which the outer context applies.

In a context where both the object identifier and the type identifier are visible, components of the record may be accessed by "component selection". The record object name followed by the component identifier constitutes the name of the component, and has all the properties of an object of the appropriate type - including the possibility of having components itself, if the component is a record within a record.

For example, in the context of the type declarations of POSITION and LENGTH, there may be data object declarations

```
P, Q: POSITION;       -- data object declaration
SCAN : LENGTH;
```

with components such as

```
P.EAST
Q.HEADING
```

Thus we might have

```
Q := POSITION'(
  EAST    => P.EAST + SCAN,
  NORTH   => P.NORTH - SCAN,
  HEADING => P.HEADING);
```

The identifiers EAST, NORTH and HEADING (the component identifier in type POSITION) are not directly visible here, and other declarations for these identifiers would be possible without confusion.

9.7.3   Formal parameters of subprograms

Within any context where a subprogram name is visible, the identifiers for the formal parameters of the subprogram are not directly visible, but may become visible in the local context of a subprogram call, for association by name with actual parameters.

A subprogram call consists of the procedure or function name followed by the list of parameter associations. This list constitutes a special

context, in which the identifiers for the formal parameter of the
ubprogram are visible on the left hand sides of name-association
arameters. They are not visible on right hand sides of name-
ssociations or in positional parameters.

For example, with the declaration

procedure INSERT (IT: **in** ITEM; LIST: **in out** ITEM_PTR);

he identifiers ITEM and ITEM_PTR must be already visible at the point
f declaration; the declaration introduces the identifier INSERT. The
dentifiers IT and LIST are not visible in that context, and if there
appen to be declarations elsewhere in the block for these identifiers
here is no confusion.

On a call of this procedure, the parameter list may contain the
dentifiers IT and LIST as parameter names.

```
declare
    A, B : ITEM;   -- inner declarations
    L : ITEM_PTR;
    IT:  INTEGER;  -- no confusion
begin
    INSERT(IT => A, LIST => L);
end;
```

oth these parameter associations are by name; the first specifies that
ormal parameter IT is to be given the value A. Similarly the second
arameter association specifies that the formal parameter LIST is to be
aken as the object L. Note the inner declaration of IT. This is
isible in parameter association by position and on the right of
arameter associations by name: it could be used in an expression of
he appropriate type. As with record aggregates, zero or more actual
arameters may be given, in the same order as in the declaration,
ollowed by any others required in any order, with their formal
dentifiers to distinguish them. Parameters with default values may be
mitted, but if values have to be given for parameters declared
ubsequently, the formal identifiers must be used since the order cannot
e maintained. A single parameter may be given alone (in contrast with
 record aggregate).

.8   Signature of subprograms

 subprogram (procedure or function) is distinguished by the combination
f its declared identifier and the properties of its parameters. The

relevant parameter properties are their types (in order), with the typ
of the result, if any. This combination is called its signature c
profile (parameter profile, parameter and result profile). As
consequence of the parameter properties being involved in the signature
it is possible for a single subprogram identifier to be "overloaded", s
that it can be declared with different bodies for different forma
parameters. This is particularly important for the input/outpu
procedures, where PUT and GET are defined for the various predefine
data types.

The signature of the subprogram is used (at compile-time) to fin
which is the appropriate subprogram declaration for each subprogra
call, and is composed of the information which must be specified in th
call. The resolution of subprogram overloading is done at compile time
so there is no run-time overhead. Section 10.3 explains how subprogram
declared in other compilation units may be used, even if they have th
same signature.

In order to give this information unambiguously, each subprogra
parameter must have its type determinable (implying the need for
qualified expression if overloaded literals are used, such as numerica
constants with user-defined types). For example, if a special outpu
procedure were needed for data of type WEIGHT, it could be declared

```
procedure PUT (X:WEIGHT) is
      -- appropriate body
end PUT;
```

This could be used with variables of type WEIGHT

```
W : WEIGHT;
PUT(W);
```

but to apply this special procedure to a constant, say 0.0E0, the typ
qualifier must be used

```
PUT(WEIGHT'(0.0E0));
```

to determine the right signature.

Exercises

1. Given

```
A : array (0 .. 100) of FLOAT;
```

write statements to find the negative element with smallest index value, and set

    I : INTEGER;

to that index value. What happens if no element is negative?

. Given character sets (which are in effect enumeration types) ASCII and EBCDIC, and a conversion array

    A_TO_E : **array** (ASCII) **of** EBCDIC;

with variables

    C : ASCII;
    D : EBCDIC;

write statements to assign to D the character corresponding to the current value of C unless it is a dollar sign, in which case assign a space. Remember that in this context, unqualified character strings would be ambiguous in type, different from both ASCII and EBCDIC.

. In the sequence of statements following the declarations of section 9.6.2, including

    P,Q : POSITION;

we have

    declare
      EAST : FLOAT;
      -- other declarations
    begin
      -- statements
      PUT (P.EAST);
    end;

Does the above declaration of EAST affect the meaning of P.EAST ? (No.)
Would any declaration there affect the meaning of P.EAST.?   (Yes: redeclaration of P)

CHAPTER 10

Separate Compilation and Generics

This chapter is concerned with compilation aspects of an Ada program, the physical structure of the program text, and the compile-time processing. The physically separate program units are called compilation units. Ada includes facilities for compile-time parametrization: as well as conventional run-time parameters for subprograms, both subprograms and packages may be written with compile time parameters; they are then called generic program units.

In order that several programmers may be able to work concurrently on a project, each must be developing a distinct and clearly defined part of the eventual large program. Each must be able to handle and test his part without unnecessary dependence on other programmers, and without making other programmers unnecessarily dependent on him.

In general, each programmer is implementing certain facilities on the assumption that certain other facilities are available. The information which he needs to know is therefore the specification of these facilities, independent of the way they are implemented.

The textual structure of the part of a program developed by an individual programmer must be such as to contain and distinguish

   a. Specification of facilities provided;

   b. Implementation details of facilities provided;

   c. Identification of facilities assumed.

Packages provide the logical structure in a program, distinguishing the specification of facilities from their implementation. Compilation nits provide the physical structure; they are disjoint program units, refixed by a heading that identifies any other unit on which they epend. The heading is called the context clause, and the units epended on must be library units. Compilation units are compiled eparately, but taking account of the specifications of their context. program is eventually formed by linking together the code from all the elevant compilation units. Most compilation units are packages, but ther kinds (see below) are possible; in particular, a main program which is a procedure that is not called by any other) will be a ompilation unit.

An Ada program is written as a collection of separately compiled rogram units, with compile-time type-checking across boundaries. Each nit may provide a set of facilities, and may use the facilities of ther units. This kind of program structure determines the order in hich units must be compiled: definition before usage. The context in hich a unit is to be used must clearly be specified first if the unit s sensitive to that context. Library units are context insensitive so an be compiled before any unit which uses them. Ada separates the mplementation part of a module from its specification part, so the pecification parts can be compiled in the required order but the mplementation parts subsequently in whatever order is convenient provided that they conform to the previously compiled specification).

Here we consider how to design and construct an Ada program from a umber of compilation units – how to express the relationship between hem, and what the consequences of these relationships are in terms of he order in which compilation units are handled.

0.1   Compilation Units

program in Ada is formed from a number of separate compilation units, hich are translated individually and then linked together to form the arget program load. If any changes have to be made to the program after he initial translation, it is only necessary to recompile the affected ompilation units (and any others which depend on the recompiled units) hen relink them with the unaffected compilation units.

Although compilation units are translated separately, consistency hecks are applied to ensure that their interfaces are compatible. This eans that communication between separate compilation units is as well-hecked as that between parts of a single compilation unit. In order to chieve this degree of security at compilation time, the translation of compilation unit is not done in isolation but is associated by the ompiler with information from other compilation units which are

relevant. Similarly, after a compilation unit has been compiled
information is maintained for subsequent use in the translation of other
compilation units which may depend on it. All this information for
inter-compilation unit checking is maintained by the Ada translation
system, forming a data base for each set of compilation units which
comprise a complete program.

The fundamental idea in Ada is that each compilation unit, although
compiled individually, is considered to be defined in some context which
determines the visibility of declarations between one compilation unit
and another. A compilation unit may use identifiers declared in that
context (perhaps in other compilation units), but of course need not do
so.

A basic distinction is drawn between compilation units that are
effectively at the outermost level of declarations in a program, and
those which are not. The former are called library units, the latter
subunits. A subunit must state which already existing unit effectively
contains it; this is called its parent unit. A library unit makes no
assumptions about declarations in the context of its definition; it
could then be taken into other contexts as required. Tasks may only be
subunits; subprograms and packages may be library units or subunits. A
library unit may be a declaration or a corresponding body. All subunits
of the same parent must have distinct names. All library units must
have distinct names.

Once a library unit has been compiled, the facilities that it
provides (by its public declarations) may be used in other compilation
units by giving a suitable context clause.

We discuss how to specify the context of effective definition of a
compilation unit; how to specify which other contexts it may refer to,
and how these relationships affect the order in which the compilation
units of a program must be compiled or recompiled after some change.

10.2   Effective context of a compilation unit

The rules of visibility of declarations apply between compilation units
in the same way as they do between program units within the same
compilation unit. Thus the identifiers declared in a separately
compiled unit are visible in the context of the declaration and any
context in which they are exposed, but nowhere else. It is of course
possible to make the context of the declaration be the main level of the
program and thereby get the identifiers visible throughout the program
(apart from redeclarations), but this is by no means necessary.

A library unit has an effective context which is the whole program,
e. all other library units. A subunit has a context which is
plicitly specified in its parent unit: another unit (either a library
it or a subunit), where the effective position of the subunit is
rked by a stub. Thus a program as a whole consists of a number of
mpilation units, of which some are library units and the rest are
bunits. Every subunit has another unit as its parent unit.

A library unit may be the declaration or body of a subprogram or a
ckage (not a task); a subunit may be the body of a subprogram,
ckage or task. Library units are effectively global for the whole
ogram, but subunits belong to particular contexts.

The context in which a particular subunit is to be effectively
fined is somewhere in the outermost declarative level of its parent
it, as given by a body stub such as

```
package body FLUSHING is separate;
procedure PRINT_HELP_FILE is separate;
```

The parent unit must always contain the complete specification of the
bunit, whether it is a package, task or subprogram. In the case of a
bprogram, the specification gives the formal parameters and result, if
y.

```
procedure DRAW2 (X, Y: FLOAT) is separate;
function ASK (QUESTION: STRING)
    return BOOLEAN is separate;
function MAT_MUL (X : MATRIX;
                  Y : COL_VEC)
    return COL_VEC is separate;
```

the subunit is a module, the parent unit must contain the
ecification explicitly. The context of a subunit is exactly that of
s stub.

Suppose CLEAN_FILTER needs a package FLUSHING, which is written
parately, then CLEAN_FILTER must contain the specification of FLUSHING
ong its local declarations:

```
-- in the declarative part of CLEAN_FILTER
package FLUSHING is      -- specification here
  procedure WATER_FLUSH ( N : NATURAL range 1 .. 2);
  procedure AIR_FLUSH;
end FLUSHING;
```

The corresponding package body must be indicated later in the sam
declarative part; it may be given either immediately here, c
substituted by a "stub" here and compiled separately as a subunit.   Th
body is given immediately thus:

```
    -- later in declarative part of CLEAN_FILTER
    package body FLUSHING is
      -- local declarations
      -- bodies of WATER_FLUSH and AIR_FLUSH
      -- initialisation
    end FLUSHING;
```

or by substituting a stub:

```
    -- later in declarative part of CLEAN_FILTER
    package body FLUSHING is separate;    -- stub
```

with the separately compiled subunit:

```
    separate (CLEAN_FILTER)       -- stating parent
    package body FLUSHING is
      -- local declarations
      -- bodies of WATER_FLUSH and AIR_FLUSH
      -- initialisation
    end FLUSHING;
```

10.3   Contexts accessible to a compilation unit

The default context for a compilation unit is the package STANDAR
(given in Appendix A), allowing the unit to access the predefine
declarations for INTEGER, NATURAL, BOOLEAN, FLOAT etc.

A compilation unit may access the declarations of other compilatio
units if they are explicitly stated in the context clause at its head
in with clauses.

The package STORE specified in section 7.1 may be compiled separatel
to form a library unit (since it needs no context beyond STANDARD)
Suppose we have another unit, GEOGRAPHY which needs to use the variable
in STORE, then GEOGRAPHY may be written

```
    with STORE;
    package GEOGRAPHY is
      -- may use STORE.ALAT etc
```

   end GEOGRAPHY;

The shorthand notation for entities specified in STORE may be used if we
write

   use STORE;

either immediately after the with clause at the head (to expose the
public declarations of STORE over all of GEOGRAPHY) or in the
declarative part of any program units nested within GEOGRAPHY (to limit
the exposure).

   Any number of library units may be specified in the context clause.
All the public declarations of these units are brought into scope for
the unit being compiled. If several have the same signature (see
section 9.8), then any subprogram call using the simple subprogram name
must resolve the ambiguity between them, by using distinct formal
parameter names. (If the formal parameter names are the same, then the
full name of the subprogram must be used to resolve the ambiguity.)

10.4   Separate subunits

Consider two program units OUTER and INNER, related such that if they
were written in a single compilation unit, then OUTER would contain
INNER. The relationship has aspects pertaining to both units, which
must be distinguished if the units are compiled separately. Each unit
must indicate the relationship for itself: with separate compilation for
the fact that OUTER contains INNER must be given in the OUTER unit, but
also must be given (if relevant) in the INNER unit.

   As a declaration in OUTER, the body stub

   package body INNER **is separate**;

expresses the fact that OUTER contains INNER, and allows any subsequent
declarations or statements in OUTER to use INNER as though the full text
of the package body were there. This also expresses the fact that INNER
is a subunit, and OUTER is its parent unit.

   The heading for INNER

   separate (OUTER)
   package body INNER **is** --

connects this compilation unit to the specification for INNER given i
OUTER; it expresses the fact that INNER may use the entities declared i
OUTER, and allows any subsequent declarations or statements in INNER t
refer to any of the other declarations of OUTER visible at the positio
of the body stub.

10.5   Order of compilation

The separate compilation units which form an Ada program may b
submitted for translation in any logical order. We here explain how th
ideas of context of effective definition and accessible context
influence the order of program construction whether by top-down o
bottom-up methods.

    The underlying principle is that if one compilation unit require
information from another compilation unit, then the unit providing th
information must be translated before that requiring the information.

    The with clause is the main influence on order of compilation.   Fo
each compilation unit governed by such a clause, the listed units
specifications must have already been compiled before the unit namin
them in a with clause, so that their declarations may be accessible
Thus if we have

    with TIME_SCALES, CHANNEL_VALUES;
    package body FILTER_OPERATIONS is
      -- text
    end FILTER_OPERATIONS;

then FILTER_OPERATIONS can not be compiled until after th
specifications of TIME_SCALES and CHANNEL_VALUES have been compiled.
subunit must always be compiled after the specification of its parent
the unit CLEAN_FILTER that contains

    package body FLUSHING is separate;

must be compiled before that which begins

    separate (CLEAN_FILTER)
    package body FLUSHING is

in order that the specification and body of FLUSHING are properl
associated.

If a compilation unit does not have a context clause, then there is no constraint on its order of compilation. This allows library modules to be compiled in advance of programs which use them,

The parent unit of a subunit contains the specification of the subunit, so may use all its facilities. The other declarations in the outermost level of the parent unit may also be used in the body of the subunit, just as though it were textually present in the parent.

In bottom-up program construction, we build the program progressively from subprograms into larger units, generally completing the body of a unit before working in detail on the unit that calls it. This allows each unit to be easily tested as all its subsidiary units have been completed by the time work on it begins. In this method, compilation units would generally be library units, which might refer to previously written library units. Perhaps a project-specific package would be written first to contain basic declarations for the project, and all subsequent units would be compiled with that package as their context.

In top-down program construction, we build the program by refinement, with increasing amount of implementation detail, generally completing the specification of entities and the body of the unit using those entities, before working in detail on the implementation of the specified entities. This allows each unit to be easily verified, as all the units are specified in advance of implementation and the implementation of each unit can be validated on its own. In this method, compilation units might well be subunits, sensitive to the context in which the unit is effectively declared.

In practice, of course, programs are constructed using both bottom-up and top-down methods, and Ada allows both to be accommodated.

10.6   Order of recompilation

If there is a change to the program, either because an error has been corrected, or some change to the specification has been taken into account, or a different programming technique is adopted, or for any other reason, one or more compilation units are immediately affected and the new versions of them must be recompiled.

There are circumstances in which other compilation units not immediately concerned are nevertheless possibly affected; these must also be recompiled, to make sure that all the consistency checks for an Ada program still hold.

The guiding principle is to maintain software interfaces as far as possible, and explicitly check changes. If a change does not affect an interface, then parts of the program beyond the interface need no attention. But if a change does affect an interface, then all other units which can access that interface are potentially affected.

If a separate subprogram is changed so that its body is different but its specification (formal parameters and result) remains the same, then recompilation of the subprogram has no effect on the other compilation units of the program.

However if a subprogram is changed and given a different specification in any respect (e.g. changing the number of parameters, or even the name of a formal parameter) then all other compilation units which refer to this subprogram are invalidated, and must be recompiled before the program load can be linked together again.

Similarly, if a module body is changed (but its specification remains the same), there are no consequential effects, but if a module specification is changed in a recompilation, then the corresponding module body (whether included explicitly or written as a separate subunit) must also be recompiled.

Any compilation unit carrying a **with** clause is also invalidated by recompilation of any of the units mentioned in this context clause. A subunit is invalidated by recompilation of the unit containing its stub.

To summarise, after a change to a compilation unit, THIS_UNIT, the recompilation of THIS_UNIT invalidates (and consequently requires recompilation of) all units with any of the following properties:

a. If THIS_UNIT is a parent unit, then all its subunits, which must begin

   separate (THIS_UNIT)

b. If THIS_UNIT is a library unit specification, then every unit with a context clause containing THIS_UNIT, i.e. every unit including

   with THIS_UNIT;

   in its heading.

c. If THIS_UNIT is a specification, then the corresponding body, if any.

After recompilation of each of these, further compilation units may be invalidated by the same rules.

Note that no consequential recompilations are necessary as a result of recompiling the _body_ of a library unit or subunit, or a subprogram declaration whose specification is not changed, provided that it has no subunits and the name is not in any unit's context clause.

10.7   Generic Program Units

A universally valuable technique in programming is to write once a piece of code which will be used many times. This underlies the ideas of loops, procedures and libraries in Ada as in other programming languages; generic program units are another case of the idea in Ada. A generic program unit is a compile-time parametric subprogram or package, that can be written once (usually as a library unit) and then used as many times as needed, as the program is being compiled. The generic program unit forms a model or pattern that may involve compile-time parameters. The technique is commonly used in macro-processors, but in only a few high-level languages.

A generic unit is not itself directly executable, but instances of the model (formed at compile-time) have the properties of the appropriate program unit. Only subprograms and packages may be made generic.

Generic program units are pieces of program which define patterns for subprograms or packages, such that the patterns can be filled out to form proper subprograms or packages by the program translator. The act of making a particular instance of the unit given generically is called instantiation.

Note that all the processing to do with generic program units takes place at translation-time. After a unit has been compiled, there is no difference in meaning between one which was written individually and one which was an instance of a generic unit.

Just as subprograms may have parameters, so may generic program units, allowing the different instances of the pattern to have individual features. Generic parameters offer a wider range of possibilities than subprogram parameters, because they are handled at translation time rather than execution time. Generic parameters may be data values or data objects (like subprogram parameters, but excluding out mode), or types or subprograms.

Whenever an instance of a generic unit is required in a program, actual entities must be specified for the generic parameters. This corresponds to giving actual subprogram parameters in a subprogram call, but takes place at compile time rather than run-time.

10.7.1   Comparison of direct, separate and generic styles

We can compare three ways of writing a program unit: directly, separately, or generically. Suppose in a certain context R we need to declare a procedure P. One way is to write

```
procedure P is     -- direct style
begin
    -- statements to be executed for P
end P;
```

In this style, the statement to be executed for P are entirely specific to the context.

Another way is to write (in the declarative part of R) a body stub

```
procedure P is separate;      -- separate style
```

with the required body given as

```
separate (R)
procedure P is  -- separate style
begin
    -- statements to be executed for P
end P;
```

In this style, the separate procedure body is again specific to its context of use, even though it is written separately from it. However, different versions of the body could produced by file editing (independent of Ada).

The third way is to write (in the declarative part of R) a generic instantiation

```
procedure P is new P_PATTERN;   -- generic style
```

with the required pattern given as

```
generic
procedure P_PATTERN is  -- generic style
```

```
   begin
      -- statements to be executed for P_PATTERN
   end P_PATTERN;
```

In this, the generic style, the body may be given in terms of parameters
whose actual meanings are specified on instantiation, and the program
can have any number of declarations containing

```
   new P_PATTERN;
```

with the same or different actual parameters.

10.8   How to use generics

A principal use for generic program units is to specify the pattern of a
package for dealing with entities of different types, where similar but
not necessarily identical actions are needed.

   This is particularly important with input/output, where similar
actions are needed to handle the types in the program. The input/output
packages defined in Ada are explained in chapter 11, but they rely
heavily on generic program units. For even a very simple program (as in
section 1.2), input/output of integer types needs generic instantiation.
Probably most installations will deal with this by having a local
library package that contains instantiations of the predefined generic
packages for the basic scalar types:

```
   with TEXT_IO;
   package LOCAL_TEXT_IO is
      package INT_IO is new TEXT_IO.INTEGER_IO ( INTEGER );
      package FLT_IO is new TEXT_IO.FLOAT_IO ( FLOAT ));
      package BOOL_IO is new TEXT_IO.ENUMERATION_IO ( BOOLEAN );
   end LOCAL_TEXT_IO;
```

so that a program can do simple input/output without complications. The
context clause at the head of the program contains

```
   with LOCAL_TEXT_IO; use LOCAL_TEXT_IO;
```

and the program text may contain

```
   use INT_IO; -- in declarative part
   begin
      GET(A);        -- LOCAL_TEXT_IO.INT_IO.GET to get an INTEGER
      ---
```

end;

As another example of a generic unit, there may be a generic package
for stack manipulation. It is necessary for all items in a stack to be
basically the same type (refinements allow a variety of types to be
represented in terms of the basic type), but different stacks may have
different base types. For each stack, operators are needed to push new
items on and pop existing items off, which will depend in detail on the
base type of the stack items, although their general pattern is the
same.

Similarly we may have a generic package for manipulating lists of
elements.   Since a list is to be such that in principle any item could
be used in place of any other, all the items on the list must be
basically of the same type. (Elaborations are possible to allow a
variety of types to be represented in terms of the base type).   In
general we will want to be able to deal with a number of lists all
containing elements of the same type, with procedures to search, append
and remove items, or move items for one list to another. These will
follow a general pattern which does not depend on the base type,
although there will be particular places where the item type is
relevant.

A generic program unit is written by prefixing a generic part to a
subprogram specification or package specification. The generic part
gives the generic parameters, which may then be used within the
specification and corresponding body. The generic program unit would
usually be a library unit, in which case the corresponding body would be
written as another library unit. However, it may be written wherever a
declaration is allowed, in accordance with the ordinary Ada rules about
specification and body.

10.8.1   Generic Parameters

The parameters of a generic program unit are given in much the same way
as those of a procedure - as identifiers in the declaration of the
generic program unit, and may then be used inside the body which
follows.   When the generic program unit is instantiated, actual
parameters are given which replace the generic parameters in the body.
There are two major differences from the formal parameters of a
procedure:

   a. The substitution is at compile-time (so that generics are in
       this respect more like macros than procedures); consequently

b. The kinds of entity which can be parametrized generically
    are more varied than those for procedures.

The parameters of a subprogram carry values of data objects at run-time;
those of a generic program unit may similarly carry data values at
compile_time, but in addition they can be used to give types or
subprograms.

If a generic parameter is defined as a data item, it may be of mode
in (the default), meaning a constant determined at compile-time, or of
mode in out, meaning an object whose identity is determined at compile-
time.

If a generic parameter is defined as a type, then the generic formal
parameter must indicate what kind of type it is, to permit strict
checking. The kinds of type recognised are indicated in the heading of
the generic unit when introducing the identifier:

    (<>)   -- discrete (enumeration or integer)
    range <>   -- integer
    delta <>   -- fixed point,
    digits <>   -- floating point,

for scalar types, or the actual definition of an array type, access
type, or private type. The notation for the formal parameter shows
which of these is intended, and allows the consistency of the contents
of the generic unit to be checked (e.g. a discrete type used as an index
for an array type). The symbol '<>' is pronounced `box'.

If a generic parameter is defined as a subprogram, the full
specification of the subprogram must be stated (introduced by the word
with). The parameter may be provided with a default, in which case the
corresponding parameter may be omitted when the program unit is
instantiated. The default is shown by writing is after the subprogram
specification.   Two forms of default are allowed: either the name of a
subprogram visible at the position where the generic program unit is
declared, or the subprogram with the same name as the formal parameter,
visible at the position where the generic program unit is instantiated.
For the first default write the required name after is; for the second
write is <>.

10.8.2   Queue Handling

The following generic package deals with a doubly-linked list of
objects, where the type of the objects is left parametric.   No

operations on the objects are carried out in the generic package, so
they can be considered to be of a private type.

```
generic
  type OBJECT is private;      -- generic parameter
package QUEUE_HANDLING is

  type ITEM;      -- incomplete, needed for access
  type POINTER is
    access ITEM;

  type ITEM is
    record
      CONTENTS : OBJECT;
      NEXT     : POINTER; -- null for last item in queue
      PREVIOUS : POINTER; -- null for first item in queue
    end record;
    -- invariant :
    -- ANY_POINTER.NEXT = null or else
    -- ANY_POINTER.NEXT.PREVIOUS = ANY_POINTER;
    -- invariant :
    -- ANY_POINTER.PREVIOUS = null or else
    -- ANY_POINTER.PREVIOUS.NEXT = ANY_POINTER;

  type QUEUE is
    record
      FIRST : POINTER;   -- null if queue is empty
      LAST  : POINTER;   -- null if queue is empty
    end record;
    -- invariant:
    -- ANY_QUEUE.FIRST = null or else
    -- ANY_QUEUE.FIRST.PREVIOUS = null;
    -- invariant:
    -- ANY_QUEUE.LAST = null or else
    -- ANY_QUEUE.LAST.NEXT = null;

  procedure STRIP (ONE, ANOTHER : QUEUE);
      -- move ONE.FIRST to become ANOTHER.LAST

end QUEUE_HANDLING;
```

The list structure uses **access** types (see section 12.5). The body of
the package shows how the queues are manipulated (see figure 10a).

```
package body QUEUE_HANDLING is
```

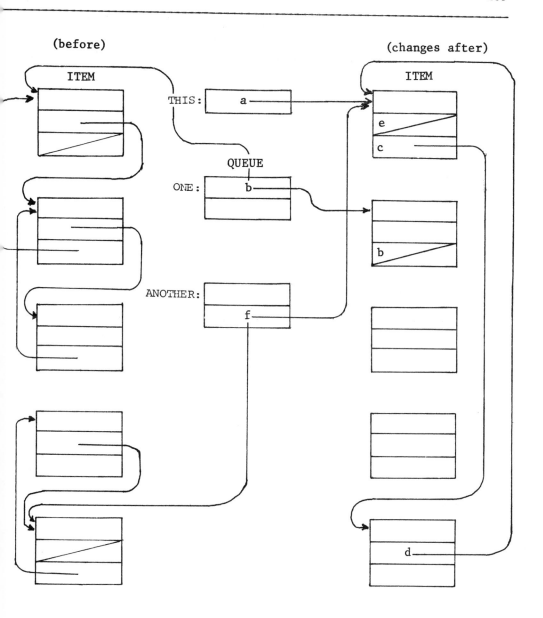

Figure 10a: Strip item from one queue to another

procedure STRIP (ONE, ANOTHER : QUEUE) **is**

```
    -- move ONE.FIRST to become ANOTHER.LAST
     -- assert ( ONE /= null );   -- something to move

    THIS : POINTER := ONE.FIRST;    -- item to be moved

begin

    ONE.FIRST := THIS.NEXT;
      -- a: new first item (may be null)

    if ONE.FIRST /= null then
       ONE.FIRST.PREVIOUS := null;
       -- b: mark it as first item in queue
    end if;

    -- Join old ANOTHER to THIS :
    -- assert ( THIS.PREVIOUS = null );
      -- since it was the first item
    THIS.PREVIOUS := ANOTHER.LAST;
       -- c: attach it to other queue (may be null)
    if THIS.PREVIOUS /= null then
       THIS.PREVIOUS.NEXT := THIS;
       -- d: adjust previous last item
    end if;

    -- Make new ANOTHER :
    THIS.NEXT := null;
       -- e: mark it as last item in queue
    ANOTHER.LAST := THIS;
       -- f: new last item

  end STRIP;

end QUEUE_HANDLING;
```

To get a version (instance) of this package called FQH suitable for use
with lists of objects of type FLOAT, we would write

```
    package FQH is new QUEUE_HANDLING (FLOAT);
```

This counts as a declaration of the package (both specification and
body), so can be followed by declarations of objects of type
FQH.POINTER, FQH.QUEUE and calls of the procedure FQH.STRIP, or after

```
    use FQH;
```

---

he short names POINTER, QUEUE and STRIP.

0.8.3   Table with keys

s a further example of a generic program unit, we give this package for
andling an indexed data set, where the key values are presumed to be
parse. (A simpler version, assuming compact keys, is given in
ASCOT_POOL in chapter 13.) This version presumes that each
nstantiation will be used in only one task.

```
generic
  type KEY is private;
  type ITEM is private;
  with function HASH(K:KEY) return INTEGER range 0..INTEGER'LAST;
  SIZE : NATURAL;

package ASSOCIATIVE_MEMORY is
  procedure ENTER(K:KEY;X:ITEM);
  procedure REMOVE(K:KEY);
  function VALUE(K:KEY) return ITEM;
  function CURRENT_KEY return KEY;
  function ADVANCE_KEY return KEY;

  NONEXISTENT, MEMORY_FULL : exception;
end ASSOCIATIVE_MEMORY;
```

The main facilities provided are to enter or remove an item with a
iven key, or to determine the value of a current item. These may raise
xceptions in certain cases. Also, in order to be able to scan the
emory, facilities allow the current key and key of the next item in the
emory to be discovered.

The implementation uses a number of working variables, set by a
ommon search procedure. These are used in the relevant procedure
odies to detect errors, and refer to relevant positions in the memory.

```
package body ASSOCIATIVE_MEMORY is
  type STATUS is (VALID,DELETED,EMPTY);
  type INDEX is 0..SIZE-1;
  type ASSOCIATION is
    record
      LOCATOR : KEY;
      CONTENTS : ITEM;
      CHECK : STATUS :=EMPTY;
```

```
      end record;
MEMORY : array (INDEX) of ASSOCIATION;
START, CURRENT, POSSIBLE : INDEX;
THIS_KEY : KEY;
FULL : BOOLEAN;          -- all memory has been examined;
GAP : BOOLEAN;           -- there is space for insertion;

procedure SEARCH(K:KEY) is
   -- on exit:
   -- THIS_KEY = K;
   --CURRENT,POSSIBLE are such that
   --(MEMORY(CURRENT).CHECK = VALID and
   -- MEMORY(CURRENT).LOCATOR = K) or else
   --(MEMORY(POSSIBLE).CHECK/= VALID and
   -- this is a suitable place to locate K);
begin
   FULL:=FALSE;
   GAP :=FALSE;
   START:=HASH(K) rem SIZE;
   CURRENT:=START;
   THIS_KEY:=K;
   while MEMORY(CURRENT).CHECK /= EMPTY loop
     if MEMORY(CURRENT).CHECK = DELETED then
        if not GAP then
          POSSIBLE := CURRENT;
          GAP := TRUE;
        end if;
     if MEMORY(CURRENT).LOCATOR /= K then
        CURRENT:=(CURRENT+1) mod SIZE;
     else -- found
        if not GAP then
          POSSIBLE:=CURRENT;
        end if;
        return;
     end if;
     if CURRENT = START then
        FULL := TRUE;
        exit; -- searched all memory
     end if;
   end loop;
   -- not found
   if not GAP then
     POSSIBLE := CURRENT;
   else
     CURRENT   := POSSIBLE;
   end if;
   return;
```

```
  end SEARCH;

  procedure ENTER ( K:KEY ; X:ITEM ) is
  begin
    SEARCH(K);
    if FULL and not GAP then
      raise MEMORY_FULL;
    end if;
    MEMORY(CURRENT).CHECK := DELETED;
    MEMORY(POSSIBLE) := (K,X,VALID);
  end ENTER;

  procedure REMOVE (K:KEY) is
  begin
    SEARCH (K);
    if MEMORY(CURRENT).CHECK /= VALID then
      raise NONEXISTENT;
    end if;
    MEMORY(CURRENT).CHECK := DELETED;
  end REMOVE;

  function VALUE (K:KEY) return ITEM is
  begin
    SEARCH (K);
    if MEMORY(CURRENT).CHECK = VALID then
      return MEMORY(CURRENT).CONTENTS;
    else
      raise NONEXISTENT;
    end if;
  end VALUE;

  function CURRENT_KEY return KEY is
  begin
    return THIS_KEY; -- may not have an entry
  end CURRENT_KEY;

  function ADVANCE_KEY return KEY is
  begin
    START := CURRENT;
    CURRENT := (CURRENT+1) mod SIZE;
    while MEMORY(CURRENT).CHECK /= VALID loop
      if CURRENT = START then -- no other entries
        return THIS_KEY;
      end if;
      CURRENT := (CURRENT+1) mod SIZE;
    end loop;
    THIS_KEY := MEMORY(CURRENT).LOCATOR;
```

```
      return THIS_KEY;
   end ADVANCE_KEY;

end ASSOCIATIVE_MEMORY;
```

Exercises

1. Write a library unit to define the type for control and stat
    registers in a PDP-11, with procedures to enable and disab.
    interrupts by adjusting bit 6 in a control and status register.

2. Package MAJOR_PHASES is a library unit. Write the heading of
    separately compiled procedure that uses the facilities provided I
    this package.

3. Package DIRECT_IO is generic with respect to the ELEMENT_TYPE.
    Write a declaration for an instance of this package to handle ca
    images, and declare a read-only files of card images called CR.

4. Function UNCHECKED_CONVERSION is generic with respect to two type
    SOURCE and TARGET. Declare a function to do unchecked conversi
    from type FP_REP to type FLOAT.

CHAPTER 11

Input/Output and representations

Ada allows the programmer to deal with input/output on any peripherals
which may be connected to a computer - not only conventional
peripherals, such as card readers, line printers and backing store
devices, but also those which are important for embedded computer
systems such as communication data-links and on-line instrumentation for
real-time monitoring and control.

Input/output is concerned with communication between internal and
external processes, using shared variables such as data buffer registers
and intercommunication stimuli which are received by the computer as
interrupts. No special features or additional program structures are
needed to deal with these in Ada, but the programmer needs the ability
to specify data structures and their representations.

It may seem paradoxical that Ada has no special facilities for
handling input/output, but this is so precisely to avoid problems that
might arise if translators were tied to particular kinds of peripherals.
The facilities required for input/output are achieved by making
extensive use of the module (package and task) features, rather than by
having many special features in the language. We can define the
input/output operations in Ada, and put them in a library for other
programmers to use.

Input/output is necessarily machine dependent, and the aim of this
style of programming in Ada is to keep the machine dependency in as
limited a context as possible. Where equivalent operations exist in
different computers, then a package specification gives the common
interface to the operations, and different computers would have
different package bodies to implement these operations in the
appropriate ways.

Each input/output operation consists of a type conversion between a
internal value and a value at the shared interface between the compute
and the peripheral. The program has to treat concrete representations
and relate the desired internal types to the hardware-determined type
of the physical devices.

The Ada Language Reference Manual defines such common Input/Outpu
facilities in five packages, which would normally be tailored b
installations to suit their particular needs. There are two general
purpose input/output packages, called SEQUENTIAL_IO and DIRECT_IO, fo
handling devices or files by streams of data values of the same type
there is one special-purpose package, TEXT_IO, for input/output o
streams of characters intended for communicating with people by tex
strings; there is a further low-level package, LOW_LEVEL_IO, definin
the basic operations that may be used for handling peripheral device
directly. Finally, there is a package called IO_EXCEPTIONS defining th
exceptions that might arise during input/output.

The input/output packages make extensive use of generic facilities
as explained in chapter 10, to ensure that the facilities are defined i
a uniform way for the great variety of input/output peripherals that ca
occur. The instantiation (see section 10.8) of the generic packages ha
to be done before the input/output facilities may be used in a program
this will often be done by each installation making library package
available to all its programmers, taking particular types for device
and data that are required for the computers and peripherals they use
An explanation of this is given in section 11.4.

There is a great deal of similarity between the three main packages
DIRECT_IO, SEQUENTIAL_IO and TEXT_IO. The basic difference between the
is the range of operations they provide for manipulating files, and th
kinds of file element they handle.

In order to handle the details of input/output transfers, or t
program application specific devices, it is necessary for the Ad
program to specify particular representations of data objects an
particular addresses in the computer where data objects are located
These are done by representation clauses.

The physical configuration of peripherals is specified by values in
data structure determined by the computer architecture (e.g. channe
number, subchannel number, device address; or unibus address o
principal control and status word). The hardware/software interface i
specified by another data structure determined by the device controlle
(e.g. structure of control registers, layout of buffer registers).

1.1   Files

da treats input/output as the transfer of sequences of data values
etween the program and some external sources or destinations. There can
e a number of logically independent sequences being operated on
oncurrently. They are called files, and are distinguished as values in
pecial types which are defined in the packages DIRECT_IO and
EQUENTIAL_IO (see Appendix A).

The primary distinction implied by these packages in Ada is whether
r not the elements of a file are considered to be accessible in
rbitrary order (by citing a number giving an element's position in the
ile). It is always assumed that they can be accessed in sequential
rder, but sometimes this is the only order of accessing the elements.
he facilities of SEQUENTIAL_IO are a strict subset of those in
IRECT_IO, so that anything available in SEQUENTIAL_IO is also available
n DIRECT_IO, but there are additional facilities in DIRECT_IO (to do
ith indexing positions of elements in the file) that are not in
EQUENTIAL_IO. We refer to the additional kind of access available in
IRECT_IO as indexed access.

Ada requires the programmer to state two fundamental facts about each
nput/output activity, which of their nature seem to imply a restriction
n the kinds of input/output that can be carried out. Each input/output
equence (file) has a particular element-type (which is permanent), and
 current file-mode which determines the direction of data transfer.

The direction indicates the permissible transfer operations: either
eading data values into the program from the external source, or
riting data values from the program to the external destination, or (in
he case of DIRECT_IO only) both reading and writing data values between
he program and the external file. We refer to the external source or
estination as the partner for the input/output operation.

A file available for read-only access (such as from a card reader)
ust be given the mode IN_FILE; a file available for write-only access
such as to a line printer) must be given as an OUT_FILE; a file
vailable for both reading and writing (such as with a CAMAC crate) must
e given as an INOUT_FILE. An INOUT_FILE can only be used with
IRECT_IO. An interactive terminal is considered to need two separate
iles: one, an IN_FILE, from the keyboard, and the other, an OUT_FILE,
or the display. Similarly, a duplex communication line is considered
s two separate sequential files, for the two directions of
ommunication. The purpose of distinguishing the direction of the file
s to allow checks that reading or writing are intended.

The order of the operations applied to a file always determines the particular data values used — thus a sequence of write operations will send to the destination the given data values in the given order. This permits the implementation of the input/output package to buffer sequences of such operations to the same file; input/output operations need not be carried out immediately, as long as the effect (i.e. the order of reading and writing) is preserved.

This rule appears trivial in the case of an IN_FILE or an OUT_FILE but it is particularly important for an INOUT_FILE. It means that a write operation (which may give a read command F(0) to a CAMAC module followed by a read operation (getting the data read by the module) will be carried out in the order stated in the program. In other words, it ensures that the write operation has been completed before the read operation is started.

Note that the the two concepts of random access and half-duplex communication are expressed together in the package DIRECT_IO; the facilities of package SEQUENTIAL_IO provide for sequential-only access and simplex communication. There is no provision in these packages for half-duplex communication without random access. (Situations needing such provision would call for further Ada packages to be written.)

Specifying the element-type for a file is the way of stating the type of the data values which will be transferred. Note that this has to be fixed in the program and cannot change during execution. This rule is consequence of the "strong typing" style of programming in Ada. Since each data object has to have a particular type known at compile-time any data object whose value is obtained by input (or which gives its value for output) must have a particular type, and consequently all the data values in the sequence which might be transferred to it during input/output must be of the same type. The rule makes logical sense when considered as a means of converting the values from their external form into a suitable internal form for use in the program. What is actually input (or output) is a bit-pattern, and the input/output procedures in the program must convert this to or from the appropriate internal values. To make this conversion, the procedures must know the type of the internal values.

Although the element-type for a file must be fixed, there is no restriction on using the file to hold values of different types provided that they can all be represented as sequences of elements of the common element-type. It is then a matter of programming appropriate conversion procedures to be used in association with the actual data transfer operations.

Ada does not specify which particular external source or destination is to be used for each file: the way of identifying the external partners and their connection is so machine-dependent that it has to be programmed explicitly.

Thus the presumption is that for any input/output package, there would be a procedure to establish the association between a file and a partner, using whatever scheme is appropriate for the machine to identify the partner.

The packages DIRECT_IO and SEQUENTIAL_IO in Ada presume a system in which files have permanent names, used to identify them when several programs may access the same file. The packages are generic, with the type of the elements in the file as the parameter. For any particular element-type, such as WORD, the appropriate package must be instantiated, by a declaration such as

    package WORD_IO is new DIRECT_IO (WORD);

This establishes all the file-types and file-operations:

    WORD_IO.FILE_MODE   -- for the directions of data transfer
    WORD_IO.COUNT   -- for the index values (0 up)
    WORD_IO.POSITIVE_COUNT -- for index values (1 up)
    WORD_IO.FILE_TYPE   -- for files of words

and the operations including indexed access. A different instantiation would be needed for files permitting only sequential access, for example for files of card images where

    type CARD_IMAGE is array (1 .. 80) of CHARACTER;
    package CARD_HANDLING is new SEQUENTIAL_IO (CARD_IMAGE);

Thus for a card reader and a card punch we would use files of this type:

    CR, CP : CARD_HANDLING.FILE_TYPE;

To operate on these we would first set the file mode (direction), e.g.

    CARD_HANDLING.OPEN (CR, IN_FILE, "CRD1");

then to transfer a card image we write:

    CARD_HANDLING.READ (FILE => CR, ITEM => IMAGE);

The input/output procedures and functions can be called using their
full names, or by

    use CARD_HANDLING;

and the local names of the package (assuming there is no ambiguity).

11.1.1   Preparing to use a file

To create a new file to receive output, the program must declare a
variable of the appropriate type, say

    DAC : WORD_IO.FILE_TYPE;

and call the procedure CREATE to set up the control block for that file,
with a permanent name (and, optionally, format information):

    WORD_IO.CREATE (DAC, OUT_FILE, "Magnet wave-form");

This would be done only once in the life of a file. If it is impossible
or illegal to create a file with the name given, an exception is raised.
STATUS_ERROR means that the file variable (DAC in this example) is
already in use (i.e. open), so is not available for a new file;
NAME_ERROR means that the permanent name specified is already in use or
is not allowed for some reason; USE_ERROR means that the file cannot be
created with the stated mode.

For a program to use a file which already exists, a variable must be
declared of the appropriate file type, say

    ADC : WORD_IO.FILE_TYPE;

and the procedure OPEN must be called to set up the control block for
the file and on the basis of the file's permanent name, to make the
connection between the external partner and the current program.

    WORD_IO.OPEN (ADC, IN_FILE, "VOLTAGE SENSOR");

If the OPEN operation cannot be carried out, an exception is raised.
These are the same exceptions as can be raised by CREATE, with slightly
different conditions applying. STATUS_ERROR again means that the file
variable (ADC here) is already in use. This exception would be raised if
by mistake the OPEN procedure was called twice in succession with
identical arguments: the second call would detect this error, even

though the file name happened to be the same. NAME_ERROR means either that there is no file in existence with the specified name, or that it exists but access to it is prohibited. USE_ERROR means that the file cannot be opened with the stated mode.

Every file used in a program must have a variable of the proper file-type which is initialised by calling one of the procedures CREATE or OPEN. No other operations may be carried out on the file until it has been opened (creation implies opening) — if any is attempted, the exception STATUS_ERROR is raised.

Other exceptions may be raised during the course of input/output operations once a file has been opened: DEVICE_ERROR means that there are difficulties in the underlying system (software or hardware — not distinguished), which prevent the operation being completed; MODE_ERROR means that the specified operation is physically impossible or prohibited. In other words, DEVICE_ERROR is something which might arise when the user program is itself correct and sensible, but MODE_ERROR indicates a fault in the logic of the user program.

After use of a file by a program, some post-processing may be necessary before the connection is actually severed. Corresponding to CREATE and OPEN, there are two procedures which reverse their effects.

    WORD_IO.CLOSE(ADC);

causes the file ADC to be closed but to remain in existence with its permanent name for future use.

    WORD_IO.DELETE(DAC);

causes the file DAC to be closed and all information about it deleted, including its permanent name.

The mode (direction of transfer) of a file may be changed by calling RESET thus:

    WORD_IO.RESET (ADC, OUT_FILE);

giving the desired new mode. This automatically resets the index for the file to 1. The index may be reset without changing the mode by omitting the second parameter.

The permanent name of a file may be discovered using the function NAME:

    S : constant STRING := WORD_IO.NAME(ADC);

Similarly the current mode and form of the file may be discovered by
functions MODE and FORM. The current state (open or closed) may be
tested using the function IS_OPEN, thus:

```
if WORD_IO.IS_OPEN(ADC) then
  -- file ADC is open
else
  -- file ADC is closed
end if;
```

11.1.2   File Positioning

As a file consists of a sequence of elements, the number of elements in
it is in principle countable. At any stage during processing, there is a
current position, which establishes the next element to be read or
written in sequential access. Unless specific instructions are given, a
series of read or write operations apply to consecutive positions in the
file.

For some kinds of file there is no possibility of working other than
sequentially. However, other kinds of file have possible control actions
to reposition them (such as backspacing a magnetic tape, or seeking a
track on a disk file). The package DIRECT_IO provides procedures to
manipulate the position of a file, but recognises that particular
operations may be physically impossible. There is no systematic
distinction between files that can or cannot have particular operations
applied to them: there is no check at compile-time on the use of
positioning procedures, but if such a procedure is executed on a file
that cannot substain the operation, the exception USE_ERROR is raised.

The positions in the file are counted from 1, with one position
occupied for each element of the file. Thus in the context of
CARD_HANDLING each card image occupies one position. The function INDEX
returns a value of type POSITIVE_COUNT giving the position of the next
element available to be read or written:

```
I1 := INDEX(CR);      -- serial number of next card
```

and the function SIZE returns an integer value of type COUNT giving the
total number of elements currently in the file

```
I2 := SIZE(CP);       -- number of cards punched
```

'hen a file has just been created, its size is 0 and its position is 1.
.s each element is written to it in sequence, its size and position both
ncrease by one. When a file is closed, its current size may be recorded
n a directory (but this is not required by the package). When a file
hat already exists is opened, its size is the same as when it was last
losed (but this information may not be available); the newly opened
ile is set at position 1.

The position of a file is changed by reading from it or writing to
t, or (if the external partner has the ability) by repositioning. The
rocedure SET_INDEX changes the position number, making the element at
he specified position be the next one available to be read or written.
onsequently

    SET_INDEX(FILE1, 1);

ets the file to position 1, in other words rewinds it;

    SET_INDEX(FILE1, INDEX(FILE1) - 1);

ets it before the previous element, as a back-space operation;

    SET_INDEX(FILE1, SIZE(FILE1) + 1);

ets it to access the next element position after the last current
lement, in other words spacing forwards to the end of the current file.
f the position given in SET_INDEX is outside the current range of
ositions for the file, there is no immediate error, but if there is an
ttempt to READ from such a position then the exception END_ERROR is
aised.

1.2   Data Transfers

he primary operations of transferring data to or from a file are done
y the procedures READ and WRITE. Each transfers a single element of the
ppropriate type. Thus with

    W1 : WORD;

e can have

    use WORD_IO;
    READ(ADC, W1);
    WRITE(DAC, W1);

to read the next value from the file controlled by ADC into the local variable W1, then to write that value to the file controlled by DAC.

Note that the use of READ and WRITE is checked against the file mode each time either is called, and the exception MODE_ERROR is raised if READ is attempted with a file of mode OUT_FILE, or WRITE is attempted with an IN_FILE. Thus READ may be used only with an IN_FILE or INOUT_FILE; WRITE may be used only with an OUT_FILE or an INOUT_FILE.

Each READ or WRITE operation carried out refers to the next element in sequence in the file, unless the file type is DIRECT_IO.FILE_TYPE and a third parameter gives the desired element position for indexed access (see section 11.1.2 above). In the simplest case, each WRITE adds one new element to the file, until an eventual CLOSE marks the end of the file. If a READ operation is executed when there are no more elements in the file, the exception END_ERROR is raised.

With an INOUT_FILE, the READ and WRITE operations with no index parameters refer to consecutive elements in sequence: WRITE adds a new element to the file and a subsequent READ takes the next element after that. (This means that if there is any buffering of elements, any READ must flush out the buffer of elements waiting to be written, and ensure that all the previous WRITEs have been completed before the READ is allowed to proceed.) In the case of indexed access, the READ or WRITE operation specifies the index value from or to which the element is to be transferred.

The READ operation implies checking that the next element in the file is a proper value of the declared element-type for the file. If the element is not of the proper type then the exception DATA_ERROR is raised.

In the presence of file positioning operations, the next position to be available for data transfer (by READ or WRITE) is stated explicitly. This means that elements may be skipped, reread, or overwritten, assuming that such operations are physically possible. If the position has been set to a value outside the range of existing positions for the file, a READ operation will raise the END_ERROR exception. In similar circumstances a WRITE operation is carried out with automatic adjustment of the file size. Any intermediate positions have indeterminate values - a subsequent READ might give an arbitrary value or might raise DATA_ERROR.

1.3   Text Input/Output

Ada includes a package providing facilities for input/output of strings
of characters, such as are needed for communication between a computer
and an operator or programmer. The principal use of this package would
be in conventional computer contexts for program development (see
section 1.6.1), rather than embedded computer systems, where each
program runs under the control of an operating system that handles its
input/output as sequences of characters, which we call streams.

The characters are considered to form lines and pages. (The number
of characters in a line, and the number of lines in a page, are
controlled by the program. They need not be fixed.)

The package presumes that a particular source and destination are by
convention used as standard input and standard output for each program.
The identification of these standard partners is not specified by Ada,
but is presumed to be arranged by the implementation, in other words by
the operating system. The package is called TEXT_IO, and provides
facilities similar to those of SEQUENTIAL_IO for file management, with
the addition of extra facilities to cover textual layout and
input/output of values in the various data types in Ada. Easy procedure
calls are provided for working with the standard input and output
streams but other files (of the right type) may be specified if
required. The specification of package TEXT_IO is given in Appendix A.

The standard input and output streams are automatically opened when
the program begins execution. If any other files are to be used with
TEXT_IO, they must be opened or created using the facilities of the
package to declare and create or open appropriate files. The files used
for these standard streams may be changed: see section 11.3.6 below,
Note that text files can be of mode IN_FILE or OUT_FILE (but not
INOUT_FILE).

The package TEXT_IO contains four generic packages, to deal with
integers, floating-point values, fixed-point values and enumeration
values respectively. These must be instantiated for particular types of
these kinds. In practice, it would be likely that each installation
would have instantiations of them for the types INTEGER, FLOAT, (no
fixed-point), and BOOLEAN in a locally defined package that might be
called LOCAL_TEXT_IO (see section 10.8). Each program unit using them
would have to include

    with LOCAL_TEXT_IO;

as well as

   with TEXT_IO;

in the context specification at its head, and

   use LOCAL_TEXT_IO;
   use TEXT_IO;

to make all the names directly visible. The inner generic packages for
integer, floating point, fixed point and enumeration types must be
instantiated if they are needed for any other program-defined type:

   package CENT_IO **is new** INTEGER_IO (CENTS);
   package ANGLE_IO **is new** FLOAT_IO (ANGLE);
   package DAY_IO **is new** ENUMERATION_IO (DAY_NAME);

for those types declared in chapter 2.

11.3.1   Simple Text Output

All text output is done by the procedure PUT, which can take parameters
of different types for the values to be output, together with parameters
defining the layout.

   The procedure PUT can be used directly to output characters or
strings. By instantiation in LOCAL_TEXT_IO as explained in section
10.8, it can be used to output integers, floating-point values or truth
values (BOOLEAN). By specific instantiation as in DAY_IO above, it is
made available for other types.

   Presuming that we had declared

   LINE_NO, TOT_CHARS : NATURAL;
   TODAY : DAY_NAME;
   use DAY_IO;

and had accumulated counts of lines and characters for the present day's
work in them, the statements

   NEW_LINE;
   PUT("Number of lines:");   -- string output
   PUT(LINE_NO, 5);   -- LOCAL_TEXT_IO.INTEGER_IO.PUT
   PUT("; average length:");
   PUT(FLOAT(TOT_CHARS)/FLOAT(LINE_NO), 3, 2);

```
PUT(" on ");
PUT(TODAY);
```

uld give on the standard output a new line containing something like

lumber of lines: 874; average length: 3.02E+01 on TUESDAY

ie string parameters are output unchanged, as many characters as given.
ie declaration of LINE_NO gives its subtype as NATURAL, which implies
iat its type is INTEGER. In the statement to output the value of
NE_NO, the version of PUT provided is therefore that with
iecification

procedure PUT (ITEM : **in** INTEGER;
                   WIDTH : **in** FIELD := DEFAULT_WIDTH;
                   BASE : **in** NUMBER_BASE := DEFAULT_BASE);

'om the generic package INTEGER_IO with type NUM being INTEGER. The
cond parameter specifies the desired field-width, that is the minimum
imber of columns to be used for this value. No BASE parameter is
iecified, so the default base of 10 is used. Thus the current value of
NE_NO is converted from internal INTEGER format to a decimal integer
i five columns (or longer if necessary to hold the value).

In the later statement, an expression is given whose value is to be
itput. This value is of type FLOAT, so extra parameters are used to
iecify the layout. The version of PUT in this case has specification

procedure PUT (ITEM : **in** FLOAT;
                   FORE : **in** FIELD := DEFAULT_FORE;
                   AFT : **in** FIELD := DEFAULT_AFT;
                   EXP : **in** FIELD := DEFAULT_EXP);

om the generic package FLOAT_IO, with the type NUM being FLOAT. The
cond parameter specifies the desired number of characters before the
cimal point, and the third parameter specifies the number of digits
ter the decimal point. No EXP parameter is specified, so by default
ree characters are used. (Note that this is different from
eliminary Ada.)

The final statement uses the instantiation of ENUMERATION_IO with
pe ENUM being DAY_NAME. Each enumeration value is output as an
entifier in upper case (unless explicitly requested to be in lower
se) or as a character literal, padded out on the right with spaces if
field-width parameter is given.

11.3.2   Simple Text Input

All text input is done by the procedure GET, which has an **out** paramete
(i.e. a variable) to receive the value input. The type of the paramete
determines what kind of conversion (if any) is done as the value
taken in.   GET takes the characters from the input stream to make
value of the required type, automatically going over line boundaries
necessary.

   Thus if we have

      I : INTEGER;
      X : FLOAT;
      J : NATURAL;

then after instantiating the packages in TEXT_IO or using   LOCAL_TEXT_
as described above, the statements

      SKIP_LINE;
      GET($\overline{I}$);
      GET(X);
      GET(J);

will start on the next line of the input file, first read the characte
to form an integer (terminated by a space or end of line), then
floating point number, and then another integer, which must not
negative.   This is free-format input, and the values are not depende
on the number of spaces or lines between them.

   The following procedure has the same effect as the default form
SKIP_LINE to force input from a new line: it reads any remaini
characters on the current line, so that a subsequent GET starts on a n
line.

      procedure READLN **is**
        CH : CHARACTER;
      begin
        loop
          GET(CH);
          exit when END_OF_LINE;
        end loop;
      end READLN;

   If an error or inconsistency is detected during input, an excepti
is raised.   If the characters read are not consistent with the type

he parameter given (for example a letter is detected instead of an nteger) then DATA_ERROR is raised. If the value of an integer or pproximate number read is outside the range implemented, then UMERIC_ERROR is raised. If the value is outside the range constraint f the parameter, then CONSTRAINT_ERROR is raised.

Similar facilities are available for Boolean input, and for rogrammer-defined fixed point or enumeration types.

For boolean and enumeration values, the characters may be in upper ase or lower case without distinction. The characters are read to form n identifier; if this is not one of the values in the expected type, hen the exception DATA_ERROR is raised.

1.3.3   Fixed format input

he GET procedures may also be used with explicit WIDTH parameters to ead in a fixed format. A string variable automatically implies the idth of the string.

Thus with the further declaration

    S : STRING(1 .. 5);

he statements

    GET (S);
    GET (I, 5);
    GET (X, 10);

ill read in five characters for S, the next five for I, and the next en for X. In each case, any line terminators or page terminators are kipped before significant characters are counted. There are no utomatic facilities for discovering what type a string might refer to and because of overloading, the value may not be unique); but when the rogram has decided what type is required - say INTEGER - the ppropriate value in that type can be obtained by a string conversion.

1.3.4   String Conversion

he procedures PUT and GET can also be used to carry out conversions to nd from character strings, in the same way as for input/output, but eeping the strings inside the computer.

To convert a value to the corresponding character string (but without
outputting it), use the procedure PUT. The appropriate package must
have been instantiated for the type concerned (integer, fixed-point,
floating-point or enumeration); we will assume LOCAL_TEXT_IO as above.
The first parameter must be a string variable (to receive the converted
value), instead of a file. The width of the resulting character string
is determined by the length of the given string variable.

Thus with LINE_NO and S defined above,

    PUT (S, LINE_NO);

has the effect of

    S := " 874";

and

    PUT (S, 3 < 4);

has the effect of

    S := "TRUE ";

If the string variable is too short to hold the converted value, the
exception LAYOUT_ERROR is raised.

To convert in the opposite direction, from a sequence of characters
to a value in a scalar type, use the procedure GET. The first parameter
must have a string value (rather than a file), and the second parameter
is a variable of the type required. A third parameter is required in
this case: an integer variable, to indicate how many characters of the
string value have been read. Thus,

    GET ("825ABC", I, J);

has the effect of

    I := 825;
    J := 3;

since the integer read from the beginning of the string is 825
comprising 3 characters. Similarly, if strings M and E have values
"3.012" and "E+01" respectively, then

    GET (M & E , X, J);

ssigns to X the floating-point value denoted by the concatenated
tring, and sets J to 9, the number of characters read.

1.3.5   Layout control

he characters in a text file consist of printable characters and
ontrol characters. The printable characters are considered to be
rranged as a series of lines of text, each line consisting of a number
f columns. Line lengths may be fixed or may be indicated by the
ontrol characters.

    The end of each line is marked by a line terminator. A sequence of
ines forms a page, whose end is marked by a page terminator immediately
fter the last line terminator. The end of the whole file is marked by
file terminator.

    Lines and pages in an output file are by default presumed to be
nbounded, but may be given particular maximum values if they are to be
f bounded size. Thus to limit the line length of file F1 (which must
e of mode OUT_FILE) to 80 columns, we must write

    SET_LINE_LENGTH(FILE => F1, N => 80);

r

    SET_LINE_LENGTH(F1, 80);

he limit may be given for the standard output file by omitting the file
arameter.

    A series of printable characters occupy consecutive columns in the
ame line; control characters affect the line or column numbers. Line
umbers and column numbers are both counted from 1. The effect of the
ackage is defined only for the printable characters: Ada does not
pecify what happens with control characters.

    At any stage during processing with a text file, there is a current
age, a current line and a current column, which establish the next
haracter to be taken or provided. With GET and PUT operations,
equences of characters occupy consecutive columns in one line, then the
ext line and so on. In some circumstances it is possible to specify
he line or the column to be used next. TEXT_IO includes procedures and
ssociated functions for doing this, but that does not guarantee that
hey can always be used - if an attempted action is not possible, the
xception USE_ERROR is raised. If the column number gets beyond the

line length, LAYOUT_ERROR is raised. The functions END_OF_LINE, END_OF_PAGE and END_OF_FILE indicate whether the appropriate terminator is next.

The current line number is set (say to 25) by

    SET_LINE(F1, 25);

Similarly the column number may be set (say to 72) by

    SET_COL(F1, 72);

and the current page, line and column numbers may be discovered by using functions PAGE, LINE and COL respectively. In all of these the file parameter may be omitted (implying the current output file), or stated explicitly.

11.3.6   Implied Streams

The procedures PUT and GET can work with either an implied file or an explicitly specified file. If the file is specified, it must have been declared as an IN_FILE for GET, and an OUT_FILE for PUT. (Remember that there are no INOUT_FILES with TEXT_IO). If the file is not specified, an implied input or output stream is used.

The implied streams are initially set to the standard input and output streams, but subsequently may be set by procedures

    SET_INPUT(NEW_SOURCE);
    SET_OUTPUT(NEW_DESTINATION);

their current values may be discovered at any stage by using statements as follows:

    SRCE := CURRENT_INPUT;
    DSTN := CURRENT_OUTPUT;

(where SRCE is a FILE_TYPE variable of mode IN_FILE and DSTN is a similar variable of mode OUT_FILE). The right hand sides of these assignments are actually calls of functions with no parameters. The functions STANDARD_INPUT and STANDARD_OUTPUT deliver the default initial values of these files.

11.4   Packaged Input/Output

General guidance for input/output can be summarised thus:

a. Identify as a data type the structure of device addresses
    determined by the computer architecture, and define the
    various peripherals by the values of this type.

b. For each kind of peripheral, identify (as a data type) the
    structures of the registers which constitute the
    hardware/software interface for communication with it, both
    for device control, status monitoring and data transfer.

c. Regard each peripheral as a task which cannot be
    reprogrammed; design a corresponding device driver as a task
    which communicates with it using variables of the defined
    types   for device addressing, device control and data
    transfer, and synchronised to it by the device interrupt.
    The driver task can only transfer data of a predetermined
    type. For other more abstract types, higher level procedures
    must include any conversions necessary to use that type as a
    concrete representation.

This approach leads to a program in which there can be representation
dependencies in certain parts, to specify hardware addresses and bit
positions for interface registers.

The input/output for special peripherals will usually be written
individually for each particular system.   However, it may be that
classes of peripherals are sufficiently common to justify library
packages being prepared. For example, CAMAC devices may be controlled
using a package which implements the CAMAC operations:

```
package CAMAC_IML is

    type CRATE_NUMBER is range 0 .. 63;
    type STATION_NUMBER is range 0 .. 31;
    type SUB_ADDRESS is range 0 .. 15;

    type CAMAC_ADDRESS is record
      C : CRATE_NUMBER;
      N : STATION_NUMBER;
      A : SUB_ADDRESS;
    end record;
```

```
type F_CODE is range 0 .. 31;
type F_READ is new F_CODE range 0 .. 7;
type F_WRITE is new F_CODE range 16 .. 23;
type F_OP1 is new F_CODE range 8 .. 15;
type F_OP2 is new F_CODE range 24 .. 31;

procedure SA ( CNA : CAMAC_ADDRESS; F : F_READ;
               DATA : out WORD);

procedure SA ( CNA : CAMAC_ADDRESS; F : F_OP1);

procedure SA ( CNA : CAMAC_ADDRESS; F : F_WRITE;
               DATA : in WORD);

procedure SA ( CNA : CAMAC_ADDRESS; F : F_OP2);

end CAMAC_IML;
```

The procedures would be implemented differently on different systems; for example with a particular crate controller on a PDP_11 we have these declarations in the package body

```
type NAF is
  record
    N : STATION_NUMBER;
    A : SUB_ADDRESS;
    F : F_CODE;
  end record;

CAR : CRATE_NUMBER;
NAFR : NAF;
DBR : WORD;
```

with representation clauses giving their hardware addresses and layout. Each procedure body is declared like this:

```
procedure SA ( CNA : CAMAC_ADDRESS; F : F_OP1) is
begin
  CAR := CNA.C;
  NAFR := NAF'(CNA.N, CNA.A, F_CODE'(F) );
end SA;
```

This selects the required crate then applies the F code for the operation to the specified station and subaddress.

11.4.1   Low-level input/output

For computers that require special instructions to initiate input/output actions, the normal technique is to make suitable procedures with code bodies. Two procedures are predefined for sending control information to a physical device, and requesting status information back from it.

```
package LOW_LEVEL_IO is    -- see Appendix A
   -- type declarations for devices
   -- type declarations for control and status
   procedure SEND_CONTROL (DEVICE : {device_type};
                    DATA : in out {control_and_status});
   procedure RECEIVE_CONTROL (DEVICE : {device_type};
                    DATA : in out {control_and_status});
end LOW_LEVEL_IO;
```

There may be several such procedures, overloaded for different device types

11.4.2   Interrupts

For programmer-defined input/output, the program sets an operation going then either has to test status repeatedly or wait for an interrupt before carrying out the next operation on the same device. The facilities for having tasks in Ada mean that the driver for the device can be written as one task, containing an **accept** statement to wait for a call of the corresponding entry, which can be set so that its representation is a hardware interrupt.

To illustrate this technique, we show a simple timer using the PDP-11 line clock. The hardware clock causes an interrupt at regular intervals (1/50 or 1/60 second) and the program increments a counter by 1 on each occasion.

```
package SIMPLE_TIMER is
   TICK_COUNT : INTEGER := 0;
end SIMPLE_TIMER;

package body SIMPLE_TIMER is
   task TIMER_CONTROL is
      entry DOIO;
      for DOIO use at 8#100#;
      pragma PRIORITY (5);
   end TIMER_CONTROL;
```

```
task body TIMER_CONTROL is
begin
  loop
    accept DOIO;
    TICK_COUNT := TICK_COUNT + 1;
  end loop;
  end TIMER_CONTROL;
end SIMPLE_TIMER;
```

(Note that this program uses a priority mechanism to ensure that TICK_COUNT cannot be accessed while it is being incremented.)

The representation clause for DOIO gives the address of the hardware interrupt to which the entry is linked. Whenever the interrupt occurs, there is an entry call to DOIO. The accept statement waits for the interrupt (indicating to the hardware its readiness for the rendezvous), in accordance with the semantics of a rendezvous. (This is probably best done by having the interrupt handler run at a higher hardware priority than the rest of the program, as shown in the following example.)

For a slightly more complicated case, consider output of a series of characters to the LA36 printer. Assigning a character to the register PBF starts the print operation; when the printing is completed there is an interrupt through location 64 octal. The important thing is to prevent a new character being assigned to PBF before the previous one has been printed. We do this as follows:

```
task SIMPLE_PRINT is
  entry PRINT (C : CHARACTER);
  entry DOIO;
  for DOIO use at 8#64#;
  pragma PRIORITY (4);
end SIMPLE_PRINT;

task body SIMPLE_PRINT is
  LA36 : OUTPUT_DEVICE;
  for LA36 use at 8#177564#;
begin
  loop
    accept PRINT (C : CHARACTER) do
      LA36.PBF := C;
    end PRINT;
    accept DOIO;
  end loop;
end SIMPLE_PRINT;
```

The task body alternates the two parts (i.e. it ensures mutual exclusion), taking the PRINT rendezvous to copy the character to the buffer with the interrupt disabled, then enabling the interrupt for the DOIO while not accepting calls to PRINT. When the interrupt arrives, the rendezvous starts, the interrupt is disabled, and on completion of the rendezvous (trivial in this case), the task body loops back.

11.5   Representation Clauses

The input/output of a real embedded computer system will have to specify not only sequences of operation but detail to the level of particular bit-patterns and particular hardware addresses which have to be used. Ada provides facilities for doing this as representation clauses.

The normal declarations in Ada are sufficient to define the logical properties of the entities involved, but do not give all the physical details. For normal purposes it is appropriate that the compiler should make choices for these, and apply them consistently. When input/output is concerned, the program has to relate to other parts of the system about which independent decisions have been taken, and the compiler is not free to choose physical representations unilaterally.

Various kinds of representation clauses may be included in a program, giving implementation details for different entities involved in the program. The most important of these are for the layout of a record type and the location of a data object (variable); in addition we can state the representation for values of an enumeration type and various details about storage allocation. All representation clauses use the keywords **for** and **use**, with various other words to denote particular details. Representation clauses must be given after all the declarations in a program unit, before any inner unit bodies or the executable part.

11.5.1   Record layout

The layout of a record type is specified by giving the positions of its components, stating for each component which location it is in (relative to the start of the record) and which range of bit positions it occupies. Ada presumes that there are addressable storage units which are used consecutively, and bit numbers which identify the bits within a storage unit (or extending to adjacent storage units). Ada (regrettably) does not specify which bit number corresponds to the most significant end of a storage unit.

The type declaration

```
type OUTPUT_DEVICE is
  record
    PSR : CSR_WORD;
    PBF : CHARACTER;
  end record;
```

would be used in connection with a PDP-11 where CSR_WORD is a previously defined type consisting of bits for special purposes.

The components in this record always occupy consecutive words starting on a multiple of 4 bytes. This is indicated by the representation clause

```
for OUTPUT_DEVICE use
  record at mod 4;
    PSR at 0 * WORD range 0 .. 15;
    PBF at 1 * WORD range 0 .. 7;
  end record;
```

where WORD has the value 2 in a PDP-11 (each word consists of two bytes, and the byte is the addressing unit : hardware addresses are given in bytes). The range specifies the bit numbers used in the stated location for the given component.

Similarly, we could give the representation for floating point values by writing

```
type FP_REP is
  record
    SIGN    : BOOLEAN;
    EXPONENT: INTEGER range -128 .. 127;
    MANTISSA: delta 16.0 ** -14
              range 0.0 .. 1.0 - 16.0 ** -14;
  end record;
```

with representation clause

```
for FP_REP use
  record
    SIGN     at 0 range 0 .. 0;
    EXPONENT at 0 range 1 .. 7;
    MANTISSA at 1 range 0 .. 55;
  end record;
```

Bit numbering extends over consecutive storage units as far as necessary.

11.5.2   Device Addresses

In the PDP-11, all devices connected to the computer communicate with it and are controlled through registers at particular Unibus addresses; in general each device is identified by the Unibus address of its principal control and status register. (The situation is more complicated for multiplexed devices, but the same principles apply.) In other computers, devices are connected to particular ports or channels, which are similarly represented.

A PDP-11 output device (e.g. LA36 printer) would be declared thus

    LA36 : OUTPUT_DEVICE;

and the actual location to be used for its control and status register could be specified by stating

    for LA36 **use at** 8#177564#;

(Note the use of the based integer to give the location in octal.)

The representation clauses thus allow devices to be referred to explicitly through ordinary Ada names, and for example a character C can be sent to the printer by the assignment

    LA36.PBF := 'C';

Checks on the status word can similarly be programmed. This is of course for direct output to the device with no hidden buffering. Any buffering needed can be programmed explicitly.

11.5.3   Enumeration representations

The idea of an enumeration type is that identifiers, rather than internal codes, are used as the values of the type. This makes it very much easier to understand and maintain the program. However, when an enumeration value is input or output directly (e.g. in a message format) a code value is required rather than an identifier. For example, messages may carry a precedence field which uses a particular code to denote the several possibilities.

To deal with this, Ada allows the code for an enumeration type to be
specified. The identifiers would still be used in the program, but their
internal representations would be as specified. The code values are
stated as integers, and the correspondence between the symbolic values
of the enumeration type and the integers are given as an aggregate,
thus:

```
type PRECEDENCE is
  (ROUTINE, PRIORITY, FLASH);

type SECURITY_CLASSIFICATION is
    (UNCLASSIFIED, RESTRICTED, CONFIDENTIAL,
     SECRET, TOP_SECRET) ;

for PRECEDENCE use
  (ROUTINE  => 1,
   PRIORITY => 2,
   FLASH    => 4);

for SECURITY_CLASSIFICATION use
  (UNCLASSIFIED => 0,
   RESTRICTED   => 1,
   CONFIDENTIAL => 2,
   SECRET       => 4,
   TOP_SECRET   => 8);
```

11.5.4   Representations affecting storage allocation

Without specifying in complete detail the layout of a record or array
type, it is possible to state that it is to be stored compactly
(possibly at the expense of access time) by writing

```
pragma PACK ( CSR_WORD );
```

Giving slightly more detail about a type, we can specify the maximum
number of bits to be allocated for objects of the type

```
for SMALL_INTEGER'SIZE use 10;
```

The representation for a fixed-point type depends on the fineness of the
approximation used. The compiler will normally choose a suitable value
(equal to or less than the declared delta), but we can if necessary
over-ride this by stating explicitly (using the attribute SMALL) the
separation between adjacent values represented in the fixed-point type:

```
for COMPASS'SMALL use 0.05;
```

We can also specify the number of storage units to be reserved for he collection of objects in an access type by writing

```
K  : constant := 1024;
for POINTER'STORAGE_SIZE use 2 * K;
```

The same format is used to specify the amount of working storage to e allocated for an activation of a task.

1.5.5   Manipulating representations

s well as allowing the programmer to state the representation to be sed for objects of specified types, Ada provides an 'escape' from the trong typing rule, for use in special situations such as input/output.

When a value has to be converted for input/output, the low-level cogram may have to manipulate the bit-patterns which represent values. n order to be able to do this, we must be able to treat representations f values of one type by the operations appropriate to another type. learly this is a very dangerous thing to do, as mistakes cannot be etected by the compiler. Manipulations like this should only be done thin the body of a package whose body is carefully checked manually.

There is a predefined library unit called UNCHECKED_CONVERSION (see ppendix A), which is a generic function to return a value in one type ich has the same representation as the value in another type. (It ctually does nothing, but satisfies the type rules.)

Any program unit which needs to use this must be headed

```
with UNCHECKED_CONVERSION;
```

access the library unit; the context specification acts as a warning the maintenance programmers that it may do strange things. Inside he unit, the generic function must be instantiated for the particular ource and target types required:

```
function FLOAT_OF_REP is
  new UNCHECKED_CONVERSION
    ( SOURCE => FP_REP,
      TARGET => FLOAT );
```

This would allow us to write

```
R : FP_REP;
X : FLOAT;
---
X := FLOAT_OF_REP(R);
```

to take the representation R as a floating point value.

11.5.6   Entry points

In the case of a subprogram or module, the code may be provided from outside the Ada program; the position at which it is loaded can be specified in the Ada program by a representation clause. Suppose there is a kernel subroutine for resetting the system clock, whose entry point is at 220 octal. We would specify the procedure thus:

```
procedure RESET_CLOCK;
for RESET_CLOCK use at 8#220#;
```

The program could then call RESET_CLOCK and thereby enter the kernel subroutine.

11.5.7   Code Statement - executable machine code

On any particular target computer, there may be useful machine instructions that are not normally generated by the Ada translator. You can program them explicitly in Ada by writing the body of a procedure as one or more code statements, giving the values for fields of the machine instruction as a qualified expression, thus:

```
MACHINE_CODE.OPCODE'(BPT);
```

where MACHINE_CODE is the name of a package that includes

```
type OPCODE is (HALT, NOP, REI, BPT, RET,
  RSB, MTPR, MFPR);
```

```
for OPCODE use
  (HALT => 0, NOP => 1, REI => 2,
   BPT => 3, RET => 4, RSB => 5,
   MTPR => 16 # DA #, MFPR => 16 # DB # );
```

the instruction needs operands, the type must express what they can
, and the code statement must include suitable values given as an
gregate value, thus

    MACHINE_CODE.OP2'(MFPR, SID, W'ADDRESS);

ing another type from package MACHINE_CODE that defines the operations
king two operands, and

    type VAX_REGISTER **is**
        (KSP, ESP, SSP, USP, ISP, SID); -- and others

    for VAX_REGISTER **use**
        (KSP => 0,
         ESP => 1,
         SSP => 2,
         USP => 3,
         ISP => 4,
         SID => 62);

For each implementation, the library package MACHINE_CODE (if it
sts) defines the record types for the allowed instructions. The
pilation unit must therefore have

with MACHINE_CODE;

its head. A procedure containing a machine code statement should not
tain any other kind of statement.

Exercises

Write statements to input two unsigned decimal integers and print
out their sum (up to three digits).

Write a function to ask the user a question, and return a Boolean
result, depending on whether the reply is yes or no.

Using the GINO_F procedure DRAW2, draw a horizontal line of length
one unit.

Write an interrupt handler for input from a keyboard, where each key
depression causes an interrupt with the character code in a hardware
register.

5. Reserve 200 blocks of storage, each sufficient to hold a tra
   image, for allocation with track pointers.

CHAPTER 12

More on types

he description of types and values in chapter 2 deliberately left out a
umber of finer points in order to concentrate on the basic ideas. In
his chapter we complete the exposition of types in Ada. There are a
umber of separate issues to be covered, which all combine to give a
ery powerful and flexible scheme.

The type specifies more than the range of possible values - it also
etermines the way the data values are represented, and which operators
re valid for a data item. Ada has a fixed set of operator symbols;
heir meanings with certain elementary types are predefined, but the
rogram may give additional meanings for an operator symbol by defining
t with other types. Thus the operator + is defined for addition of
ntegers and real values, as used in

```
3 + 2      -- 5
4.1 + 3.3  -- 7.4 (approximately)
```

r other expressions involving similar values, but not immediately for
alues of other types, such as in 'A' + 'x' (i.e. unless the programmer
as taken steps to define + applied to characters).

Every type has a representation (such as a series of distinct bit
atterns for an enumeration type). Different types sometimes have the
ame representation, but are nevertheless kept distinct by the
ranslator. The representation is usually chosen by the translator, but
n some circumstances (particularly in connection with input/output) it
ay be necessary to specify explicit details. Section 11.6 explains
his.

The fundamental "strong typing" idea means that programs should
ontain distinct types for all the different kinds of data item with

171

which they deal. Ada allows new types to be introduced easily. Derive
types (section 12.1) take their properties from already existing types
so that there are similar values in the new type, and the operation
applicable to them are the same. Abstract data types (section 12.2) ar
more general, in that the new type has an explicitly specified set o
properties - the programmer gives the complete set of operation
applicable to values of the new type. Variant records (section 12.3
are more flexible, in that different values of the type may hav
different components.

Further sections in this chapter deal comprehensively with the ide
of constraints on types (section 12.4), and dynamic objects which ar
the values of access types (section 12.5). Finally, we discuss ho
types may be used to clarify ideas during the design stage of a progra
(section 12.6).

12.1   Derived Types

There may be occasions when we wish to use the typing rules of Ada t
maintain a distinction between similar values - such as betwee
measurements in different units, or of different kinds such as length
and weights. We want to be able to add lengths together, but not to ad
a length to a weight. The way of doing this in Ada is to use derive
types.

```
type METRES is new FLOAT;
type FEET is new FLOAT;
type POUNDS is new FLOAT;
```

The fact that the types are distinct means that even though they ar
all handled as floating point quantities, they are logically different
Although we can add together floating point values, we can not add
quantity in metres to one in feet, or a length to a weight.

We can construct a new type as a derivative of another, so that th
new type "inherits" all properties of the original one (in particula
its literals and the operators which may be applied to it) ye
nevertheless the values in the new type are treated as distinct, an
assignments between different types are prevented.

So with

```
L1, L2 : FEET;
W1, W2 : POUNDS;
```

e can have

```
L1 := 5.0;          -- literal of type FEET
L2 := L1 + 1.0;     -- addition of type FEET
W1 := 2.2;          -- literal of type POUNDS
W2 := 0.5 * W1;     -- multiplication of type POUNDS
```

ut not for example L1 + W1 or W1 := L2 or a comparison W2 < L1 — all
f which are clearly nonsense and in Ada are detected at compile-time.

(Note that the checking which Ada provides is not a full dimensional
nalysis: there would be no challenge to the physically meaningless
tatement

```
W1 := W1 * W2;
```

ince there is no infringement of the type matching rules).

A derived type is introduced by writing the word **new** before the
riginal type name, and then possibly putting a constraint. The derived
ype is given a name by introducing it in a type declaration

type NEW_TYPE **is new** OLD_TYPE;

o allow objects and parameters to be introduced for this type.

Any type (predefined or user-defined) may be used as the basis for
erived types, including arrays and records. However, the most useful
ases are likely to be derivatives of the predefined scalar types FLOAT
nd INTEGER. These are explained below, in the section on Constraints
nd Derived Types.

2.2   Private data types

or some purposes it is necessary to control access to the values in a
ype, to provide security between one part of a program and another. For
xample, a system may have several input/output channels with a package
o handle the physical input/output using a control block for each
hannel. It is important that the rest of the program should not
nterfere with the control blocks, or even with the control block for
he channel which it might be using. It might even be important to
revent unauthorised copying of control blocks. We deal with this
ituation in Ada using a private data type, in which the type is given a
ame and operations on objects of the type are defined, but nothing is
hown about the implementation details for the type.

12.2.1   Visible part

A private data type in Ada is declared thus:

type CHANNEL **is private;**

The private type must always be introduced in the visible part of
package module, and the same visible part must contain the declaration
for all the other information related to that type - any constant value
of the type that may be used, and the subprograms that can manipulat
objects of that type. Several private data types may be introduced i
the same module if required, by appropriate private type declarations
The rest of the program (wherever the package is visible) can use th
private type - declaring objects of that type, and using them a
parameters to the given subprograms. But the rest of the program canno
directly investigate or interfere with the values of any object of th
private type, or even determine what its structure is (i.e. whether
scalar, a record or an array).

So if the package consists of

package IO_HANDLING **is**
  type CHANNEL **is private;**
  INACTIVE : **constant** CHANNEL:
  procedure CONNECT (C : **out** CHANNEL);
  procedure DISCONNECT (C : CHANNEL);
    -- further declarations, including private part

then the program elsewhere can contain

  use IO_HANDLING;
  C1, C2 : CHANNEL;

  C1 := INACTIVE;
  CONNECT (C2);
  CONNECT (C1);

If the private type is introduced as shown above, then it i
permitted for objects of that type to be copied using assignmen
statements, and compared for equality. However, the assignment an
equality operations can be eliminated by declaring

type SPECIAL_CHANNEL **is limited private;**

here the word **limited** indicates that only the operations defined by the
subprograms in the visible part of the package are available for objects
f the private type. Objects of a limited private type may not be
ssigned (copied) using assignment statements, nor may they be compared
with one another, unless suitable relational operators are given in the
ame visible part as the type definition.

A common use for limited private type would be when the values are
ecords containing linkages to other records, and cross references have
o be maintained, so copying by assignment would bypass the maintenance
f the cross references.

Private types in Ada separate the essential logical properties of the
ype from its implementation, like abstract data types. However, the
perations applicable to a private type are defined only so far as their
ames and parameters are concerned: the effects on the parameters are
ot stated.

2.2.2   Private part

package specifying a private data type must contain a further part
iving implementation details of the type and associated constants,
alled its private part. Although this is written and handled with the
isible part, the information it contains is not openly available to any
nit using the package. (It is needed for compilation of such units, so
hat variables of the type can be allocated the right amount of space.)

As well as a full type declaration (of any kind) for each type
pecified as private, the private part must contain the full declaration
or any constant value of the type, such as INACTIVE above. The earlier
eclaration is called a deferred constant declaration, since it
ntroduces the identifier and its type, but does not state the value in
he visible part. After the full type declaration in the private part,
he constant declaration must be given (in the normal way, as described
n section 2.4), in terms of the private type details.

For example, we might complete the above example with

```
private
  type CHANNEL is
  record
    ACTIVE : BOOLEAN;
    IO_UNIT : NATURAL;
  end record;
```

```
    INACTIVE : constant CHANNEL := CHANNEL(FALSE, 0);
  end IO_HANDLING;
```

Several private types may be introduced in the same package: the private
part must contain the full details for all of them. The full type
declaration in the private part may be of a record with variants.

12.3   Records with variants

A record may have variants in which certain components are only present
in particular circumstances. For example, in a message switching
system, we might have a directory which will give the disposition of
messages according to their destination address - some local (for
immediate delivery), and some remote (for passing to a neighbouring
node). The record for each destination address must contain information
for either local or remote destinations, together with some common
information. The whole directory would be an array of such records,
indexed by the telephone number of the relevant entry.   Each entry in
the directory would have components as shown, according to whether it
was local or remote.

```
    type TRUNK is range 1 .. 9;
    type LINE is range 1 .. 99;
    type WHERE is (LOCAL, REMOTE);
    type DIRECTORY_ENTRY (PROXIMITY: WHERE := LOCAL) is
      record
        ANSWER_BACK : STRING(1..5);
        case PROXIMITY is
          when LOCAL =>
            LINE_NUMBER : LINE;
          when REMOTE =>
            TRUNK_NUMBER : TRUNK;
        end case;
      end record;
```

Similarly, in an air traffic control system there will be observed
tracks, flight plans, and advance warning of tracks from adjacent
geographical areas; each track will require a record with some common
information plus some further specialised information depending on which
kind of track it is. Variants allow the value of the record to take
account of the possibility that certain components may sometimes be "not
applicable" or "not relevant".

    In general, a record consists of a fixed part or a variant part or
both. The variant part may contain several mutually exclusive variants;

each variant contains any number of components (which may themselves contain inner variants). The several variants in a variant part are distinguished by the value of a special component called the discriminant: PROXIMITY in the above example. The discriminant is introduced as a special component in the heading of the type declaration; the heading also usually gives a default value for the discriminant. All the variants are collected together in a **case** clause which uses values of the discriminant to select each particular variant.

The value of the discriminant determines the storage allocated for the record; this may be either fixed when an object is declared to be of the variant record type, or left variable so that values of any variant can be assigned to the object. The difference is expressed by the use of a default value for the discriminant in the type declaration.

If, as above, a default value (LOCAL) is given for the discriminant PROXIMITY), then each declared object of this type may take any value of the type, including different variants; the default determines the initial value of the discriminant.

As usual with a **case** clause, the values given for the discriminant to select the different variant parts must be all different. Any number of components may be introduced for each variant; if it happens that a particular variant has no components, then **null** must be written to indicate this explicitly. Usually the discriminant is an enumeration type, and the selections in the case clause correspond to the values of that enumeration type, as with LOCAL and REMOTE in the above example. A number of special forms are possible for the cases where several values for the discriminant all determine the same variant, as in a **case** statement (section 4.3.2): the list of values or a range denotation for a compact set of values may be given as the selection.

In any value of type DIRECTORY_ENTRY, there is the PROXIMITY component (the discriminant), which specifies whether the particular value is LOCAL or REMOTE, and always a component called ANSWER_BACK which is a string of five characters; if PROXIMITY is LOCAL then there is a further component called LINE_NUMBER, whose value is an integer in the range 1 to 99; but if the PROXIMITY is REMOTE the DIRECTORY_ENTRY contains a component called TRUNK_NUMBER, whose value is an integer in the range 1 to 9. The notation of the variant record ensures that a line-number exists for a local directory-entry and a trunk number only exists for a remote directory-entry. (In practice, the implementation may use the same storage location for these components, but they are logically distinct).

Thus with

```
    D1, D2: DIRECTORY_ENTRY;
```

we could have assignments to the complete record:

```
  D1 := (LOCAL, "CMDHQ", 1);
        -- by position

  D2 := (ANSWER_BACK => "DIVN5";
         PROXIMITY => REMOTE;
         TRUNK_NUMBER => 5);
         -- by name
```

and to individual components for the appropriate variant:

```
  D1.LINE_NUMBER := 91;
  D2.TRUNK_NUMBER := 6;
```

(with appropriate range checks on the integer values given). Note that
assignments are always complete objects (never partial records, with
some components missing).

An alternative, less general form, is to give no default value for
the discriminant in the heading. In this case, each object declared to
be of the type must have its discriminant value given in the object
declaration, thus constraining the object always to have that particular
discriminant value.

A similar notation is used to denote a record containing an array of
variable length; the length is the discriminant. Each value of the
record must have a particular length, but different records may have
different lengths. This is illustrated by the component SRC in
WAIT_CONTROL_BLOCK, whose length is given by S_COUNT.

```
  PROC_MAX : constant := 5;
            -- maximum number of processes

  type PROC_NO is range 1 .. PROC_MAX;

  type SOURCE is
    record
      HOST : BYTE;
      NAME : BYTE;
    end record;

  type WAIT_CONTROL_BLOCK (S_COUNT : range 0 .. PROC_MAX := PROC_MAX)
    record
      W_TYPE : W_CODE;
```

```
      SRC : array (PROC_NO range 1 .. S_COUNT) of SOURCE;
   end record;
```

A record may contain several variable-length arrays, but the bounds on their indices must be simple (not expressions), and all variable bounds must be written in the heading as discriminants. This is to ensure that each object of the record type is allocated the right amount of space when it is declared.

The variants of a record always come after the non-variant components. However, any component (including those in variants) may be of any type, so may itself be a record containing variants. Thus with

```
   type OP_CODE is (MODIFY, OPEN, CLOSE,
                       RESET_LINK,
                       RESET_VC,
                       RESTART);

   type DETAILS (OP_CMD : OP_CODE := MODIFY) is
      record
        case OP_CMD is
          when MODIFY =>
            MODIF : ADDRESS;
          when OPEN .. RESET_LINK =>
            LINK : LINK_NO;
          when RESET_VC =>
            L_C : L_CHANNEL_NO;
          when RESTART =>
            SUBSCRIBER : SUBSCR_NO;
        end case;
      end record;
```

we can have

```
   OP1, OP2 : DETAILS;
```

which means that these variables can take values with different variants on different occasions: we may assign

```
   OP1 := (MODIFY, 201);    -- by position
   OP2 := DETAILS'( OP_CMD => OPEN, LINK => 5 ); -- by name
```

Note that a constant value is given as the complete aggregate, including the value of the discriminant. The aggregate may be written as a qualified expression, if necessary to avoid ambiguity.

A nested variant structure is possible. This is illustrated in type
MESSAGE below, where the component OP itself has variants.

```
type TIMER_IDENTIFIER is range 0 .. 255;

type TIMER_TIME is range 0 .. 64 * K - 1;

type NET_B_PTR is range 0 .. NET_BUF_MAX;

type M_CODE is (OPERATOR, IN_DONE, OUT_DONE,
                DO_OUTPUT, TIMER, LOCAL, NET_IO,
                BUFF_MAN);

type MESSAGE (M_TYPE : M_CODE := OPERATOR) is
  record          -- use array (1 .. 4) of BYTE
    case M_TYPE is
      when OPERATOR =>
        OP : DETAILS;
      when IN_DONE .. DO_OUTPUT =>
        STATUS : S_CODE;
        BUFF : NET_B_PTR;
      when TIMER =>
        ID : TIMER_IDENTIFIER;
        T : TIMER_TIME;
      when others =>
        null;  -- to be defined
    end case;
  end record;
```

Also, inner variant parts may be written in each variant; but the
discriminant must be given in the main heading.

```
type LINE_STATUS ( DEFINED, IN_USE : BOOLEAN := FALSE ) is
  record
    case DEFINED is
      when FALSE =>
        null;
      when TRUE =>
        SUBSCRIBER : SUBSCR_NO;
        case IN_USE is
          when FALSE =>
            null;
          when TRUE =>
            PARTNER : SUBSCR_NO;
        end case;
    end case;
  end record;
```

e section 12.4.3 for details of constraints that can apply to records th variants.

.4   Constraints and subtypes

thin the set of values comprising a type, there may be useful subsets, ich we may want to use in the program. This can be used to give names a particular range of values relevant to the problem, e.g. for fferent parts of a week:

```
subtype WEEKDAY is DAY_NAME range MONDAY .. FRIDAY;
subtype WEEKEND is DAY_NAME range SATURDAY .. SUNDAY;
```

that a variable could be declared to hold values in a weekend

```
SS : WEEKEND;
```

d this would be always in the specified range.

We often require particular ranges of integers. The type INTEGER cludes all whole-number values from an extreme negative value to a rge positive value; but there are many cases when only certain ranges e sensible. There are two useful predefined subtypes of INTEGER:

```
subtype NATURAL is INTEGER range 0 .. INTEGER'LAST;
subtype POSITIVE is INTEGER range 1 .. INTEGER'LAST;
```

eaders who had studied earlier definitions of Ada should note this vised definition of NATURAL). With this, we can write

```
TRACK_COUNT : NATURAL;
```

is means that TRACK_COUNT is a variable whose values will be of type TEGER but always constrained to the range 0 up to the largest integer lue. Since its type is INTEGER, all the usual integer operations can used with it, but whenever there is an assignment of a new value to ACK_COUNT, an implicit check is made that the value is in the proper nge. If this check fails, the exception CONSTRAINT_ERROR is raised.

The object declaration could have been written equally well

```
TRACK_COUNT : INTEGER range 0 .. INTEGER'LAST;
```

th the type given explicitly, and the constraint to be applied for is object. The subtype declaration is simply a shorthand notation, giving a simple name for the type and constraint.

The values in a range constraint need not be constants or even stat
expressions: the values will be calculated if necessary when tl
declaration is met in the course of executing the program. So we migl
have a subprogram with a formal parameter MAX and a local declaration

    subtype INDEX **is** INTEGER **range** 1 .. MAX;

12.4.1　Range constraints

There are various kinds of constraint which are used with differei
types.　We have already met a range constraint used with type INTEGEI
it can equally apply to other scalar types.　Thus we can have subtyp
declarations:

    subtype UC_LETTER **is** CHARACTER
                     range 'A' .. 'Z';
    subtype LC_LETTER **is** CHARACTER
                     range 'a' .. 'z';
    subtype HIGH_GRADE **is** SECURITY_CLASSIFICATION
                     range CONFIDENTIAL .. TOP_SECRET;

and object declarations

    START_DAYLIGHT : MONTH **range** FEB .. MAY;
    END_DAYLIGHT   : MONTH **range** AUG .. NOV;

A range constraint may be used by itself to form an implied deriv
type, for numerical values (integer or floating-point). The bounds
the range must be of the same type, and the range implies a derivati
of that type. Thus

    range 1 .. 10;

as a type definition implicitly means

    new SHORT_INTEGER **range** 1 .. 10;

(on a computer with SHORT_INTEGER covering this range).

A range constraint may be given for a floating point type and <u>must</u> l
given for a fixed point type. It is needed to determine tl

presentation for values of the type. The actual range implemented will
over the specified range, but need not exactly match it. A value
utside the specified range will raise CONSTRAINT_ERROR. A value
utside the implemented range will raise NUMERIC_ERROR.

2.4.2   Accuracy constraints

or a real type (i.e. fixed or floating point), we use accuracy
onstraints. The sets of abstract values concerned are approximations
o mathematical real numbers (for example, measurements of continuous
hysical quantities such as length, voltage, temperature or weight). A
undamental distinction is made in Ada between approximations which are
elative and those which are absolute. This is shown by the accuracy
onstraint given in the declaration. You either specify the number of
ecimal digits of precision needed (indicating that the approximation is
elative) or the magnitude of the acceptable error bound for the
pproximation (indicating that the approximation is absolute).

. Relative precision: Floating point.

   The type declaration

      type SPEED **is digits** 5;

   says that the possible values for SPEED are approximations to real
   numbers, with a relative accuracy of at least five decimal digits.
   (It is left to the compiler to decide for each computer whether this
   needs single precision or double precision floating point.)

   We could then use this type to declare objects

   AIR_SPEED : SPEED;
   GROUND_SPEED, WIND_SPEED : SPEED;

or components of records:

   record
      MAGNITUDE : SPEED;
      ORIENTATION : ANGLE;
   end record;

   The predefined environment of Ada includes the built-in
floating-point types SHORT_FLOAT, FLOAT and LONG_FLOAT; the
particular number of digits of precision in each depends on the

computer concerned. Any floating-point type is effectively derive
from one of these, appropriate for the constraint:

type SPEED **is new** FLOAT **digits** 5;

(on a computer with at least five decimal digits of precision i
FLOAT).

b. Absolute precision: Fixed point.

The type declaration

type COMPASS **is delta** 0.1 **range** 0.0 .. 360.0;

says that the possible values for COMPASS are approximations to rea
numbers, with an absolute precision of 0.1 (and the rang
specified). In other words, the possible values of COMPASS wil
cover the range and will allow discrimination between real values a
least 0.1 apart. (It is left to the compiler to decide for eac
computer whether to use more finely spaced approximations: usuall
it will choose a suitable power of 2 to achieve an efficien
representation.)

Every object declared with absolute precision must have its rang
specified. This might be done in the type declaration itself a
above, or in two stages:

type POTENTIOMETER **is delta** 0.0001;

followed by

X, Y : POTENTIOMETER **range** 0.0 .. 1.0;

or by using an intermediate subtype:

subtype LOW_POT **is** POTENTIOMETER **range** 0.0 .. 0.1;
Q : LOW_POT;

There are no predefined fixed point types in Ada: any absolut
precision quantities needed must have an explicit type definition.

4.3   Discriminant constraints

type defined as a record with variants (section 12.3) may have
scriminant constraints. For example, the type DIRECTORY_ENTRY implies
at we can have local or remote values with appropriate line numbers or
ink numbers. There will be an occasion when we wish to deal only with
lues of that type which are local; to specify this we can declare

subtype LOCAL_ENTRY **is** DIRECTORY_ENTRY
                    (PROXIMITY => LOCAL);

d declare objects such as

Ll : LOCAL_ENTRY;

combine the declarations together as in

Rl : DIRECTORY_ENTRY (PROXIMITY => REMOTE);

The objects so declared have all the components of the stated variant
   the base type (including of course the discriminant and all the
mponents in the fixed part of the record). This fixes the
scriminant value for the objects declared in this way, irrespective of
y default value for the discriminant in the type declaration.   These
mponents may be accessed in just the same way as those of an object of
e base type, but any assignment of a new value to Ll is checked to
sure that the component PROXIMITY has the value LOCAL. If this check
ils, the exception CONSTRAINT_ERROR is raised.

The discriminant constraint is written after the name of the type (or
btype) to which it applies, and consists of an aggregate specifying
e required value of the discriminant. Notice the crucial importance
   the default value for the discriminant in the type declaration. If
ere is no default value, then every object declaration (whose type is
e record with variants) must include a discriminant constraint, thus
eventing the object from taking values in other variants. If we want
e greater generality of allowing the object values to be able to range
er all variants, then we **must** give a default value for the
scriminant(s) in the type declaration.

This is necessary because, in principle, the size of each variant may
   different, so the amount of space needed to store the object depends
  its longest variant. The language is designed to allow the space
location to be handled properly.

A discriminant constraint may also be applied to an access typ where the base type is a record with variants. (In this case t constraint refers to the objects in the collection denoted by the valu in the access type.)

12.4.4   Index constraints

A type defined as an array may have index constraints. These give t lower and upper bounds (and hence the type) of each index of the arra Index constraints are particularly important with array parameters f subprograms, and for arrays whose sizes are not fixed in the ty definition.

For example, the predefined declaration

    type STRING **is array** (POSITIVE **range** <>) **of** CHARACTER;

defines STRING as a one-dimensional array but does not give the boun for the index. Any object declaration for a string must specify t bounds to be used, either by attaching an index constraint or by givi an initial value:

    CARD_IMAGE : STRING (1 .. 80);
    PROMPT : **constant** STRING := "TYPE NEXT VALUE";

Since array indexes may be of any discrete type (not just integers), index constraint must be of the same type as is given in the arr definition. For example, with the unconstrained array

    type RATE **is array** (DAY_NAME range <>, POSITIVE range <>) **of** FLOAT;

we could have constrained arrays defined as

    DAY_RATE : RATE (DAY_NAME **range** MONDAY .. FRIDAY, 9..18);
    WEEKEND_RATE : RATE
              (DAY_NAME **range** SATURDAY .. SUNDAY, 0..24);

An index constraint is written after the name of the type (subtype) to which it applies, and consists of one or more discre ranges that specify the bounds for the array indices. For each ind position, the discrete range is written either

        LOWER .. UPPER

ere the expressions for LOWER and UPPER are of the proper type (and
ere is no ambiguity, which is usually the case with indices of type
TEGER), or

INDEX_TYPE **range** LOWER .. UPPER

ving the index type explicitly.

If a parameter of a subprogram is specified as an array, the formal
rameter may leave the bounds unspecified so that the subprogram body
n be applied to any array of the appropriate dimensionality and
ement type. (The types of the indices must also be fixed, in order
at statements in the subprogram body can manipulate them.) So we can
ve

type VECTOR **is array** (POSITIVE **range** <>) **of** FLOAT;
function SCALAR_PRODUCT(X, Y : VECTOR) **return** FLOAT;

ere the procedure can be applied to any two vectors. On each occasion
e function is called, there is an implied index constraint applied to
e parameters, taking the bounds of the actual parameters.

.4.5   Constraints and Derived Types

type may be defined by a constraint clause (or combination of
nstraint clauses) on its own. This is implicitly taken to be derived
om an appropriate built-in type, chosen by the implementation to
tisfy the constraint. Depending on the constraints given, this could
an integer, a floating-point type or a fixed-point type.

A **range** constraint with integer values for its range bounds, say

range 0 .. 5280;

s the effect of

new INTEGER **range** 0 .. 5280;

perhaps SHORT_INTEGER or LONG_INTEGER, to cover the stated range.

A **digits** constraint, say

digits 5;

is taken as a type definition for a floating point type

    new FLOAT **digits** 5;

or perhaps SHORT_FLOAT or LONG_FLOAT, to provide at least the stat
number of digits of precision.

    A digits constraint may be followed by a range constraint with re
bounds, such as

    digits 5 **range** -1.0 .. 1.0;

this is taken as

    new FLOAT **digits** 5 **range** -1.0 .. 1.0;

    A **delta** constraint may not be given by itself, but both a **delta** and
range may be given together to define a new fixed-point type: f
example

    delta 0.125 **range** 0.0 .. 255.0;

There are no built-in fixed-point types, and this is the comple
definition of such a type.

    Types which are derived from these numeric types may have furth
constraints applied, provided that the additional constraint does n
try to extend the set of possible values in the type.

    Thus if an additional range constraint is given for an existi
scalar type S_TYPE, the new bounds must be contained in

    S_TYPE'FIRST .. S_TYPE'LAST

If an additional **digits** constraint is given for an existing floatin
point type, the new precision must have no more digits than the existi
type. If an additional delta constraint is given for an existing fix
part type, the new delta must be no finer than that of the existi
type.

    The values in accuracy constraints may be given by expressions, b
they must be static, that is independent of any dynamically comput
value, so that they are determinable when the program is translated.

    In general, if a derived type definition is given with constraint
the effect is as though a new type had been set up by definition, th

he constraints applied to that. Thus the type definition

    new W_VALVE range WATER_INLET .. FLUSH_WATER;

akes a distinct type with the same operators and literals as for
_VALVE, but only the given range of values in it.

We may use these ideas to show constraints on values returned by
unctions, such as

    subtype POSITIVE_FLOAT is FLOAT
            range FLOAT'SMALL .. FLOAT'LARGE;

    subtype UP_TO_ONE is FLOAT range -1.0 .. 1.0;

    function SIN(X:FLOAT) return UP_TO_ONE;

    function SQRT(X:POSITIVE_FLOAT) return POSITIVE_FLOAT;

another use for constraints and derived types is to deal with possible
ndex values in an array containing cross references:

    MAX_SIZE : constant := 200;

    type POSSIBLE is range 0 .. MAX_SIZE;

    subtype DEFINITE is POSSIBLE range 1 .. POSSIBLE'LAST;

    type LIST_ITEM is
      record
        PREV, NEXT : POSSIBLE;   -- value 0 means none
        VALUE : FLOAT;
      end record;

    A : array (DEFINITE) of LIST_ITEM;

12.5   Access Types

An access type is used for a collection of objects, all of the same type
(usually a record) where the number of objects currently relevant can
change during the execution of the program, and it is necessary to note
relationships between one object in the collection and another. For
example, in an air defense system, there will be a collection of tracks
(changing as aircraft pass through the region under surveillance) and

relationships between them, such as between targets and interceptors
The type of the individual objects in the collection is called the base
type; the linkages between them are held as pointers or references (i.e.
internal addresses of the data objects).

The access type both establishes the collection, and introduces the
possibility of values (which would be pointers) denoting particular
members of the collection. Each access type establishes a collection of
a particular base type; all the objects in the collection have values of
the base type, and any value of that access type can denote (i.e. point
to) one of the objects currently in that collection, or be **null** denoting
no object at all. (Note that there may be other objects having values
of the base type, which are not in the collection; these can not be
denoted by values of the access type.)

For example, with

```
type TRACK_IMAGE is
   record                     -- basic components
      TRACK_NAME : STRING(1 .. 5);
      X_COORD : DISTANCE;
      Y_COORD : DISTANCE;
      HEIGHT  : KFEET;
   end record;
```

The corresponding access type is

```
type TRACK_POINTER is
   access TRACK_IMAGE;
```

This establishes a collection of objects of type TRACK_IMAGE. The
type TRACK_POINTER may then be used to access objects in that
collection. We can show this by drawing the access-value as an arrow,
pointing at the appropriate object of the base-type (or a diagonal line
for **null**). We might have values of these types as shown in figure 12a.

The key point in understanding access types is to appreciate that the
access type definition itself implies the collection of base-objects,
and that the set of possible values in that access type consists of **null**
and the collection of base-objects so implied. (In other words, the
access type definition causes space for the collection to be allocated,
with its own local storage manager called for each **new** object in the
collection. The access values themselves are pointers to such objects.)

Thus with

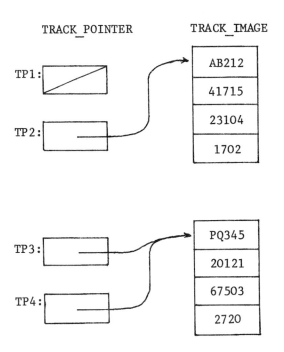

Figure 12a: Track pointers and track images

type POINTER **is access** BASE_TYPE;

he declaration itself implies a collection of objects of type
ASE_TYPE, which can be referred to only by objects of type POINTER.
ccess objects may be isolated, such as

   P1, P2 : POINTER;

r be components of a record (including the BASE_TYPE to which they
efer).

   The rules of type-matching apply as usual, so if we have several
ccess type definitions, they are distinct types, having different
ollections of base-objects, even though the base-types may be the same.

   Any number of access-type objects (including components in records)
ay denote the same base object. This means that if any of them is a
ariable which makes a change to the object it denotes, then all other
ariables necessarily denote the changed object. This is an important
ifference from the normal behaviour of variables, and is a possible
ource of errors in programs. For variables not of an access type, and

not shared between different tasks, the value of the variable is that
which was most recently assigned to it. In the case of access types, it
is true that the object denoted by the variable is the same as that
which was most recently assigned to it, but the properties of that
object are not necessarily the same. Since when dealing with access
types we normally think directly of the properties of the object
denoted, this can be confusing.

12.5.1   Access objects

We can introduce access objects to denote possible objects of the base
type by an ordinary object declaration, specifying the required access
type:

    TP1, TP2 : TRACK_POINTER;

The variables TP1 and TP2 will have values which in general may denote
objects in the collection, not necessarily different objects, and
perhaps denoting no objects at all. The top pointer in figure 12a might
have been the result of

    TP1 := **null**;

whereas the bottom pointer could have been made to point to the same
object as the third by

    TP4 := TP3;

    The notation for a component of a record can also be used for the
component of an object denoted by an access value: thus

    TP1.TRACK_NAME

means the value of the TRACK_NAME component in the object currently
denoted by TP1, in this case "AB212". The special notation

    TP1.**all**

means all components of the base object currently denoted by TP1.

    There is a crucial difference between values of a base type and
values of a corresponding access type. Consider:

    T1, T2 : TRACK_IMAGE;

then

    T1 := T2;

assigns all the current value of T2 to T1, making two identical copies
of that value. Any subsequent change to T2 or any of its components such
as T2.X_COORD has no effect on T1.

    In contrast, the assignment

    TP1 := TP2;

sets TP1 to denote the same object as is denoted by TP2: two identical
references to the same object. Any subsequent change to a component of
that object such as TP2.X_COORD necessarily implies the same change to
TP1.X_COORD. However, if TP2 is changed so that it denotes a different
object than there is no effect on TP1.

    If we want to copy the value of an object denoted by an access value,
we must write

    TP1.all := TP2.all;

this sets all the components of the object denoted by TP1 to have the
same values as the components of the object denoted by TP2, making the
objects equal but not necessarily identical (see figure 12b).

12.5.2   Constructing new objects

A new object in the collection is formed by allocation in an expression
(see section 3.5d). An allocator consists of the word **new** followed by an
appropriate typed expression to give the value of the allocated object.
Each new object is different from all previously allocated objects in
the collection, even though the value of the object may be the same as
that of another object. The allocator both creates the new object, and
gives an access value denoting that object as its result. Thus

    TP1 := **new** TRACK_IMAGE (T1);
    TP2 := **new** TRACK_IMAGE ("AB212", X, Y, H);

generates two new objects in the TRACK_POINTER collection (since that is
the type of TP1 and TP2), and assigns values denoting them to TP1 and
TP2.

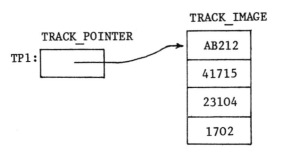

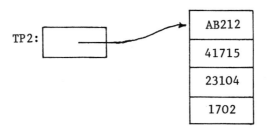

Figure 12b: Pointers to equal objects

Notice the significance of each **new** allocating a distinct object: the
two statements

    TP1 := **new** TRACK_IMAGE (T1);
    TP2 := **new** TRACK_IMAGE (T1);

allocate two objects with the same values (figure 12b), whereas

    TP1 := **new** TRACK_IMAGE (T1);
    TP2 := TP1;

allocates one object with two access values denoting it.

12.5.3   Access values as record components

The principal use of access types is for working with inter-
relationships between the objects in the collection. For each such

relationship an object might have, its record has a component of the appropriate access type, denoting the object (if any) with which it has the relationship. Thus a track may be that of an interceptor, which may be associated with a target.

We can link any track with another if we include a component for the link in the type for TRACK_IMAGE:

```
record
     -- basic components plus
     ASSOCIATED_TRACK: TRACK_POINTER;
end record;
```

We make the link by assigning the required track pointer to the ASSOCIATED_TRACK component. The link may be changed during the course of execution, or broken by

```
TP1.ASSOCIATED_TRACK := null;
```

There is a notational problem that follows from the rule that every identifier in Ada must be declared before it may be used. Since the declaration of an access type must specify the type of the objects in the collection, and the type of the objects is usually a record containing components whose type is the access type, each declaration depends on the other, and therefore (according to the rules of scope for declarations), must be written after it. The way to write the declarations in the right order is to give the base type a name, but not to specify its details until after the access type has been declared, thus:

```
type TRACK_IMAGE_LINKED;         -- with no details yet
type TRACK_POINTER_LINKED is
   access TRACK_IMAGE_LINKED;
type TRACK_IMAGE_LINKED is       -- now with details
   record
       TRACK_NAME : STRING (1..5);
       ASSOCIATED_TRACK : TRACK_POINTER_LINKED;
   end record;
```

Notice that there are two declarations for TRACK_IMAGE_LINKED; the first is incomplete: it simply says that this identifier refers to a type, without giving the type definition; the second gives the necessary type definition. A similar technique of splitting name and details is used for private types (see section 7.4).

12.5.4   Relations between access objects

Components which are themselves access values are the crucial ones for dealing with the inter-relationships.

TP1.ASSOCIATED_TRACK

denotes the track (if any) associated with TP1.

Suppose TP1 denotes the linked track image with name PQ345, and that TP2 denotes track XY678, neither having an associated track. We can establish the association between these two tracks (see figure 12c) as follows:

```
TP1.ASSOCIATED_TRACK := TP2;   -- make link a
TP2.ASSOCIATED_TRACK := TP1;   -- make link b
```

The two tracks now stand associated in both directions, and the variables TP1 and TP2 could be used for other purposes without affecting these track images.

Similar techniques are used to express inter-relationships between objects of different types, for example tracks of interceptors and their controllers. Now we need an access type for each distinct collection of objects, and the record for any of the objects may include components of an access type corresponding to the kind of related object.

Thus we may also have

```
type CONTROLLER;

type CONTROLLER_POINTER is
  access CONTROLLER;

type TRACK_IMAGE_CONTROLLED is
  record
    -- basic components plus
    TRACK_CONTROLLER : CONTROLLER_POINTER;
  end record;

type CONTROLLER is
  record
    INTERCEPTOR : TRACK_IMAGE_CONTROLLED;
    TARGET : TRACK_IMAGE_CONTROLLED;
  end record;
```

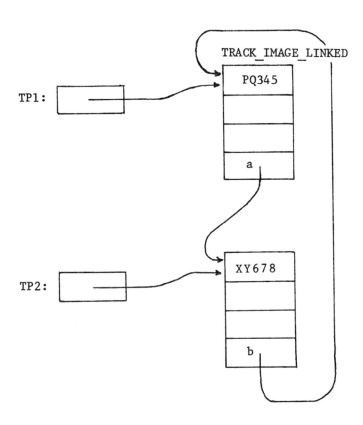

Figure 12c: Links between tracks

This allows each controller to be able to refer to two distinct tracks, an interceptor and a target, while each track can denote the controller responsible for it (in either capacity). A typical situation is shown in figure 12d.   In the second case a target is linked to a controller but an interceptor has not yet been set up.

Another arrangement might be

type POSSIBLE_TRACKS **is** (NORMAL, TARGET, INTERCEPTOR);

type TRACK_IMAGE_SPLIT (TRACK_TYPE : POSSIBLE_TRACKS) **is**
   record
       -- basic components
      case TRACK_TYPE **is**
       when NORMAL =>

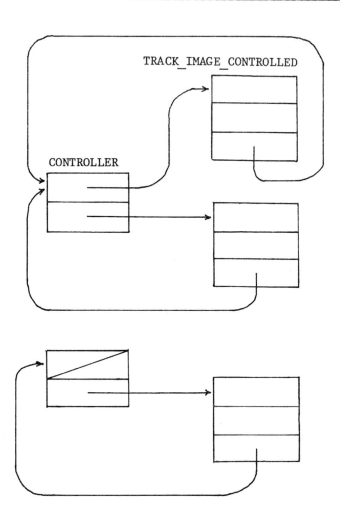

Figure 12d: Track controller links

```
      null;
    when TARGET =>
      ASSOCIATED_TRACK : TRACK_POINTER;
    when INTERCEPTOR =>
      TRACK_CONTROLLER : CONTROLLER_POINTER;
    end case;
  end record;
```

or the pointers could be kept distinct by

```
type NORMAL_TRACK is
  record
      -- basic components
  end record;

type TARGET_TRACK;

type INTERCEPTOR_TRACK;

type NORMAL_POINTER is
  access NORMAL_TRACK;

type INTERCEPTOR_POINTER is
  access INTERCEPTOR_TRACK;

type TARGET_POINTER is
  access TARGET_TRACK;

type TARGET_TRACK is
  record
      -- basic components plus
      ASSOCIATED_TRACK : INTERCEPTOR_POINTER;
  end record;

type INTERCEPTOR_TRACK is
  record
      -- basic components plus
      TRACK_CONTROLLER : CONTROLLER_POINTER;
  end record;
```

2.5.5   List processing

he same linking technique is used for maintaining a list (of varying
ength) of items for processing. The relationship in this case is the
rdering of the list: each item (except the last) has a successor.
uppose we have queues of messages awaiting transmission along several
runks, we would make a collection of message items as follows (see
igures 12e and 12f):

```
type MESSAGE_ITEM;       -- without details
type MESSAGE_PTR is
  access MESSAGE_ITEM;
type MESSAGE_ITEM is      -- details now
  record
```

MESSAGE ITEM

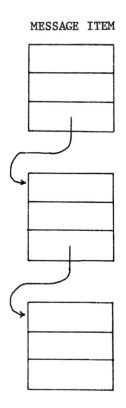

Figure 12e: Sequence of messages

```
    DESTINATION : PORT;
    CONTENTS : STRING (1..80);
    SEQUEL : MESSAGE_PTR := null;      -- default for last item
end record;
```

```
DIRECTORY   : array (PORT) of TRUNK;
PENDING : array (TRUNK) of MESSAGE_PTR;
    -- first element in queue
NEW_MESSAGE : MESSAGE_PTR;      -- with SEQUEL = null
```

NDING points to the first message (if any) for each trunk, and we wish
attach a new message to the pending queue for its destination.

The SEQUEL component in MESSAGE_ITEM allows a chain of these items to
formed, each containing a pointer to the next (and the last in the
ain containing null), as shown in figure 12e.

Note that since an access-object may have the value null there might
no object component denoted by a name such as TP1.TRACK_NAME or
SEQUEL. This possibility cannot be detected at compile time, and if
occurs during execution then the exception ACCESS_ERROR is raised.
y use of an access value with a component selector implies the
ssibility of ACCESS_ERROR, and the programmer should specify the
tion to be taken in the case of this error by writing an appropriate
ception handler.

The possibility can be avoided by explicit programming, thus (see
gure 12f):

```
    -- attach NEW_MESSAGE to appropriate queue
    M : MESSAGE_PTR;
    T : TRUNK;
  begin
    T := DIRECTORY (NEW_MESSAGE.DESTINATION);
            -- find trunk to use.
    M := PENDING (T);
            -- start of queue pending transmission on
            -- this trunk.

    if M = null then
        -- a: no messages pending
      PENDING (T) := NEW_MESSAGE;
    else
        -- b: attach message
      while M.SEQUEL /= null loop
        -- assume that few repetitions are needed
        M := M.SEQUEL;
      end loop;
        -- advance to the last current message
      -- assert ( M.SEQUEL = null );
      M.SEQUEL := NEW_MESSAGE;
        -- c: attach message
```

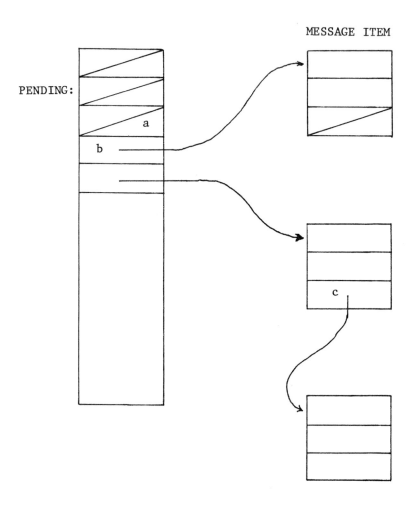

Figure 12f: Attach message to queue

```
      end if;
      NEW_MESSAGE.SEQUEL := null;
            -- d: mark end
   end;
```

Notice that M.SEQUEL always occurs in positions where M is not **nul**
thus avoiding the possibility of ACCESS_ERROR.

.5.6   Limited number of objects

principle, the number of objects in a collection for an   access   type
y change during execution without limit. In practice, because a finite
ount of storage must be reserved for the collection, there is a   limit
the number of new objects which may be allocated in each collection.

If the program tries to allocate an object when   there   is   no   space
ailable for it in the collection, then the exception STORAGE_ERROR is
ised. Any use of an allocator (with **new** in an expression) implies   the
ssibility of a STORAGE_ERROR, and the programmer should specify the
tion to be taken in case of this   error   by   writing   an   appropriate
ception handler.

The representation for an   access   type   should   include   a   length
ecification, which gives the amount of storage space to be reserved
r all objects of that access type. (The space reserved   may   have   to
ntain special variables for the allocator, so the maximum number of
ssible objects is not precisely determined).   The   attribute
ORAGE_SIZE is measured in system storage units, whereas the SIZE of an
ject is measured in bits; hence they have to be combined in   a   rather
mplicated way. For example

  for TRACK_POINTER'STORAGE_SIZE **use** 200 *
     TRACK_IMAGE'SIZE/SYSTEM.STORAGE_UNIT;

ovides space for nearly 200 new track images. The number   of   objects
ich can be allocated in the collection is independent of how many
riables are declared for the access type, and also of the   possibility
at any object of the access type may cease to be relevant. When any
riable or record component of the access type is given a new value   by
assignment, the old value is lost, but the object denoted by that
lue continues to exist.

If as a result of such an assignment there is no access value at   all
noting some particular object, then there is no way of ever
bsequently referring to that object: it has in effect ceased to exist.
e storage space is still occupied by the object, however, and there is
t necessarily any automatic recovery of the inaccessible   space   (i.e.
garbage collection). Once a new object has been allocated, it
ntinues to occupy space until the whole collection is   lost   when   the
rogram reaches the end of the block in which the access type is
clared.

12.5.7   Storage control with access types

When objects are entering and leaving the collection dynamically, som
improvement is needed on the primitive technique by which storage i
allocated for a new object but never recovered. The program must itsel
control the use of storage for these objects.

The simplest technique is to maintain a list of all the objects whic
are currently unused, called a free list, and arrange that when a
object enters the collection, the first free object is used for it, an
when an object leaves the collection, it is attached to the free list.

To maintain a list of objects, the usual method is for each record t
contain a component which is an access value denoting the next object i
the list (or **null** for the last object in the list).

```
type OBJECT;
type OBJECT_REF is
   access OBJECT;
type OBJECT is
   record
      -- details of object
      NEXT : OBJECT_REF;
   end record;
```

A variable of the access type is needed to denote the first object :
the free list. (A second variable of the access type may also be used t
denote the last object in the free list. This spreads the usage o
objects throughout the collection).

```
FIRST,THIS : OBJECT_REF;
```

To initialise the list, new objects must be constructed and linke
together:

```
FIRST := null;  -- marks end of list
for I in 1 .. 200 loop
   FIRST := new OBJECT (FIRST);
             -- sets object with link to previous one
end loop;
```

The body of the loop is executed once for each object to be put on t
free list, each time using the previous value of FIRST as its NE
component, and setting FIRST to point to the newly created objec
Initialising FIRST to **null** causes the list to be properly terminate
(It is constructed from the end, so that the last one actually allocat

ill be denoted by FIRST.)

When an object is needed for use, the first one from the free list is
nlinked and denoted by THIS:

```
THIS := FIRST;        -- get object
FIRST := THIS.NEXT;   -- adjust free list start
THIS.NEXT := null;
```

Similarly when an object is no longer needed, it is put on the free
.ist (before the variable denoting it is changed). Suppose THIS denotes
.he object to be freed:

```
THIS.NEXT := FIRST;   -- attach free list to it
FIRST := THIS;        -- adjust free list start
```

Iow THIS can be changed without damaging the list.

The following sequence of statements manipulate a list, exchanging
:he head items of lists A and B (see figure 12g).

```
THIS := A.NEXT;       -- save rest of A list (object Q)
A.NEXT := B.NEXT;     -- a. attach rest of B list to A
B.NEXT := THIS;       -- b. attach rest of A list to B
THIS := A;
A := B;               -- c.
B := THIS;            -- d.
```

(Notice the structure: the first three statements exchange A.NEXT and
3.NEXT; the second three statements exchange A and B.)

The set of procedures for obtaining and freeing objects can
:onveniently be formed into a package, so that all changes to the
aembership of the collection would be carried out properly.

The allocation of space for a new object is normally permanent,
within the scope of the access type. This is a safe rule, since there
aay be references to the object at any time after its allocation, as
long as the access declaration is visible. A consequence is that the
space allocated gradually (for individual access objects) is deallocated
totally, only when the program reaches the end of the block enclosing
the access declaration. In some circumstances this is undesirable, and
the programmer may wish to deallocate space for individual objects,
taking responsibility for ensuring that there are no refences to an
object about to be deallocated. To provide for this, Ada provides a
generic procedure, UNCHECKED_DEALLOCATION. This must be instantiated

(before)

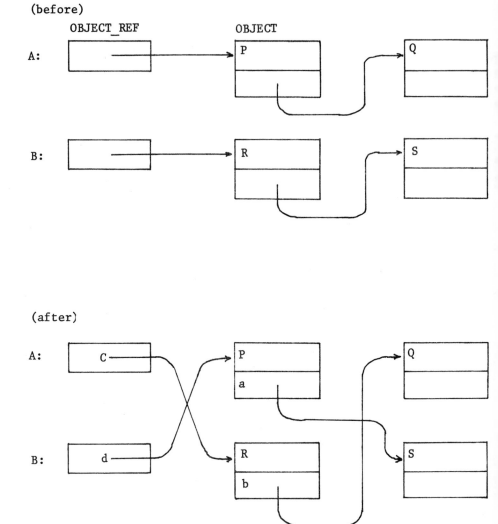

Figure 12g: Exchange list head items

for the particular access type concerned, and it then may be called to deallocate the space occupied for a given access object. No internal checks are made: the programmer must make sure that there are no references to this object before deallocating the space.

2.6   Use of types in program design

he notation of a type definition gives valuable assistance in program
esign, by allowing the programmer to show the contents of tables and
ontrol blocks (as records) and the possible values for coded fields (as
numeration types). While the program is partially designed, it is
ikely that many types will be declared using type names which are
ntroduced but not yet declared. The following example illustrates
his, in which some types (such as AB_CODE) are given in full, but
thers use type names which have not yet been declared (such as L_S_CODE
n LINK_STATUS)

```
    type AB_CODE is (          -- CCITT X25, sections
       TIMER_RECOVERY,        -- 3.7.10
       DTE_BUSY,              -- 3.7.8
       DCE_BUSY,              -- 3.7.9
       FC_REJECT,            -- 2.3.20,  3.10,  table 2.7
       RETRANSMISSION         -- 2.4.3,  3.7.5  (ii),  3.7.7
       RESET);

    type LINK_STATUS is
       record              -- ref CCITT definition of X 25 sections
          STATE     : L_S_CODE;   -- 1.7 to 1.9
          AB_COND   : AB_CODE;
          MODE_B    : B_CODE;
          V_S, V_R  : SR_STATE;   -- 2.2.2, 2.2.4
          TRIES     : SHORT_INTEGER range 0 .. MAX_TRIES;    -- II-40
          UNACK_I   : SHORT_INTEGER range 0 .. MAX_UNACK_I;  -- II-40
          U_I_Q     : QUEUE;      -- of unacknowledged I frames
          T_I_Q     : QUEUE;      -- of I for transmission
          GOING     : DEFINITE;   -- frame being output
          NEXT_F    : SHORT_NETWORK_BUFFER;
                          -- piggy-back for next frame

       end record;

    type MESSAGE_CONTROL_BLOCK is
       record
          PRIORITY  : PRI_CODE;
          BUFFERING : BUF_CODE;
          SENDER    : PROC_NO;
          TARGET    : PROC_NO;
          USER_DATA : MESSAGE;
       end record;

    type NETWORK_BUFFER_HEADER is
```

```
   record
     NEXT   : POSSIBLE;
     VCN    : VIRTUAL_CCT_NO;
     IN_USE : BOOLEAN;
     LINK   : LINK_NO;
     FRAME_LENGTH : SHORT_INTEGER range 0 ..  MAX_FRAME_LENGTH;
   end record;

type NETWORK_BUFFER_FRAME is
   record
     ADR_FIELD : BYTE;
     CTR_FIELD : BYTE;
     PKT       : PACKET;
   end record;

type BUFFER is
     record
       HDR : NETWORK_BUFFER_HEADER;
       FRAME : NETWORK_BUFFER_FRAME;
     end record;

POOL : array (DEFINITE) of BUFFER;

procedure SEND_MSG(M : MESSAGE_CONTROL_BLOCK)
     return STATUS range SUCCESS .. NO_IPM_BUFF;

procedure WAIT_MSG(W : WAIT_CONTROL_BLOCK;
                   B : DEFINITE)
     return STATUS range SUCCESS .. NO_MESSAGE;

procedure GET_BUFF(B : DEFINITE) return STATUS;

procedure RELEASE_BUFF(B : DEFINITE) return STATUS;
```

Such text would of course give rise to diagnostic messages if submitted
for compilation before all the types had been defined – but these
messages could be a useful aid for the program designer. As a temporary
expedient, types that have not yet been considered could be declared
thus:

```
type WAIT_CONTROL_BLOCK is (NOT_DEFINED_YET);
```

to satisfy compiler checks, and to be a visible reminder in the   program
text.   With this technique, each set of types and associated operations
can be written as a package, leading to an 'object-oriented' style of
programming.

Exercises

1. Write the type declarations for a track image which may be normal, a
   target or an interceptor; if it is a target it must be able to be
   associated with another track (its interceptor), and if it is an
   interceptor, it must be able to denote a controller. A normal track
   needs none of these.

2. Write three separate type declarations for normal tracks, targets
   and interceptors as in exercise 1, and declare separate access types
   for collections of each. What are the differences between the two
   techniques, regarding (a) storage for each track, (b) flexibility
   between the number of tracks of each type, (c) possibility of
   execution-time errors?

3. A message switching system handles messages of type

   ```
   type MESSAGE is
     record
       DESTINATION : PORT;
       CONTENTS : STRING (1..80);
     end record;
   ```

   At a node with no local lines, destinations are interpreted using

   ```
   DIRECTORY : array (PORT) of TRUNK;
   ```

   to determine which trunk is to be used for forwarding. Messages
   arrive spontaneously; they have to be sorted according to their
   trunk number into queues pending onward transmission. Assume they
   are forwarded sufficiently quickly that queues are short. Write a
   suitable declaration for the collection of messages, capable of
   holding a list of messages for each trunk number, and appropriate
   variables to define the queue of messages for each trunk number.
   Write a sequence of statements to add a new message to the
   appropriate queue.

4. To maintain a list in order as a queue, with new items arriving at
   one end and items being taken off the other end for further
   processing, it is common to include with each item a pointer to the
   next item in the queue and also another pointer to the previous item
   in the queue. Define a type for the queued items (assuming that the
   information to be carried is of type OBJECT) and an access type for
   a collection of them. Define a queue control type to denote the
   first and last items in a queue (which may be empty). Write a
   sequence of statements to take the first item from one (non-empty)
   queue and put it as the last item in another queue.

CHAPTER 13

More on Tasking

In this chapter we deal with advanced tasking facilities, mainly
concerned with writing the passive tasks used to provide communication
media between sibling active tasks. We cover grouping techniques,
non-determinism, and faults. The grouping techniques provide for
handling similar tasks (section 13.1), or similar entries within a task
(section 13.2). These are basically notational matters, that are not
intrinsically novel. Non-determinism, on the other hand, introduces an
entirely new principle into programming (section 13.3). Failures
(section 13.4) are particularly tricky in multi-task systems, because of
the dangers of a domino effect between tasks communicating with one
another. We illustrate how to write tasks for two kinds of
communication, including the use of a generic package, in section 13.5.
Section 13.6 concludes the book.

13.1   Task types

When a number of tasks have similar properties (specifically the same
body with corresponding entries), they may be written together as a task
type. The notation here draws on the ideas of task declarations and
object declarations: the task declaration is treated like a type rather
than an object, and an object declaration must be given (with the task
type as its type) for each particular task with the given properties.
(Remember that there is no provision in Ada for generic tasks.)

    The specification of a task type is written just as for an individual
task, except for the introductory words:

    task type SIMPLE_CHANNEL **is**
      entry GIVE (M : **in** MESSAGE);

```
    entry TAKE (M : out MESSAGE);
  end SIMPLE_CHANNEL;
```

The body is written exactly as for an individual task

```
  task body SIMPLE_CHANNEL is
    MESS : MESSAGE; -- local
  begin
    loop
      accept GIVE (M : MESSAGE) do
        MESS := M;  -- caller gives M to channel
      end GIVE;
      accept TAKE (M : out MESSAGE) do
        M := MESS; -- caller takes M from channel
      end TAKE;
    end loop;
  end SIMPLE_CHANNEL;
```

The idea is that the several instances of the task type may use
reentrably the same code for the body (although this is not guaranteed
by the language). The task body may be written separately as a
subunit, with a stub in its place in the program unit containing the
specification.

Having declared a task type, we can introduce task objects:

```
    C1, C2 : SIMPLE_CHANNEL;
```

and refer to their entries by the dot notation:

```
    C1.TAKE (M1);  -- take M1 from channel C1
    C2.GIVE (M1);  -- give M1 to channel C2
```

Task objects may also be declared as components of records or arrays.

13.2   Families of entries

When a number of entries to a task have similar properties
(specifically, the same formal part), they can be written together as a
family. In effect this is like an array of entries, although it is not
officially called an array to avoid giving the impression that it has
general array properties. A family of entries has a single dimension;
the members of the family are distinguished by the index value.

The entry declaration for a family is written with the discrete range for the family index:

```
task TRUNK_MONITOR is
  entry CHECK_TRUNK (TRUNK);        -- see section 12.3
  ---
end TRUNK_MONITOR;
```

Any formal parameters are given in the usual way after the family index:

```
task SETTLE is
  entry VALVE_STABLE (VALVE)        -- name with index
    (STATE : out VALVE_STATUS);     -- parameters
  ---
end SETTLE;
```

The two parts in parentheses here are entirely different, giving the index and parameters respectively. The notation for entry calls and accepts are similar.

To call an entry in a family, we must give the particular index value and relevant parameters, thus

```
TRUNK_MONITOR.CHECK_TRUNK (T1);     -- no parameters
SETTLE.VALVE_STABLE (CLEAN_WATER) (S); -- parameter S
```

There is no notational distinction between the parameters for an ordinary entry call and the index for a member of a family. When the family entry takes parameters, there are two adjacent parts in parentheses. The first is always evaluated to establish which member of the family is called; the second may be evaluated, according to the mode of the formal parameters.

Within the body of the task declaring the family of entries, accept statements specify the rendezvous actions for members of the family. The index may be a constant or a variable (of the right type), and its value determines which member of the family is accepted by that statement. Thus for a particular value E of type TRUNK

```
accept CHECK_TRUNK (E);
```

will accept a call of CHECK_TRUNK for that index value, and no other. The value E could be given as a constant, but most commonly would be a loop index covering all the members of the family. This is explained in the section on conditional rendezvous (13.3.5).

3.3   Non-determinism

he facilities described previously are all deterministic: the actions
n the program are determined by the previous actions that have taken
lace. We now turn to non-determinism in programs, in which the actions
n one task depend not only on the previous actions in the task, and the
ata communicated to it from other tasks, but on the relative timings of
ctions taking place in other tasks.   In general non-deterministic
rograms are not precisely repeatable, so are particularly difficult to
ebug.   This is of course characteristic of real-time embedded computer
ystems.

The most vivid form of non-determinism is the time-out.   A task
ontains a series of actions to be carried out, but if a certain action
annot be done by a given time, then an alternative action may be
ttempted.   We have met this in Chapter 8. Non-determinism also arises
ith buffer handling: one task may be producing items for the buffer,
nother task consuming items from the buffer, but the precise order of
roducing and consuming may be arbitrary and unrepeatable.

The statement in Ada used to indicate non-determinism is **select**.   It
s used in a variety of forms, which we describe here. A select
tatement is a compound statement, which contains several sequences of
tatements, one of which is executed.

The principal form of select statement introduces a set of accept
tatements, to achieve mutual exclusion between the execution of the
orresponding bodies. Other forms are used to achieve time-outs and
onditional rendezvous.

3.3.1   Selective rendezvous

task may have several entries, and at a certain stage be prepared to
ave a rendezvous with any of them, whichever might be called first.

```
    loop
      select
        accept READ (X : out ITEM) do
            X := STORED;
        end READ;
      or
        accept WRITE (X : ITEM) do
            STORED := X;
        end WRITE;
```

```
  end select;
end loop;
```

This uses a local variable STORED, of type ITEM, presumed to b
initialised in some way, which can be read or written in any order
either to READ the current value or to WRITE a new value.

A select statement frequently occurs in a loop, so that each REA
gives the value of the most recent WRITE.

Notice the important difference between this and a program wit
procedures for READ and WRITE.   Because procedures are reentrable
there is nothing to stop a task calling one procedure while the same o
an associated procedure is in the course of execution for another task
The loop select construct gives disjoint execution of the several accep
statements.

If the relevant entries have been called before the select statemen
is reached, one (only) of the accept statements is executed, chose
arbitrarily.

Each arm of a select statement must begin with a special kind o
statement, so that the appropriate choice can be made.   As well a
accept (described above), the possibilities are an entry call (describe
in section 8.4.2), **delay**, or **terminate**. The delay is used to give
time-out on the accepting side (similar to time-out on the calling side
see section 8.4); the terminate is used to indicate that the task may b
terminated at this point.   A further form provides for alternativ
action if no task is ready for a rendezvous when the select statement i
executed. We explain these in detail below.

13.3.2   Watchdog timer

We can check that an entry is called within a prescribed time a
follows:

```
select
  accept OK;
or
  delay 3.0;
  PUT ("something wrong here");
end select;
```

This will expect the entry OK to be called within the next 3.0 seconds
if this happens, the statement is executed and the delay is ignored

ut if the delay expires, the second arm of the statement is executed
nd the message is output: the entry OK is no longer acceptable.

There may be several delay arms, but only the one with the shortest
uration can be effective. They can be used with any number of accept
rms.

3.3.3   Conditional task termination

n the loop select construct, we have to be able to allow the task to be
leanly terminated in case the enclosing task needs to be terminated.
Remember the rule that when a task reaches its end, all its child tasks
ave to terminate before the parent task can finish.) Typically a child
ask may offer a number of entries by the loop select, and may properly
erminate between executing any of the corresponding accept statements,
ut not within an accept statement. We express this by writing
erminate; as another arm of the select statement, being an option that
s chosen if another task is trying to terminate this one when the
elect statement is executed.

```
loop
  select
    accept READ (X : out ITEM) do
      X := STORED;
    end READ;
  or
    accept WRITE (X : ITEM) do
      STORED := X;
    end WRITE;
  or
    terminate;
  end select;
end loop;
```

There may not be more than one terminate arm, or a terminate arm with
ny delay arms in the same select statement.

3.3.4   Inhibition

The arms of a select statement may be preceded by clauses which inhibit
he possibility of those arms being executed.

```
select
  when SET =>
    accept READ (X : out ITEM) do
       X := STORED;
    end READ;
or
  accept WRITE (X : ITEM) do
     STORED := X;
     SET := TRUE;
  end WRITE;
or
  terminate;
end select;
```

This uses a BOOLEAN variable SET, which is initially FALSE, to ensur
that READ will not be accepted until a WRITE has been given.

The same technique is used when working with a buffer to ensure tha
the producer cannot give more data when the buffer is full, nor th
consumer take more out when the buffer is empty:

```
loop
  select
    when COUNT < MAX =>
      accept GIVE (X: DATA) do
        --
      end GIVE;
  or
    when COUNT > 0 =>
      accept TAKE (X : out DATA) do
        --
      end TAKE;
  or
    terminate;
  end select;
end loop;
```

This assumes that the bodies of GIVE and TAKE make suitable adjustment
to COUNT.   The inhibition conditions are evaluated each time the selec
statement is executed.   Any arms for which the condition is false ar
not considered eligible for execution.

If all of the arms of a select statement are inhibited, so that ther
is no entry which it can ever accept, the exception PROGRAM_ERROR i
raised, unless there is an else part.

___

.3.5   Conditional rendezvous

further possibility in the select statement is to give an   alternative
quence of statements to be executed if, at the time the select
atement is met, no other task is ready to rendezvous with it.   This
   used to give a conditional rendezvous: performing the rendezvous if
other task is immediately ready, but taking other action if not.
ere are two forms of this, depending on whether the condition is put
  the calling side or the accepting side of the rendezvous.   We have
ready introduced (in Chapter 8) the selection in an active task
alling an entry);   here we describe selection in a passive task, where
entry is accepted.

For conditional acceptance of a rendezvous, we write

```
select
  accept SEIZE do
     --
  end SEIZE;
else
  AVAILABLE := TRUE;
end select;
```

other task could have called SEIZE, but if none has, then AVAILABLE is
t TRUE.   (It is presumably set FALSE elsewhere.)

Logically, the else arm in a select statement is the same as

delay 0.0;

it the different notation is used to show a different intent.

A typical situation when this might be necessary would be to   select
om entries in a family:

```
for E in TRUNKS loop
  select
    accept CHECK_TRUNK (E) do
       --
    end CHECK_TRUNK (E);
  else
     null;
  end select;
end loop;
```

Each time round the loop, any call already waiting for the correspondi
entry CHECK_TRUNK (E) will be accepted, but no further time is wasted
it has not been called. The same technique is used to provide one
several resources.

The accept arms may be preceded by inhibition clauses, in which ca
the else arm is executed if none of the uninhibited entries is calle
This includes the case where all the arms are inhibited: if there is
else part, it is executed rather than raising the exception.

In general, an else part, if used, must be the last arm of a sele
statement. There may be any number of other arms beginning with acce
statements, or a single arm beginning with an entry call. A selecti
entry may not be optional or inhibited. (An else arm may not be used
a select statement with a terminate arm or any delay arms.)

13.4   Task and rendezvous failures

As any action might fail, it is possible that a task may fa
unexpectedly, even while it is in rendezvous with another task. He
we discuss what happens, arranged to minimise the spread of damage.

There may be faults during the execution of a task (as in any oth
part of a program), and the mechanism of exception handling allo
appropriate actions to be taken after internally detected errors.
general, a failure in a task may be detected within the task (shown
raising an exception) or by another task to which it is visible.

The normal rules of exception propagation and handling apply when
failure is detected within a task, with special cases only when t
propagation passes out of an accept statement or when it reaches t
complete task body (when there is no handler at the outermost level f
the exception that has arisen). These two cases are explained in t
following subsections.

13.4.1   Controlling a task

One task may decide that another task is faulty, and try to stop i
The preferred way is to call an entry (e.g. CLOSE_DOWN). This is
ordinary rendezvous, so takes place when the faulty task is at
appropriate accept (or select) statement.

If the faulty task is dangerous, the task that discovers this may
ort it, causing it to be terminated abruptly with no chance of
aceful close-down. If the fault is detected during a rendezvous, the
sk in communication is protected from adverse effects as far as
ssible.

It is of course possible that the suspected task was not really
ulty, but the mistake was in the task that tried to stop it. This
nd of program error cannot be detected automatically. Another
ssibility is that two tasks watch one another, and both decide that
e other is faulty. On a single-processor machine, one task (non-
terministically) is likely to succeed in stopping the other before it
uld itself be stopped, so would survive. On a multi-processor
chine, both attempts could be successful: no survival would be
aranteed.

Other error conditions arise if a task terminates when another task
trying to make a rendezvous with it.

.4.2   Exception propagation out of an accept statement

 accept statement is executed when another task calls the entry: the
ndezvous then takes place. If an exception is raised during the
ndezvous, there might be a handler for it so that the rendezvous can
ke place normally. But if the exception propagates past the accept
atement, the rendezvous has failed. In this case, the propagation
reads to both tasks involved in the rendezvous, from the accept
atement in the accepting task, and from the entry call in the calling
sk.

.4.3   Exceptions at the outermost level of a task

en an exception propagates to the outermost level of a task, and there
 no handler there for it, the task is terminated with no further
tion - the exception is not propagated any further.

It may be thought that this is rather an unsatisfactory action:
parently ignoring the exception. The reason for it is that the
tion to be taken must depend on the application concerned, and should
erefore be programmed in Ada. In other words, it is the programmer's
sponsibility to ensure that there is a handler at the outermost level
 a task: every task body should contain

```
      exception
        when others =>
           TERMINATION_ACTION;
```

For example, CONTROL_LIFT must take steps to ensure safety in t
case of failure, or indeed of any other exception not handl
internally:

```
      task CONTROL_LIFT is
        entry GO;
        entry CLOSE_DOWN;
      end CONTROL_LIFT;

      task body CONTROL_LIFT is
      begin
        loop
          select
            accept GO;
            -- normal execution
          or
            accept CLOSE_DOWN;
            DISPLAY ("Please use other lift");
            exit;
          end select;
        end loop;
      exception
        when others =>
          EMERGENCY_STOP;
          DISPLAY ("OUT OF ORDER");
      end CONTROL_LIFT;
```

The termination action may be to report the fault or to close down t
part of the application system covered by this task. (The same argume
applies to an exception reaching the outermost level of a program,
illustrated in the example in section 1.3). The termination action
known as the task's 'last wishes', to be carried out before it finishe
Additional modes of control are possible, however, by one ta
influencing another: typically a parent controlling its children.

13.4.4   Stopping a faulty task

As a last resort, if a misbehaving task does not respond to the ent
call, the task watching it may abort it:

    abort CONTROL_LIFT;

Several tasks may be aborted together. If the task is currently engaged
in a rendezvous, the rendezvous is handled as explained below.
Otherwise it is stopped abruptly, as an abnormal termination.

    This is a drastic action, and prevents the task from carrying out any
last wishes.   Before it is aborted, a task should be given a chance to
carry out its last wishes by a previous entry call

    CONTROL_LIFT.CLOSE_DOWN;

The abort statement is available in case this is ineffective.

    Aborting a task also causes abnormal termination of all tasks
dependent on it, including those dependent on subprograms and blocks
currently being executed in it.

13.4.5   Faulty rendezvous

Faults may arise (or be detected) in either task involved in a
rendezvous. In general a fault in the calling task has no effect on the
accepting task, but a fault in the accepting task will always affect the
calling task.

    If the calling task is stopped before the rendezvous has started
(i.e. before the entry call has been accepted), then the attempted
rendezvous is simply ignored. If the calling task is actually in the
rendezvous when the task is aborted, the rendezvous is allowed to
complete normally, so that the accepting task can continue.

    If the accepting task is stopped, then any other tasks awaiting or
attempting to rendezvous with it are notified by raising the predefined
exception TASKING_ERROR (see section 6.6) in each.

13.5   Inter-task communication in Mascot

Mascot is a technique for developing embedded computer systems, in which
the several activities in a system are distinguished, with two
prescribed kinds of communication between them: channels and pools.   A
channel passes data in order from one activity to another; a pool
allows data to be shared between several activities.

To write a program in Ada designed in this style, each Mascot
activity corresponds to an active Ada task, and the channels and pool
for inter-task communication are given as passive Ada tasks.   In the
next two subsections we give the Ada programs for these.

13.5.1   Implementation of Mascot channels

A channel in Mascot is a means of sequential communication between two
or more tasks.   The type of data items communicated would be fixed for
any particular channel, but any tasks could use it.   There is an
implication of a buffer within the channel, containing data items in the
course of communication.

We write the channel as a task type, where the data item will be
declared in the surrounding environment.   This would probably be a
generic package, with parameters ITEM and BUFFER_LENGTH.

```
task type MASCOT_CHANNEL is
   entry GIVE (D : in ITEM);
   entry TAKE (D : out ITEM);
end MASCOT_CHANNEL;

task body MASCOT_CHANNEL is
   type BUFFER_POSSIBLE is new INTEGER range 0 .. BUFFER_LENGTH;
   subtype BUFFER_ACTUAL is BUFFER_POSSIBLE range 1 .. BUFFER_LENGTH;
   BUFFER : array (BUFFER_ACTUAL) of ITEM;
   INX,OUTX : BUFFER_ACTUAL := 1;
   CONTAINS : BUFFER_POSSIBLE := 0;
   -- invariant:
   -- (CONTAINS - INX + OUTX) mod BUFFER_LENGTH = 0;
begin
   loop
     select
       when CONTAINS < BUFFER_LENGTH =>
         accept GIVE (D : in ITEM) do
            BUFFER (INX) := D;
         end GIVE;
       INX := INX mod BUFFER_LENGTH + 1;
       CONTAINS := CONTAINS + 1;
     or
       when CONTAINS > 0 =>
         accept TAKE (D : out ITEM) do
            D := BUFFER (OUTX);
         end TAKE;
       OUTX := OUTX mod BUFFER_LENGTH + 1;
```

```
         CONTAINS := CONTAINS - 1;
      or
         terminate;
      end select;
   end loop;
end MASCOT_CHANNEL;
```

...is structure is characteristic of a server task.   The specification
‘ovides entries for communication between the user tasks.   The server
.sk body consists of a loop select that covers the several entry points
.nd terminate).

.5.2   Implementation of Mascot pools

pool in Mascot is an indexed dataset, accessible by several tasks,
.pable of   random   access with protection against interference during
.ch read or write.   The types of data items in the pool and the keys
.ed to distinguish them would be fixed for any particular pool.   The
.cilities imply memory within the pool, containing the current data
.ems, with markers distinguishing valid from invalid memory elements.
. this implementation, we assume that the possible key values are
.mpact, so that an array is a suitable format for the memory.   An
.ternative, where the key values are sparse, would follow the lines of
.e generic package ASSOCIATIVE_MEMORY given in chapter 10.

We write the pool as a generic package, whose body uses a server task
. ensure   mutual   exclusion   between access from different user tasks.
.emember that procedures in Ada are reentrable.)

```
generic
   type KEY is (<>);
   type ITEM is private;
package MASCOT_POOL is
   procedure READ (K :KEY; D : out ITEM);
   procedure WRITE (K : KEY; D : in ITEM);
   procedure UPDATE (K : KEY;
       REVISED : in ITEM;
       PREVIOUS : out ITEM);
   procedure DELETE (K : KEY);
   function IS_THERE (K : KEY) return BOOLEAN;
   NONEXISTENT, OVERWRITTEN : exception;
end MASCOT_POOL;

package body MASCOT_POOL is
```

```
task POOL_MANAGER is
  entry EXAMINE (K : KEY; D : out ITEM; PRESENT : out BOOLEAN);
  entry SET (K : KEY; D : in ITEM; PRESENT : out BOOLEAN);
  entry CHANGE (K : KEY; REVISED : in ITEM;
        PREVIOUS : out ITEM; PRESENT : out BOOLEAN);
  entry REMOVE (K : KEY; PRESENT : out BOOLEAN);
  entry X_IS_THERE (K : KEY; PRESENT : out BOOLEAN);
end POOL_MANAGER;

procedure READ (K : KEY ; D : out ITEM) is
  IS_THERE : BOOLEAN;
begin
  POOL_MANAGER.EXAMINE (K, D, IS_THERE);
  if not IS_THERE then
    raise NONEXISTENT;
  end if;
end READ;

procedure WRITE (K : KEY; D : in ITEM) is
  WAS_THERE : BOOLEAN;
begin
  POOL_MANAGER.SET (K, D, WAS_THERE);
  if WAS_THERE then
    raise OVERWRITTEN;
  end if;
end WRITE;

procedure UPDATE (K :KEY; REVISED : in ITEM;
                PREVIOUS : out ITEM) is
  WAS_THERE : BOOLEAN;
begin
  POOL_MANAGER.CHANGE (K, REVISED, PREVIOUS, WAS_THERE);
  if not WAS_THERE then
    raise NONEXISTENT;
  end if;
end UPDATE;

procedure DELETE (K :KEY) is
  WAS_THERE : BOOLEAN;
begin
  POOL_MANAGER.REMOVE (K, WAS_THERE);
  if not WAS_THERE then
    raise NONEXISTENT;
  end if;
end DELETE;

function IS_THERE (K :KEY) return BOOLEAN is
```

```
      WAS_THERE : BOOLEAN;
begin
   POOL_MANAGER.X_IS_THERE (K, WAS_THERE);
   return WAS_THERE;
end IS_THERE;

task body POOL_MANAGER is
   POOL_VALUES : array (KEY) of ITEM;
   EXISTS      : array (KEY) of BOOLEAN
                 := (KEY => FALSE);
begin
  loop
    select
      accept EXAMINE (K : KEY ; D : out ITEM;
                  PRESENT : out BOOLEAN) do
        if EXISTS (K) then
           D := POOL_VALUES (K);
        end if;
        PRESENT := EXISTS (K);
      end EXAMINE;
    or
      accept SET (K : KEY; D : in ITEM;
                  PRESENT : out BOOLEAN) do
        PRESENT := EXISTS (K);
        POOL_VALUES (K) := D;
        EXISTS (K) := TRUE;
      end SET;
    or
      accept CHANGE (K : KEY; REVISED : in ITEM;
              PREVIOUS : out ITEM; PRESENT : out BOOLEAN) do
        if EXISTS (K) then
              PREVIOUS := POOL_VALUES (K);
        end if;
        PRESENT := EXISTS (K);
        POOL_VALUES (K) := REVISED;
        EXISTS (K) := TRUE;
      end CHANGE;
    or
      accept REMOVE (K : KEY; PRESENT : out BOOLEAN) do
        PRESENT := EXISTS (K);
        EXISTS (K) := FALSE;
      end REMOVE;
    or
      accept X_IS_THERE (K : KEY; PRESENT : out BOOLEAN) do
        PRESENT := EXISTS (K);
      end X_IS_THERE;
    or
```

```
            terminate;
        end select;
      end loop;
    end POOL_MANAGER;

  end MASCOT_POOL;
```

Note the way the server task communicates with the procedures which provide the externally visible facilities, in particular the exceptions. The server gives a status flag to the calling procedure, which then decides whether to raise the exception. Many tasks may have access to the package, and provide their own handlers for the exceptions.

13.6   Conclusion

The rendezvous technique of Ada is one of the most novel features of the language, and there is very little actual experience of using it. Similar remarks also apply to the use of generics, exceptions, and (to a lesser extent) private types. The examples given here have been tested with an experimental Ada compiler, but not tried out in practice, they are therefore as tentative as any programs in Ada at this early period of its life. If they are found useful as guides to the development of real programs, the purpose of this book will have been achieved.

APPENDIX A

Predefined specifications

Certain packages and generic units are predefined in Ada, providing a standard environment from which others may be developed. There are eleven such predefined units, which are:

```
CALENDAR
DIRECT_IO
IO_EXCEPTIONS
LOW_LEVEL_IO
MACHINE_CODE (optional)
SEQUENTIAL_IO
STANDARD
SYSTEM
TEXT_IO
UNCHECKED_CONVERSION
UNCHECKED_DEALLOCATION
```

Their specifications are given in this appendix. Corresponding bodies would be provided (not usually in Ada) in the implementation. Package STANDARD is available to every compilation unit automatically, and does not have to be mentioned in the context specification. If any of the other units are needed, their names must be written in the context specification of the unit being compiled. In particular, this rule applies to the units with 'dangerous' possible effects, such as MACHINE_CODE and UNCHECKED_DEALLOCATION; any compilation unit using them must clearly say so at the top.

227

A.1   Calendar date and time

```
package CALENDAR is
  type TIME is private;

  subtype YEAR_NUMBER is INTEGER range 1901 .. 2099;
  subtype MONTH_NUMBER is INTEGER range 1 .. 12;
  subtype DAY_NUMBER is INTEGER range 1 .. 31;
  subtype DAY_DURATION is DURATION range 0.0 .. 86_400.0;

  function CLOCK return TIME;

  function YEAR (DATE : TIME) return YEAR_NUMBER;
  function MONTH ( DATE : TIME) return MONTH_NUMBER;
  function DAY (DATE : TIME) return DAY_NUMBER;
  function SECONDS (DATE : TIME) return DAY_DURATION;

  procedure SPLIT ( DATE : in TIME;
                    YEAR : out YEAR_NUMBER;
                    MONTH : out MONTH_NUMBER;
                    DAY : out DAY_NUMBER;
                    SECONDS : out DAY_DURATION);

  function TIME_OF (YEAR : YEAR_NUMBER;
                    MONTH : MONTH_NUMBER;
                    DAY : DAY_NUMBER;
                    SECONDS : DAY_DURATION) return TIME;

  function "+" (LEFT : TIME;     RIGHT : DURATION) return TIME;
  function "+" (LEFT : DURATION; RIGHT : TIME)     return TIME;
  function "-" (LEFT : TIME;     RIGHT : DURATION) return TIME;
  function "-" (LEFT : TIME;     RIGHT : TIME) return DURATION;

  function "<"  (LEFT, RIGHT : TIME) return BOOLEAN;
  function "<=" (LEFT, RIGHT : TIME) return BOOLEAN;
  function ">"  (LEFT, RIGHT : TIME) return BOOLEAN;
  function ">=" (LEFT, RIGHT : TIME) return BOOLEAN;

  TIME_ERROR : exception;  -- can be raised by TIME_OF, "+", "-".
private
  type TIME is {implementation_dependent};
end CALENDAR;
```

A.2   Direct access input/output


```
with IO_EXCEPTIONS;
generic
 type ELEMENT_TYPE is private;
package DIRECT_IO is

 type FILE_TYPE is limited private;
 type FILE_MODE is (IN_FILE, INOUT_FILE, OUT_FILE);

 type COUNT is range 0 .. {implementation-defined};
 subtype POSITIVE_COUNT is COUNT range 1 .. COUNT'LAST;

-- File Management

 procedure CREATE(FILE: in out FILE_TYPE;
                  MODE: in FILE_MODE := INOUT_FILE;
                  NAME: in STRING := "";
                  FORM: in STRING := "");

 procedure OPEN(FILE: in out FILE_TYPE;
                MODE: in FILE_MODE;
                NAME: in STRING;
                FORM: in STRING := "");

 procedure CLOSE(FILE: in out FILE_TYPE);
 procedure DELETE(FILE: in out FILE_TYPE);
 procedure RESET(FILE: in out FILE_TYPE) ;
 procedure RESET(FILE: in out FILE_TYPE;
                 MODE : in FILE_MODE);

 function MODE(FILE: in FILE_TYPE) return FILE_MODE;
 function NAME(FILE: in FILE_TYPE) return STRING ;
 function FORM(FILE: in FILE_TYPE) return STRING;

 function IS_OPEN(FILE: in FILE_TYPE) return BOOLEAN ;

-- Input and Output operations

 procedure READ (FILE: in FILE_TYPE;
                 ITEM : out CHARACTER;
                 FROM : in POSITIVE_COUNT);
 procedure READ (FILE: in FILE_TYPE;
                 ITEM : out CHARACTER);
```

```
procedure WRITE (FILE: in FILE_TYPE;
                 ITEM:  in CHARACTER;
                 TO : in POSITIVE_COUNT);
procedure WRITE (FILE: in FILE_TYPE;
                 ITEM: in CHARACTER);

procedure SET_INDEX (FILE: in FILE_TYPE;
                     TO: in POSITIVE_COUNT) ;

function INDEX (FILE: in FILE_TYPE) return POSITIVE_COUNT;
function SIZE (FILE: in FILE_TYPE) return COUNT;

function END_OF_FILE (FILE:in FILE_TYPE) return BOOLEAN ;

-- exceptions

STATUS_ERROR : exception renames IO_EXCEPTIONS.STATUS_ERROR;
MODE_ERROR   : exception renames IO_EXCEPTIONS.MODE_ERROR;
NAME_ERROR   : exception renames IO_EXCEPTIONS.NAME_ERROR;
USE_ERROR    : exception renames IO_EXCEPTIONS.USE_ERROR;
DEVICE_ERROR : exception renames IO_EXCEPTIONS.DEVICE_ERROR;
END_ERROR    : exception renames IO_EXCEPTIONS.END_ERROR;
DATA_ERROR   : exception renames IO_EXCEPTIONS.DATA_ERROR;

private
  type FILE_TYPE is {implementation_dependent};
end DIRECT_IO;
```

A.3   Input/output exceptions

```
package IO_EXCEPTIONS is

  STATUS_ERROR : exception;
  MODE_ERROR : exception;
  NAME_ERROR : exception;
  USE_ERROR : exception;
  DEVICE_ERROR : exception;
  END_ERROR : exception;
  DATA_ERROR : exception;
  LAYOUT_ERROR : exception;

end IO_EXCEPTIONS;
```

A.4   Low level input/output

```
package LOW_LEVEL_IO is
 type DEVICE_TYPE is {implementation_defined};
 type DATA_TYPE   is {implementation_defined};
 -- declarations of overloaded procedures for these types:
 procedure SEND_CONTROL    (DEVICE : DEVICE_TYPE;
                            DATA : in out DATA_TYPE);
 procedure RECEIVE_CONTROL (DEVICE : DEVICE_TYPE;
                            DATA : in out DATA_TYPE);
 end LOW_LEVEL_IO;
```

A.5   Machine code formats

```
package MACHINE_CODE is
  -- implementation-dependent
end MACHINE_CODE;
```

A.6   Sequential access input/output

```
with IO_EXCEPTIONS;
generic
  type ELEMENT_TYPE is private;
package SEQUENTIAL_IO is

 type FILE_TYPE is limited private;
 type FILE_MODE is (IN_FILE, OUT_FILE);

-- File Management

 procedure CREATE(FILE: in out FILE_TYPE;
                  MODE: in FILE_MODE := OUT_FILE;
                  NAME: in STRING := "";
                  FORM: in STRING := "");
```

```
procedure OPEN(FILE: in out FILE_TYPE;
               MODE: in FILE_MODE;
               NAME: in STRING;
               FORM: in STRING := "");

procedure CLOSE(FILE: in out FILE_TYPE);
procedure DELETE(FILE: in out FILE_TYPE);
procedure RESET(FILE: in out FILE_TYPE) ;
procedure RESET(FILE: in out FILE_TYPE; MODE: in FILE_MODE);

function NAME(FILE: in FILE_TYPE) return STRING ;
function FORM(FILE: in FILE_TYPE) return STRING;
function MODE(FILE: in FILE_TYPE) return FILE_MODE;

function IS_OPEN(FILE: in FILE_TYPE) return BOOLEAN ;

-- Input and Output operations

procedure READ(FILE: in FILE_TYPE; ITEM : out ELEMENT_TYPE) ;
procedure WRITE(FILE: in FILE_TYPE; ITEM:  in ELEMENT_TYPE) ;

function END_OF_FILE(FILE:in FILE_TYPE) return BOOLEAN ;

-- Exceptions

STATUS_ERROR : exception renames IO_EXCEPTIONS.STATUS_ERROR;
MODE_ERROR   : exception renames IO_EXCEPTIONS.MODE_ERROR;
NAME_ERROR   : exception renames IO_EXCEPTIONS.NAME_ERROR;
USE_ERROR    : exception renames IO_EXCEPTIONS.USE_ERROR;
DEVICE_ERROR : exception renames IO_EXCEPTIONS.DEVICE_ERROR;
END_ERROR    : exception renames IO_EXCEPTIONS.END_ERROR;
DATA_ERROR   : exception renames IO_EXCEPTIONS.DATA_ERROR;

private
  type FILE_TYPE is {implementation_dependent};
end SEQUENTIAL_IO;
```

.7   System-specific characteristics

```
package SYSTEM is
  type ADDRESS is {implementation_defined};
  type NAME is {implementation_defined}; -- targets possible
  -- The current actual target system is:
  SYSTEM_NAME : constant NAME := {implementation_defined};
  -- with the following properties:
  STORAGE_UNIT  : constant := {implementation_defined};
  MEMORY_SIZE   : constant := {implementation_defined};
  MIN_INT       : constant := {implementation_defined};
  MAX_INT       : constant := {implementation_defined};
  MAX_DIGITS    : constant := {implementation_defined};
  MAX_MANTISSA  : constant := {implementation_defined};
  FINE_DELTA    : constant := {implementation_defined};
  TICK          : constant := {implementation_defined};
  subtype PRIORITY is INTEGER range {implementation_defined};
end SYSTEM;
```

.8   Standard entities

```
package STANDARD is

type BOOLEAN is (FALSE, TRUE);

-- Relational operators for this type are:

-- function "=" (LEFT, RIGHT : BOOLEAN) return BOOLEAN;
-- function "/=" (LEFT, RIGHT : BOOLEAN) return BOOLEAN;
-- function "<" (LEFT, RIGHT : BOOLEAN) return BOOLEAN;
-- function "<=" (LEFT, RIGHT : BOOLEAN) return BOOLEAN;
-- function ">" (LEFT, RIGHT : BOOLEAN) return BOOLEAN;
-- function ">=" (LEFT, RIGHT : BOOLEAN) return BOOLEAN;

-- Logical operators are:

-- function "and" (LEFT,RIGHT:BOOLEAN) return BOOLEAN;
-- function "or" (LEFT,RIGHT:BOOLEAN) return BOOLEAN;
-- function "xor" (LEFT,RIGHT:BOOLEAN) return BOOLEAN;
```

```
-- function "not" (RIGHT:BOOLEAN) return BOOLEAN;

-- There is a universal type universal_integer

type INTEGER is {implementation_defined};
-- whose operators are:

-- function "=" (LEFT, RIGHT : INTEGER) return BOOLEAN;
-- function "/=" (LEFT, RIGHT : INTEGER) return BOOLEAN;
-- function "<" (LEFT, RIGHT : INTEGER) return BOOLEAN;
-- function "<=" (LEFT, RIGHT : INTEGER) return BOOLEAN;
-- function ">" (LEFT, RIGHT : INTEGER) return BOOLEAN;
-- function ">=" (LEFT, RIGHT : INTEGER) return BOOLEAN;
-- function "+" (RIGHT: INTEGER) return INTEGER;
-- function "-" (RIGHT: INTEGER) return INTEGER;
-- function abs (RIGHT: INTEGER) return INTEGER;

-- function "+" (LEFT,RIGHT: INTEGER) return INTEGER;
-- function "-" (LEFT,RIGHT: INTEGER) return INTEGER;
-- function "*" (LEFT,RIGHT: INTEGER) return INTEGER;
-- function "/" (LEFT,RIGHT: INTEGER) return INTEGER;
-- function "rem" (LEFT,RIGHT: INTEGER) return INTEGER;
-- function "mod" (LEFT,RIGHT: INTEGER) return INTEGER;

-- function "**" (LEFT: INTEGER;
                  RIGHT: INTEGER ) return INTEGER;

-- There may be other integer types,
-- particularly SHORT_INTEGER and LONG_INTEGER

-- There is a universal type universal_real

type FLOAT is digits  {implementation_defined};

-- whose operators are:

-- function "=" (LEFT, RIGHT : FLOAT) return BOOLEAN;
-- function "/=" (LEFT, RIGHT : FLOAT) return BOOLEAN;
-- function "<" (LEFT, RIGHT : FLOAT) return BOOLEAN;
-- function "<=" (LEFT, RIGHT : FLOAT) return BOOLEAN;
-- function ">" (LEFT, RIGHT : FLOAT) return BOOLEAN;
-- function ">=" (LEFT, RIGHT : FLOAT) return BOOLEAN;
-- function "+" (RIGHT:FLOAT) return FLOAT;
-- function "-" (RIGHT:FLOAT) return FLOAT;
-- function abs (RIGHT:FLOAT) return FLOAT;

-- function "+" (LEFT,RIGHT:FLOAT) return FLOAT;
```

```ada
-- function "-" (LEFT,RIGHT:FLOAT) return FLOAT;
-- function "*" (LEFT,RIGHT:FLOAT) return FLOAT;
-- function "/" (LEFT,RIGHT:FLOAT) return FLOAT;
-- function "**" (LEFT:FLOAT;RIGHT: INTEGER) return FLOAT;

-- There may be other floating point types,
-- particularly SHORT_FLOAT and LONG_FLOAT

-- Further operators for universal types:

-- function "*" (LEFT : universal_integer; RIGHT : universal_real)
--               return universal_real;
-- function "*" (LEFT : universal_real; RIGHT : universal_integer)
--               return universal_real;
-- function "/" (LEFT : universal_real; RIGHT : universal_integer)
--               return universal_real;

-- There is a type universal_fixed, whose only operators are:
-- function "*" (LEFT : any_fixed_point_type;
--               RIGHT: any_fixed_point_type)
--               return universal_fixed;
-- function "/" (LEFT : any_fixed_point_type;
--               RIGHT: any_fixed_point_type)
--               return universal_fixed;

-- The following characters comprise the standard ASCII character set.
-- The first 32 character literals correspond to control characters;
-- they are not identifiers,
-- and are indicated in lower case in this definition:

type CHARACTER is

(nul, soh, stx, etx, eot, enq, ack, bel,
 bs, ht, lf, vt, ff, cr, so, si,
 dle, dcl, dc2, dc3, dc4, nak, syn, etb,
 can, em, sub, esc, fs, gs, rs, us,

 ' ', '!', '"', '#', '$', '%', '&', ''',
 '(', ')', '*', '+', ',', '-', '.', '/',
 '0', '1', '2', '3', '4', '5', '6', '7',
 '8', '9', ':', ';', '<', '=', '>', '?',

 '@', 'A', 'B', 'C', 'D', 'E', 'F', 'G'
 'H', 'I', 'J', 'K', 'L', 'M', 'N', 'O',
 'P', 'Q', 'R', 'S', 'T', 'U', 'V', 'W',
 'X', 'Y', 'Z', '[', '\', ']', '^', '_',
```

```
'`', 'a', 'b', 'c', 'd', 'e', 'f', 'g'
'h'. 'i', 'j', 'k', 'l', 'm', 'n', 'o',
'p', 'q', 'r', 's', 't', 'u', 'v', 'w',
'x', 'y', 'z', '{', '|', '}', '~', del;

package ASCII is
-- Control characters:

NUL : constant CHARACTER := nul;
SOH : constant CHARACTER := soh;
STX : constant CHARACTER := stx;
ETX : constant CHARACTER := etx;
EOT : constant CHARACTER := eot;
ENQ : constant CHARACTER := enq;
ACK : constant CHARACTER := ack;
BEL : constant CHARACTER := bel;
BS  : constant CHARACTER := bs;
HT  : constant CHARACTER := ht;
LF  : constant CHARACTER := lf;
VT  : constant CHARACTER := vt;
FF  : constant CHARACTER := ff;
CR  : constant CHARACTER := cr;
SO  : constant CHARACTER := so;
SI  : constant CHARACTER := si;
DLE : constant CHARACTER := dle;
DC1 : constant CHARACTER := dc1;
DC2 : constant CHARACTER := dc2;
DC3 : constant CHARACTER := dc3;
DC4 : constant CHARACTER := dc4;
NAK : constant CHARACTER := nak;
SYN : constant CHARACTER := syn;
ETB : constant CHARACTER := etb;
CAN : constant CHARACTER := can;
EM  : constant CHARACTER := em;
SUB : constant CHARACTER := sub;
ESC : constant CHARACTER := esc;
FS  : constant CHARACTER := fs;
GS  : constant CHARACTER := gs;
RS  : constant CHARACTER := rs;
US  : constant CHARACTER := us;
DEL : constant CHARACTER := del;

-- Other characters

EXCLAM    : constant CHARACTER := '!';
SHARP     : constant CHARACTER := '#';
DOLLAR    : constant CHARACTER := '$';
```

```
QUERY       : constant CHARACTER := '?';
AT_SIGN     : constant CHARACTER := '@';
L_BRACKET   : constant CHARACTER := '[';
BACK_SLASH  : constant CHARACTER := '\';
R_BRACKET   : constant CHARACTER := ']';
CIRCUMFLEX  : constant CHARACTER := '^';
GRAVE       : constant CHARACTER := '`';
L_BRACE     : constant CHARACTER := '{';
BAR         : constant CHARACTER := '|';
R_BRACE     : constant CHARACTER := '}';
TILDE       : constant CHARACTER := '~';

-- Lower case letters

LC_A : constant CHARACTER := 'a';
   ---
LC_Z : constant CHARACTER := 'z';

end ASCII;

-- Predefined subtypes

subtype NATURAL is INTEGER range 0 .. INTEGER'LAST;
subtype POSITIVE is INTEGER range 1 .. INTEGER'LAST;

-- Predefined string type

type STRING is array (POSITIVE range <>) of CHARACTER;
pragma PACK ( STRING );
-- whose operators are:

-- function "=" (LEFT, RIGHT : STRING) return BOOLEAN;
-- function "/=" (LEFT, RIGHT : STRING) return BOOLEAN;
-- function "<" (LEFT, RIGHT : STRING) return BOOLEAN;
-- function "<=" (LEFT, RIGHT : STRING) return BOOLEAN;
-- function ">" (LEFT, RIGHT : STRING) return BOOLEAN;
-- function ">=" (LEFT, RIGHT : STRING) return BOOLEAN;

-- function "&" (LEFT : STRING ; RIGHT : STRING) return STRING;
-- function "&" (LEFT : CHARACTER; RIGHT : STRING) return STRING;
-- function "&" (LEFT : STRING ; RIGHT : CHARACTER) return STRING;
-- function "&" (LEFT : CHARACTER; RIGHT : CHARACTER) return STRING;

type DURATION  is delta {implementation_defined}
                  range {implementation_defined};

-- The predefined exceptions
```

```
CONSTRAINT_ERROR : exception;
NUMERIC_ERROR    : exception;
PROGRAM_ERROR    : exception;
STORAGE_ERROR    : exception;
TASKING_ERROR    : exception;

for CHARACTER use -- 128 ASCII character set without holes

(0,1,2,3,4,5,..., 125, 126, 127);

end STANDARD;
```


A.9   Text input/output


```
with IO_EXCEPTIONS;

package TEXT_IO is

   type FILE_TYPE is limited private;
   type FILE_MODE is (IN_FILE, OUT_FILE);

   type COUNT is range 0 .. {implementation-defined};
   subtype POSITIVE_COUNT is COUNT range 1 .. COUNT'LAST;
   UNBOUNDED : constant COUNT := 0; -- line and page length

   subtype FIELD is INTEGER range 0 .. {implementation-defined};
   subtype NUMBER_BASE is INTEGER range 2 .. 16;

   -- file management

   procedure CREATE (FILE : in out FILE_TYPE;
                     MODE : in FILE_MODE      := OUT_FILE;
                     NAME : in STRING         := "";
                     FORM : in STRING         := "");

   procedure OPEN   (FILE : in out FILE_TYPE;
                     MODE : in FILE_MODE;
                     NAME : in STRING;
                     FORM : in STRING := "");

   procedure CLOSE (FILE : in out FILE_TYPE);
   procedure DELETE (FILE : in out FILE_TYPE);
```

```
procedure RESET (FILE : in out FILE_TYPE;
                 MODE : in FILE_MODE);
procedure RESET (FILE : in out FILE_TYPE);

function  MODE (FILE : in FILE_TYPE) return FILE_MODE;
function  NAME (FILE : in FILE_TYPE) return STRING;
function  FORM (FILE : in FILE_TYPE) return STRING;

function  IS_OPEN (FILE : in FILE_TYPE) return BOOLEAN;

-- control of default input and output files

procedure SET_INPUT (FILE : in FILE_TYPE);
procedure SET_OUTPUT (FILE : in FILE_TYPE);

function  STANDARD_INPUT     return FILE_TYPE;
function  STANDARD_OUTPUT    return FILE_TYPE;

function  CURRENT_INPUT      return FILE_TYPE;
function  CURRENT_OUTPUT     return FILE_TYPE;

-- specification of line and page lengths

procedure SET_LINE_LENGTH    (FILE : in FILE_TYPE;
                              TO   : in COUNT);
procedure SET_LINE_LENGTH    (TO   : in COUNT);

procedure SET_PAGE_LENGTH    (FILE : in FILE_TYPE;
                              TO   : in COUNT);
procedure SET_PAGE_LENGTH    (TO   : in COUNT);

function  LINE_LENGTH        (FILE : in FILE_TYPE) return COUNT;
function  LINE_LENGTH        return COUNT;

function  PAGE_LENGTH        (FILE : in FILE_TYPE) return COUNT;
function  PAGE_LENGTH        return COUNT;

-- column, line and page control

procedure NEW_LINE  (FILE : in FILE_TYPE;
                     SPACING : in POSITIVE_COUNT := 1);
procedure NEW_LINE  (SPACING : in POSITIVE_COUNT := 1);

procedure SKIP_LINE (FILE : in FILE_TYPE;
                     SPACING : in POSITIVE_COUNT := 1);
procedure SKIP_LINE (SPACING : in POSITIVE_COUNT := 1);
```

```
function  END_OF_LINE (FILE : in FILE_TYPE) return BOOLEAN;
function  END_OF_LINE return BOOLEAN;

procedure NEW_PAGE (FILE : in FILE_TYPE);
procedure NEW_PAGE;

procedure SKIP_PAGE (FILE : in FILE_TYPE);
procedure SKIP_PAGE;

function  END_OF_PAGE (FILE : in FILE_TYPE) return BOOLEAN;
function  END_OF_PAGE return BOOLEAN;

function  END_OF_FILE (FILE : in FILE_TYPE) return BOOLEAN;
function  END_OF_FILE return BOOLEAN;

procedure SET_COL (FILE : in FILE_TYPE;
                   TO   : in POSITIVE_COUNT);
procedure SET_COL (TO   : in POSITIVE_COUNT);

procedure SET_LINE (FILE : in FILE_TYPE;
                    TO   : in POSITIVE_COUNT);
procedure SET_LINE (TO   : in POSITIVE_COUNT);

function  COL (FILE : in FILE_TYPE) return POSITIVE_COUNT;
function  COL return POSITIVE_COUNT;

function  LINE (FILE : in FILE_TYPE) return POSITIVE_COUNT;
function  LINE return POSITIVE_COUNT;

function  PAGE (FILE : in FILE_TYPE) return POSITIVE_COUNT;
function  PAGE return POSITIVE_COUNT;

-- character input-output

procedure GET (FILE : in FILE_TYPE;
               ITEM : out CHARACTER);
procedure GET (ITEM : out CHARACTER);

procedure PUT (FILE : in FILE_TYPE;
               ITEM : in CHARACTER);
procedure PUT (ITEM : in CHARACTER);

-- string input-output

procedure GET (FILE : in FILE_TYPE;
               ITEM : out STRING);
procedure GET (ITEM : out STRING);
```

```
    procedure PUT (FILE : in FILE_TYPE;
                   ITEM : in STRING);
    procedure PUT (ITEM : in STRING);

    procedure GET_LINE (FILE : in FILE_TYPE;
                        ITEM : out STRING;
                        LAST : out NATURAL);
    procedure GET_LINE (ITEM : out STRING;
                        LAST : out NATURAL);

    procedure PUT_LINE (FILE : in FILE_TYPE;
                        ITEM : in STRING);
    procedure PUT_LINE (ITEM : in STRING);

    -- Generic package for Input-Output of Integer Types

    generic
      type NUM is range <>;
    package INTEGER_IO is
        DEFAULT_WIDTH   : FIELD := NUM'WIDTH;
        DEFAULT_BASE    : NUMBER_BASE := 10;

        procedure GET (FILE  : in FILE_TYPE;
                       ITEM  : out NUM;
                       WIDTH : in FIELD        := 0);

        procedure GET (ITEM  : out NUM;
                       WIDTH : in FIELD        := 0);

        procedure PUT (FILE  : in FILE_TYPE;
                       ITEM  : in NUM;
                       WIDTH : in FIELD       := DEFAULT_WIDTH;
                       BASE  : in NUMBER_BASE := DEFAULT_BASE);

        procedure PUT (ITEM  : in NUM;
                       WIDTH : in FIELD       := DEFAULT_WIDTH;
                       BASE  : in NUMBER_BASE := DEFAULT_BASE);

        procedure GET (FROM  : in STRING;
                       ITEM  : out NUM;
                       LAST  : out POSITIVE);

        procedure PUT (TO    : out STRING;
                       ITEM  : in NUM;
                       BASE  : in NUMBER_BASE := DEFAULT_BASE);
    end INTEGER_IO;
```

```
-- Generic packages for Input-Output of Real Types
generic
  type NUM is digits <>;
package FLOAT_IO is
    DEFAULT_FORE    : FIELD := 2;
    DEFAULT_AFT     : FIELD := NUM'DIGITS - 1;
    DEFAULT_EXP     : FIELD := 3;

    procedure GET (FILE   : in FILE_TYPE;
                   ITEM   : out NUM;
                   WIDTH  : in FIELD := 0);

    procedure GET (ITEM   : out NUM;
                   WIDTH  : in FIELD := 0);

    procedure PUT (FILE   : in FILE_TYPE;
                   ITEM   : in NUM;
                   FORE   : in FIELD := DEFAULT_FORE;
                   AFT    : in FIELD := DEFAULT_AFT;
                   EXP    : in FIELD := DEFAULT_EXP);

    procedure PUT (ITEM   : in NUM;
                   FORE   : in FIELD := DEFAULT_FORE;
                   AFT    : in FIELD := DEFAULT_AFT;
                   EXP    : in FIELD := DEFAULT_EXP);

    procedure GET (FROM   : in STRING;
                   ITEM   : out NUM;
                   LAST   : out NATURAL);

    procedure PUT (TO     : out STRING;
                   ITEM   : in NUM;
                   AFT    : in FIELD := DEFAULT_AFT;
                   EXP    : in FIELD := DEFAULT_EXP);
end FLOAT_IO;

generic
  type NUM is delta <>;
package FIXED_IO is
    DEFAULT_FORE    : FIELD := NUM'FORE;
    DEFAULT_AFT     : FIELD := NUM'AFT;
    DEFAULT_EXP     : FIELD := 0;

    procedure GET (FILE   : in FILE_TYPE;
                   ITEM   : out NUM;
                   WIDTH  : in FIELD := 0);
```

```
      procedure GET (ITEM    : out NUM;
                     WIDTH   : in FIELD := 0);

      procedure PUT (FILE    : in FILE_TYPE;
                     ITEM    : in NUM;
                     FORE    : in FIELD := DEFAULT_FORE;
                     AFT     : in FIELD := DEFAULT_AFT;
                     EXP     : in FIELD := DEFAULT_EXP);

      procedure PUT (ITEM    : in NUM;
                     FORE    : in FIELD := DEFAULT_FORE;
                     AFT     : in FIELD := DEFAULT_AFT;
                     EXP     : in FIELD := DEFAULT_EXP);

      procedure GET (FROM    : in STRING;
                     ITEM    : out NUM;
                     LAST    : out POSITIVE);

      procedure PUT (TO      : out STRING;
                     ITEM    : in NUM;
                     AFT     : in FIELD := DEFAULT_AFT;
                     EXP     : in FIELD := DEFAULT_EXP);

end FIXED_IO;

-- Generic package for Input-Output of Enumeration Types

generic
   type ENUM is (<>);
package ENUMERATION_IO is

   DEFAULT_WIDTH : FIELD := 0;
   DEFAULT_SETTING : TYPE_SET := UPPER_CASE;

   procedure GET (FILE    : in FILE_TYPE;
                  ITEM    : out ENUM);

   procedure GET (ITEM    : out ENUM);

   procedure PUT (FILE    : in FILE_TYPE;
                  ITEM    : in ENUM;
                  WIDTH   : in FIELD := DEFAULT_WIDTH;
                  SET     : in TYPE_SET := DEFAULT_SETTING);

   procedure PUT (ITEM    : in ENUM;
                  WIDTH   : in FIELD := DEFAULT_WIDTH;
                  SET     : in TYPE_SET := DEFAULT_SETTING);
```

```
        procedure GET (FROM   : in STRING;
                       ITEM   : out ENUM;
                       LAST   : out POSITIVE);

        procedure PUT (TO     : out STRING;
                       ITEM   : in ENUM;
                       SET    : in TYPE_SET := DEFAULT_SETTING);
     end ENUMERATION_IO;

     -- Exceptions

     STATUS_ERROR          : exception renames IO_EXCEPTIONS.STATUS_ERROR;
     MODE_ERROR            : exception renames IO_EXCEPTIONS.MODE_ERROR;
     NAME_ERROR            : exception renames IO_EXCEPTIONS.NAME_ERROR;
     USE_ERROR             : exception renames IO_EXCEPTIONS.USE_ERROR;
     DEVICE_ERROR          : exception renames IO_EXCEPTIONS.DEVICE_ERROR;
     END_ERROR             : exception renames IO_EXCEPTIONS.END_ERROR;
     DATA_ERROR            : exception renames IO_EXCEPTIONS.DATA_ERROR;
     LAYOUT_ERROR          : exception renames IO_EXCEPTIONS.LAYOUT_ERROR;

  private

     -- implementation dependent

  end TEXT_IO;
```

A.10   Unchecked conversion between types

```
  generic
     type SOURCE is limited private;
     type TARGET is limited private;
  function UNCHECKED_CONVERSION (S : SOURCE) return TARGET;
```

11   Unchecked deallocation of space

```
generic
   type OBJECT is limited private;
   type NAME   is access OBJECT;
procedure UNCHECKED_DEALLOCATION (X : in out NAME);
```

APPENDIX B

Notes for Fortran Programmers

There are several aspects of Ada which the experienced FORTRA
programmer will find strange; however he will soon learn that the ne
features in the language actually help to minimise problems, and catc
many errors at compile-time. It is evident that the Ada text is longe
than the corresponding Fortran. The extra information that has to b
given is used for checking. This reflects the fact that Ada is designe
to be easier to <u>read</u>, accepting the price that it is not so quick t
write.

The most fundamental difference between the languages is in the are
of data types. Fortran has only a few data types (INTEGER, REAI
LOGICAL, DOUBLE PRECISION, COMPLEX and now CHARACTER), and althoug
consistency checks are applied within each subprogram, there are man
ways of breaking the rules (e.g. with COMMON, EQUIVALENCE and subroutin
parameters), to work with data of one type as though it were anothe
Experience has shown that this area of Fortran is the most frequen
source of serious errors. These are difficult to detect, particular
when a program is modified by someone else after the original design
is no longer available. For this reason the Fortran programmer shou
view the Ada typing rules as a way of preventing logical mistakes fr
getting into the running program. The opportunities in Fortran to sa
space by the techniques are avoided by the different visibility rules
Ada.

The following are detailed differences between the languages:

1. You must get used to using the semicolon and assignment symbol
   Remember that the semicolon is needed at the end of almost eve
   line; broadly speaking, those which do <u>not</u> have a semicolon a
   those ending with

is loop select begin then else of record

or of course where the statement is too long to fit on one line.

The assignment symbol := is used in assignment statements. It is a good idea to think of the colon-equals combination as the 'becomes' symbol, and to read it as 'becomes' when you see it.

2. You must declare every variable you use (except loop indexes). There are a number of points to bear in mind about this. You do of course in Fortran have to declare any arrays you need, or any variables with initial letters inconsistent with their type, or anything in COMMON or EQUIVALENCE. In Fortran you collect the information of the same kind together (DIMENSION, REAL, LOGICAL etc.) so that the details of any particular array or variable are spread over several declarations. In Ada, all the information about a particular variable comes together, and there is a natural place to put any comment about it.

3. The treatment of COMMON is easier with Ada: you do not have to repeat the COMMON declarations in every subprogram. Use a package for each block of COMMON (which can include initial values, instead of a separate BLOCK DATA). As an illustration of this, some of the package given in section 7.1 corresponds to the following in Fortran:

```
      BLOCK DATA
      COMMON /STORE/ SCALE, K, JUMP, A, SM,
     1  INPUT, IFM, ALAT, ALONG, EORW, NORS,
     2  CHANGE, FRACT, SIG, VAL, LEG
      INTEGER EORW
      COMMON /FORMAT/ FMT
      REAL * 8  FMT(10)
      COMMON /NSEW/ N, S, E, W
      INTEGER N, S, E, W
      DATA N, S, E, W/'N', 'S', 'E', 'W'/
      DATA FRACT, SIG, CHANGE/3 * .FALSE./
      DATA JUMP /11/
      DATA FMT/ '(2(F9.0,', 'A1),', 'T1,F5.0)', 7*' '
      END
```

Notice that with a little more work the package NSEW could have been changed into an enumeration type, probably leading to a slightly more compact program.

4. There is nothing in Ada quite like EQUIVALENCE, but most of the occasions where you have to use it in Fortran can be dealt with

using other facilities in Ada, such as application specific type
and renames declarations. Fortran programmers who are usin
EQUIVALENCE to give the same storage area more than one type (sa
REAL and LOGICAL) should rearrange the program so that the part
dealing with the different variables are in separate blocks - th
storage will then be allocated properly without the danger o
misuse.

5. Ada does not allow subprograms to be parameters at run-time (i.e
    as dummy arguments of functions or subroutines). They can be give
    as generic parameters, fixed at compile-time, so a Fortran progra
    that uses EXTERNAL dummy arguments must be changed so that eithe
    the arguments are static (with improved efficiency over the Fortra
    form), or selected dynamically in a specially-written procedur
    containing all the subprograms that can be called from that point.

6. Numerical constants need not distinguish the precision:

    1.0E+3

    can serve as a literal for SHORT_FLOAT, FLOAT or LONG_FLOAT (i
    available). The Fortran programmer can forget all about the
    exponent number form. Similarly there is no need to use DSQRT etc.

7. Ada input/output is very different from that in Fortran, but th
    official input-output packages are not mandatory, and facilities lik
    those of FORTRAN are likely to be developed as library packages.

APPENDIX C

Notes for Pascal Programmers

ot surprisingly, in view of its ancestry, Ada contains a subset which
s very close to Pascal. For this reason a Pascal programmer should have
ittle difficulty in converting to Ada. However there are a number of
etailed differences which must be appreciated by the Pascal programmer
hen writing in Ada.

• Ada uses terminating keywords where Pascal uses a compound
statement. Thus the Pascal compound statement

```
    IF x > y THEN
       BEGIN
          x := y;
          r := s
       END;
```

is replaced in Ada by

```
    if X > Y then
       X := Y;
       R := S;
    end if;
```

with no BEGIN, but the end marked as a terminator for the if
statement. Similar considerations arise in Pascal wherever a
statement can be replaced by one or more statements between BEGIN
and END. The corresponding Ada structure always has an explicit
closing keyword. This change makes it much easier to amend a
program when you have to add an extra statement into a loop or
conditional statement.

• The semicolon is used in Ada to terminate statements, instead of for

249

statement separation. This is most strikingly illustrated by th
Pascal statement

```
IF p > q THEN
    x := 0      (* N.B.  No semicolon *)
ELSE
    y := 0;
```

whose Ada equivalent has a semicolon before the **else**:

```
if P > Q then
    X := 0;     -- semicolon needed here
else
    Y := 0;
end if;
```

3. For array indexes, Ada uses round brackets.

4. Ada expressions have more precedence levels than Pascal. This make
   it easier to combine relations such as:

   X < Y **and** P = Q

   which must be written as subexpressions in Pascal.

5. In a type declaration, where Pascal uses an equals sign, Ada use
   the word **is**. Similarly, in a procedure declaration, where Pasca
   separates the specification from the body with a semicolon, Ad
   connects them with the word **is**.

6. Pointers in Pascal and access variables in Ada are very similar, bu
   they are declared in a different way. The main difference is tha
   no pointer symbol is used in Ada: dereferencing is implicit. Also
   space allocation is done in an expression in Ada (not in a specia
   statement).

7. There is no special mechanism for sets in Ada. An array of BOOLEA
   objects is used to represent a set, but there are no specia
   notations for set-types, set-values or set-operations. In thi
   respect, the features of Ada are not so convenient as those i
   Pascal.

8. Ada contains no equivalent to the more complicated forms of "read
   and "write" statements in Pascal, where they take several actua
   parameters. A sequence of calls must be written.

Ada takes a different approach on procedures or functions as parameters, since it has generic program units as well as subprograms. Where a Pascal program has procedure (or function) formal parameters, Ada distinguishes the cases where the binding is static (as in a library procedure) when the corresponding Ada program should use a generic procedure with a generic formal parameter, from that in which there are different subprograms chosen in different states of the program, when an intermediate procedure has to be written to make the dynamic selection.

Several irritating restrictions in Pascal are removed in Ada:

Enumeration literals can be overloaded.

Procedure parameters may be arrays with variable bounds.

The order of declarations in Ada is less rigid. (No LABEL, CONST, TYPE, VAR ordering imposed.)

Compile-time constants may be given as expressions. For example, Ada allows:

```
PI    : constant  := 3.14159265;
TWOPI : constant  := 2.0 * PI;  -- impossible in Pascal
```

APPENDIX D

Notes for Coral 66 Programmers

Coral 66 and Pascal were both derived from Algol 60, so many of the notes for Pascal programmers in Appendix C apply for Coral 66 as well. The following are some further points, based on the Official Definition of Coral 66 by Woodward, Wetherall and Gorman (HMSO 1974).

1. Sequences of statements are widely used, so that `begin` and `end` no longer act as brackets. (Ada uses fewer `begin`s and more `end` than Coral.) Semicolons terminate statements and declarations; **begin** is used to mark the end of the declarations and the beginning of the statements.

2. Many more types are used, defined in the Ada program. They can be for part-words as well as ordinary variables or arrays, and include fixed point and floating point values.

3. A Coral TABLE corresponds to an Ada array of records. Declare a record type for an entry of the table (using appropriate types for the fields in the entry, including NATURAL for unsigned and **delta** for fixed point components), then declare an array for as many of these as required. (You will have to invent an extra name for the type of the table entry, which will be used if you need to specify the internal representation.) For example, the table defined in the Official Definition (page 13) would be:

```
type DAY_DETAILS is
 record
  TICKETS : INTEGER;
  WEIGHT : delta 2**(-20)
          range -2**(-4) .. 2**(-4) - 2**(-20);
  RAIN : delta 2**(-2)
          range 0.0 .. 3.75;
```

252

```
      SUNSHINE : NATURAL range 0 .. 15;
      HUMIDITY : delta 2**(-6)
                 range 0.0 .. 1.0 - 2**(-6);
      TEMPERATURE : delta 2**(-2)
                    range -2**8 .. 2**8 - 2**(-2);
    end record;
  type APRIL is array (1 .. 30) of DAY_DETAILS;
```

o refer to a particular element in the table, combine the index and
elector notations, thus:

```
  APRIL(6).RAIN
```

or the rain on April 6th (avoiding the confusion in Coral caused by
ero-origin arrays).

. Absolute addresses are used in Coral 66 for a number of purposes
hat are distinguished in Ada, to emphasise logical relationships. It
s not essential to give the bit numbers and field sizes for part-words
n a table (although the physical layout can be specified when
ecessary, by a representation clause). It is not necessary to use
OCATION and anonymous references to make list structures: Ada provides
ccess types for this. The ABSOLUTE communicator corresponds to an
ddress specification in a representation clause. OVERLAY is
nnecessary for economising storage, but if it is needed to break the
ype-checking rule, the effect can be obtained by UNCHECKED_CONVERSION.

. The main difference concerning expressions is that Ada actually
efines how the operands and operators are evaluated, whereas Coral
eaves it to the implementation. In most cases of fixed point, this
eans that the programmer must explicitly specify the scaling of every
ixed point multiplication or division, stating the required result-
ype.   Ada has operators for dealing with bit patterns, using the same
otation as for Booleans (with and, or, xor corresponding to Coral's
ASK, UNION, DIFFER).

. The FOR statement in Coral can take a list of elements, as well as
he usual forms for iteration and repetition. To write this in Ada, you
ould store the list of values in an array (using an array aggregate),
r make the body of the loop into a procedure with the loop index as a
arameter. The switched GOTO statement in Coral is replaced by a case
tatement in Ada, bringing together the related parts of the program.

. Parameters of procedures require some attention. Coral's VALUE mode
s like Ada's in mode. Where Coral has LOCATION, in Ada you could write
n out for the general case, but out may be better, depending on the use
f the formal parameter. An ARRAY or TABLE parameter can be given as in

out, but again, a more precise mode would be better, depending on how the formal parameter is used. Coral allows labels and switches to be used as parameters, usually for denoting abnormal conditions or special return points; Ada provides exceptions for this purpose. Coral also allows procedures to be passed as parameters; in Ada, a procedure with such a parameter must be generic, and its parametric procedure bound at compile-time.

8. Macros are used in Coral for several purposes. Simple text substitution of a subprogram body is done automatically if you say pragma IN_LINE. Definitions of constant values are given by number declarations. Control of access to sensitive or tricky parts of a program is achieved by using packages.

9. Ada provides important facilities for real-time programming that are lacking in Coral 66: tasks and input/output. Supporting facilities such as application libraries can be specified as Ada packages, using pragma INTERFACE to link parts on Ada to existing bodies. This technique is illustrated by the description in Ada of Mascot channels and pools in section 13.5.

10. Ada has been found useful for designing programs that are eventually coded in Coral 66, particularly for the program structure and data structures. It is easy to write 'pseudo-code' in Ada, without needing a further language.

APPENDIX E

Pragmas and Attributes

Ada limits the ways in which implementations are allowed to extend the language, to facilitate portability: only pragmas and attributes may be so extended. Standard Ada defines the following, but implementations are permitted to add further pragmas or attributes within the same syntax.

E.1 Pragmas

Pragmas concern details not affecting the logic of the program. Pragmas may be written between statements or declarations unless there are special rules; in general, they are allowed before alternatives, clauses, exception handlers and variants, and after statements and declarations. A pragma may have arguments which may be identifiers, strings or numbers; the arguments are written in parentheses after the pragma name. The following pragmas are defined in standard Ada:

CONTROLLED   Takes an access type name as argument. It must appear in the same declarative part as the access type definition. It specifies that automatic storage reclamation should not be performed for objects of the access type except upon leaving the scope of the access type definition.

ELABORATE   Takes a list of (simple) names of library units as arguments. It must appear immediately after the context clause at the head of a compilation unit, and the context clause must mention the cited library units. It specifies that the stated library units' bodies must be made ready for execution (elaborated) before the present compilation unit.

INLINE   Takes a list of subprogram names as arguments. It must appear in the same declarative part as the named subprograms. It specifies that the subprogram bodies should be expanded in-line at each call.

INTERFACE   Takes a language name and subprogram name as arguments. It must appear after the subprogram specification in the same declarative part or in the same package specification. It specifies that the body of the subprogram is written in the given other language, whose calling conventions are to be observed.

LIST   Takes ON or OFF as argument. This pragma can appear anywhere. It specifies that listing of the program unit is to be continued or suspended until a LIST pragma is given with the opposite argument.

MEMORY_SIZE   Takes a numeric literal as argument. This pragma can only appear before a library unit. It establishes the required number of storage units in memory: the value of SYSTEM.MEMORY_SIZE.

OPTIMIZE   Takes TIME or SPACE as argument. This pragma can only appear in a declarative part and it applies to the block or body enclosing the declarative part. It specifies whether time or space is the primary optimization criterion.

PACK   Takes a record or array type name as argument. The position of the pragma is governed by the same rules as for a representation specification. It specifies that storage minimization should be the main criterion when selecting the representation of the given type.

PAGE   Takes no arguments, and may appear anywhere a pragma is allowed. It specifies that the compiler must start a new page, if it is listing the program.

PRIORITY   Takes a static expression as argument, of subtype
    SYSTEM.PRIORITY. It must appear in a task (or task type)
    specification or the outermost declarative part of a main program.
    It specifies the priority of the task (or tasks of the task type)
    or the main program.

SHARED   Takes a (simple) variable name as argument, where the
    variable is a scalar or access object, declared immediately before
    the pragma. It specifies that every read or update of the variable
    (even in different tasks) is immediately effective in all the tasks
    using the variable.

STORAGE_UNIT   Takes an integer number as argument. This pragma can
    only appear before a library unit. It establishes the number of
    bits per storage unit: the value of SYSTEM.STORAGE_UNIT.

SUPPRESS   Takes a check name (see section 6.6) and optionally also
    either an object name or a type name as arguments. It must appear
    in the declarative part of a unit (block or body).   It specifies
    that the designated check is to be suppressed in the unit. In the
    absence of the optional name, the pragma applies to all operations
    within the unit.   Otherwise its effect is restricted to operations
    on the named object or to operations on objects of the named type.

SYSTEM_NAME   Takes an argument which is an enumeration literal of
    type SYSTEM.NAME, defining the target machine for which compilation
    is to be carried out: the value of SYSTEM.SYSTEM_NAME. It may only
    occur at the start of a compilation.

E.2   Attributes in general

    The various kinds of entity in an Ada program have attributes which
    are described here. The entity may be anything named in the
    program, and the attribute gives a particular feature of it,
    written ENTITY'ATTRIBUTE. There are 49 attributes defined in
    standard Ada, governed by the kind of entity to which they are
    applied.   Implementations may add further attributes. Remember
    that an attribute qualifier is never used alone, but always as a
    suffix to a corresponding entity name. For attributes providing a
    data value, we show the type of that value as in an object

declaration, with some special (conceptual) types. These indicate
values which are implicitly converted to the appropriate type when
used in an expression.

E.3   Attribute of any type or subtype T

BASE   --   type

    Applied to a subtype, yields the base type; applied to a type,
    yields the type itself. This attribute may be used only to obtain
    further attributes of a type, e.g. T'BASE'FIRST.

SIZE : universal_integer;

    The minimum number of bits needed to represent any value in T.

E.4   Attributes of any scalar type or subtype T

FIRST : T;

    The minimum value in T.

LAST   : T;

    The maximum value in T.

E.5   Attributes of any discrete type or subtype T

IMAGE   --   function (X : T) return STRING;

If X is a value of type T, T'IMAGE(X) is a string representing the value in a standard display form. For an enumeration type, the values are represented, in minimum width, as either the corresponding enumeration literal, in upper case, or as the corresponding character literal, within quotes. For an integer type, the values are represented as decimal numbers of minimum width.

POS   -- function (X : T) return universal_integer;

If X is a value of type T, T'POS(X) is the integer position of X in the ordered sequence of values in the base type T'FIRST .. T'LAST; the position of T'FIRST being itself for integer types and zero for enumeration types.

PRED   -- function (X : T) return T;

If X is a value of type T, T'PRED(X) is the preceding value in the base type. The exception CONSTRAINT_ERROR is raised if X = T'FIRST.

SUCC   -- function (X : T) return T;

If X is a value of type T, T'SUCC(X) is the succeeding value in the base type. The exception CONSTRAINT_ERROR is raised if X = T'LAST.

VAL   -- function (J : any_integer_type) return T;

If J is an integer, T'VAL(J) is the value of enumeration type T whose POS is J. If no such value exists, the exception CONSTRAINT_ERROR is raised.

VALUE   -- function (S : STRING) return T;

If S is a string, T'VALUE(S) is the value in T that can be represented in display form by the string S. If the string does not denote any possible value, or if the value lies outside the range of T, the exception CONSTRAINT_ERROR is raised. All legal lexical forms are legal display forms.

WIDTH : universal_integer;

The number of characters in the longest image, considering all
values in T (which must be a subtype).

E.6   Attributes of any real subtype T

LARGE   : universal_real;

The largest model number of T.

MACHINE_OVERFLOWS : BOOLEAN;

True if, when a computed value is too large to be represented
correctly by the underlying machine representation of T, the
exception NUMERIC_ERROR is raised.

MACHINE_ROUNDS : BOOLEAN;

True if the machine performs every predefined operation on values
of type T either exactly or with rounding.

MANTISSA : universal_integer;

The number of bits in the mantissa of the representation of model
numbers of T.

SAFE_LARGE : universal_real;

The largest positive safe number in T'BASE.

SAFE_SMALL : universal_real;

The smallest positive non-zero safe number in T'BASE.

SMALL   : universal_real;

The smallest positive model number of T.

E.7   Attributes of any fixed point subtype T

AFT: universal_integer;

>   The number of decimal digits needed after the decimal point for the
>   precision of T.

DELTA   : universal_real;

>   The delta specified in the declaration of T.

FORE : universal_integer;

>   The minimum number of characters needed before the decimal point
>   for reresenting any value of T in decimal.

E.8   Attributes of any floating point type or subtype T

DIGITS   : universal_integer;

>   The number of digits specified in the declaration of T.

EMAX   : universal_integer;

>   The largest exponent value of the representation of model number of
>   T.   The smallest exponent value is $-$ EMAX.

EPSILON   : universal_real;

>   The difference between 1.0 and the smallest model number of T
>   greater than 1.0.   Both 1.0 and T'EPSILON are model numbers of T.

MACHINE_EMAX : universal_integer;

>   The largest exponent value of the underlying machine representation
>   of T.

MACHINE_EMIN : universal_integer;

> The smallest exponent value of the underlying machine representation of T.

MACHINE_MANTISSA : universal_integer;

> The number of bits in the mantissa of the underlying machine representation of T.

MACHINE_RADIX : universal_integer;

> The radix of the underlying machine representation of T.

SAFE_EMAX : universal_integer;

> The largest (binary) exponent value of the safe representation of any value in T, for which the implementation calculates results within model interval bounds. The smallest exponent is -SAFE_EMAX.

E.9   Attributes of any array or constrained array subtype A

FIRST : A'RANGE;

> The lower bound of the first index.

FIRST(J) : A'RANGE(J);

> The lower bound of the J'th index, where J must be a static integer expression.

LAST : A'RANGE;

> The upper bound of the first index.

LAST(J) : A'RANGE(J);

The upper bound of the J'th index, where J must be a static integer expression.

LENGTH   : universal_integer;

The number of elements in the first dimension of A.

LENGTH(J)   : universal_integer;

The number of elements in the J'th dimension, where J must be a static expression.

RANGE   -- subtype

The subtype A'FIRST .. A'LAST, whose base type is the first index type of A.

RANGE(J)   -- subtype

The subtype A'FIRST(J) .. A'LAST(J), whose base type is the J'th index type of A, and where J must be a static integer expression.

E.10   Attribute of any access type or subtype P

STORAGE_SIZE   : universal_integer;

The total number of storage units reserved for the collection of all objects of type P, within which individual objects are allocated.

E.11   Attribute of any private type or subtype P

CONSTRAINED : BOOLEAN;

    True if P is a private type (not a generic formal parameter), whose
    corresponding full type is an array with an index constraint or a
    record with a discriminant constraint; or if P is a generic formal
    private type for which the associated actual subtype has a
    constraint.

E.12   Attribute of any object P

SIZE : universal_integer;

    The number of bits required to hold the object.

E.13   Attributes of any component C of a record object

FIRST_BIT : universal_integer;

    The number of bits from the start of C'POSITION to the first bit
    used to hold the value of C.

LAST_BIT : universal_integer;

    The number of bits from the start of C'POSITION to the last bit
    used to hold the value of C. C'LAST_BIT need not lie within the
    same storage unit as C'FIRST_BIT.

POSITION : universal_integer;

    The number of storage units from the start of the record to the
    first unit of storage occupied by C.

E.14   Attribute of any record object R with discriminants

CONSTRAINED : BOOLEAN;

> True if and only if R is constant or subject to a discriminant constraint. (The discriminant values of R cannot then be modified).

E.15   Attributes of any task object T

CALLABLE : BOOLEAN;

> True unless T is completed or terminated (normally or abnormally).

STORAGE_SIZE : universal_integer;

> The number of storage units allocated for the execution of T. (Also applies to a task type.)

TERMINATED : BOOLEAN;

> True if T is terminated.

E.16   Attribute of any entry E

COUNT : universal_integer;

> The number of calling tasks currently waiting on E.

E.17   Attribute of any object, program unit, label or entry X

ADDRESS   : SYSTEM.ADDRESS;

The address of the first storage unit allocated for X.

APPENDIX F

Glossary

Access type, access value

An access type is a type in which the values denote dynamically created objects. These objects are created by execution of an allocator. An access value designates such an object.

Aggregate

An aggregate is a written form denoting a composite value. An array aggregate denotes a value of an array type; a record aggregate denotes a value of a record type. The components of an aggregate may be specified using either positional or named association.

Allocator

An allocator creates a new object associated with an access type, and returns an access value designating the created object.

Attribute

An attribute is a predefined characteristic of a named entity.

Body

A body is a program unit defining the implementation of a subprogram, package or task. A body stub stands for a body that is compiled

267

separately.

Compilation Unit

A compilation unit is a program unit presented for compilation as an independent text, possibly preceded by a context clause, naming other compilation units on which it depends. A compilation unit may be a library unit or a subunit.

Component

A component is a part of a composite object. An indexed component is a component in an array or an entry in an entry family, named by giving expressions denoting index values. A selected component is a component in a record, block or program unit, named by giving its identifier.

Composite type, composite value

A value of a composite type comprises several components, which together form the corresponding value. In an array type, all the components are of the same type and subtype; individual components are selected by their indices. In a record type, the components may be of different types; individual components are selected by their identifiers.

Constraint

A constraint is a restriction on the set of possible values in a type. A range constraint specifies lower and upper bounds of the values in a scalar type. An accuracy constraint specifies the relative or absolute error bound of values in a real type. An index constraint specifies lower and upper bounds for an array index. A discriminant constraint specifies particular values of the discriminants in a record type.

Context clause

A context clause, prefixed to a compilation unit, defines the other compilation units upon which it depends.

Declarative part

A declarative part is a sequence of declarations and related information

bodies and representation specifications) that apply over a region of a
rogram text: their <u>scope</u>.

erived <u>type</u>

derived type is a type whose operations and values are copies of those
f an existing type.

iscrete <u>type</u>

discrete type has an ordered set of distinct scalar values. The
iscrete types are the enumeration and integer types. Discrete types
ay be used for indexing and iteration, and for choices in case
tatements and record variants.

iscriminant

discriminant is a syntactically distinguished component of a record.
he presence of some other record components may depend on the value of
discriminant.

laboration

laboration is the process by which a declaration achieves its effect.
or example it can associate a name with a program entity or initialize
newly declared variable.

ntity

n entity is anything that can be named or denoted in a program.
bjects, types, exceptions, subprograms and program units are all
ntities.

ntry

n entry is used for communication between tasks. Externally an entry
s called in the same way as a subprogram; its internal behaviour is
pecified by one or more accept statements specifying the actions to be
erformed when the entry is called.

Enumeration type

An enumeration type is a discrete type whose values are given explicitl
in the type definition. These values may be either identifiers o
character literals.

Exception

An exception is a situation that prevents further normal progra
execution. Recognising that an exception has occurred is called raisin
the exception. An exception handler is a piece of program tex
specifying a response to the exception. An exception that has bee
raised is propagated through a program to discover the relevant handler

Expression

An expression is a part of a program to compute a value.

Generic program unit

A generic program unit is a template for a subprogram or package. I
may have parameters determined at compile time. A generic claus
contains the declaration of generic parameters. Instances of th
template can be obtained by generic instantiation. Such instantiate
program units define subprograms and packages that can be used directl
in a program. (There are no generic tasks; instead there are tas
types.)

Lexical unit

A lexical unit is one of the basic syntactic elements making up
program. It may be an identifier, a number, a character literal,
string, a delimiter, or a comment.

Library unit

A library unit is a compilation unit that is at the outermost level i
the whole program. A library unit may be the declaration or body of
subprogram or package.

Literal

A literal denotes an explicit value of a scalar type, for example a number, an enumeration value or a character.

Model number

A model number is an exactly representable value of a real numeric type. Operations of a real type are defined in terms of operations on the model numbers of the type. The properties of the model numbers and of the operations are the minimal properties preserved by all implementations of the real type.

Object

An object is a variable or a constant of a specified (sub)type. An object has a value of the appropriate (sub)type; if the object is a variable, its value may be changed during execution of the program.

Overloading

Overloading refers to the fact that literals, identifiers and operators may have several alternative meanings within the same scope. For example an overloaded enumeration literal is a literal appearing in two or more enumeration types; an overloaded subprogram is a subprogram whose designator can denote one of several subprograms, depending upon the kind of its parameters and returned value.

Package

A package is a program unit that defines a set of facilities for use by the rest of the program. It characteristically contains a number of related entities such as constants, variables, types and subprograms. The specification of a package contains all the information needed outside the package; the body of a package contains the implementations of the entities specified.

Parameter

A parameter is one of the named entities on which a subprogram, entry, or generic program unit may depend. A formal parameter is an identifier used to denote the named entity in the unit body. An actual parameter is an entity given in a subprogram call, entry call, or generic instantiation. A parameter mode specifies whether the parameter is used for input, output or input-output of data. A positional parameter is an actual parameter which matches the formal parameter in the same position. A named parameter is an actual parameter which matches the formal parameter whose name is given.

Pragma

A pragma is an instruction to the compiler, which has no effect on the meaning of the program.

Private type

A private type is a type whose structure and set of values are not disclosed to the user of the type. A private type is known only by its name (possibly with discriminants) and by the set of operations defined for it. A private type and its applicable operations are defined in the visible part of a package. Assignment and comparison for equality or inequality are also defined for private types, unless the private type is marked as **limited**.

Program Unit

A program unit is a major structural unit; it may be a subprogram, package or task. Program units may be nested.

Range

A range is a contiguous set of values of a scalar type. A range is specified by giving the lower and upper bounds for the values.

Rendezvous

A rendezvous is the interaction that occurs between two parallel tasks when one task has called an entry of the other task, and a corresponding accept statement is being executed by the accepting task on behalf of the calling task.

Representation clause

Representation clauses specify the mapping between program entities and features of the underlying machine that executes a program.

Scalar type

A scalar type is a type whose values have no components.   Scalar types comprise discrete types (that is, enumeration and integer types) and real types.

Scope

The scope of a declaration is the region of text over which the declaration has an effect.

Static expression

A static expression is an expression whose value can be explicitly calculated at compile-time.   It must depend only on literal numbers or combinations of them using predefined operators or names of such literal expressions.

Subprogram

A subprogram is a program unit whose execution is invoked explicitly. It may have parameters for communication between the subprogram and its caller. A subprogram declaration specifies the name of the subprogram and its parameters; a subprogram body specifies its execution. A subprogram may be a procedure, which performs an action, or a function which returns a result.   Subprograms may be concurrently executed in several tasks.

Subtype

A subtype characterizes a set of values by constraining the set of possible values of a base type. The operations over a subtype are the same as those of the type on which the subtype is based.

Subunit

A subunit is a compilation unit that conceptually belongs inside another compilation unit, at a position indicated by a body stub. A subunit may be a subprogram specification or the body of a package or task.

Task

A task is a program unit that may be executed in parallel with other tasks. A task specification establishes the name of the task and the names and parameters of its entries; a task body defines its execution. A task type is a specification that permits the subsequent declaration of any number of similar tasks.

Type

A type characterizes a set of values and a set of operations applicable to those values. A type definition is a language construct introducing a type. A type declaration associates a name with a type introduced by a type definition.

Universal

A numeric type with unlimited range and precision. Universal integer is an integer type with effectively an infinite range; universal real is a real type with effectively an infinite number of digits and an infinite range. A universal expression has a result that is one of these types, and (if static) is calculated accurately at compile-time.

Use clause

A use clause makes the declarations in the visible part of a package directly visible.

Variant

A record has variants if its components are at all optional. Components that are present or absent together constitute a variant. The collection of the several variants is called the variant part of the record. The selection of a variant is by the value of a discriminant.

Visibility

An identifier may be used at one point in a program text, with a meaning defined by a declaration given elsewhere. The declaration is said to be visible from the points where the declared entity is accessible. A declaration is directly visible from the points where the declared identifier may be used.

APPENDIX G

Ada syntax

The textual structure of an Ada program is shown in the following diagrams. Each part of a program text is called a phrase, and is illustrated by a diagram showing the phrases and atomic elements of which it is composed. The lines in the diagrams show the order in which the constituents of a phrase have to be written.

abort_statement

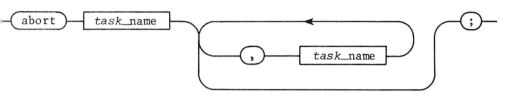

accept_alternative

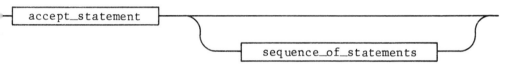

access_type_definition

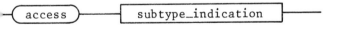

accept_statement

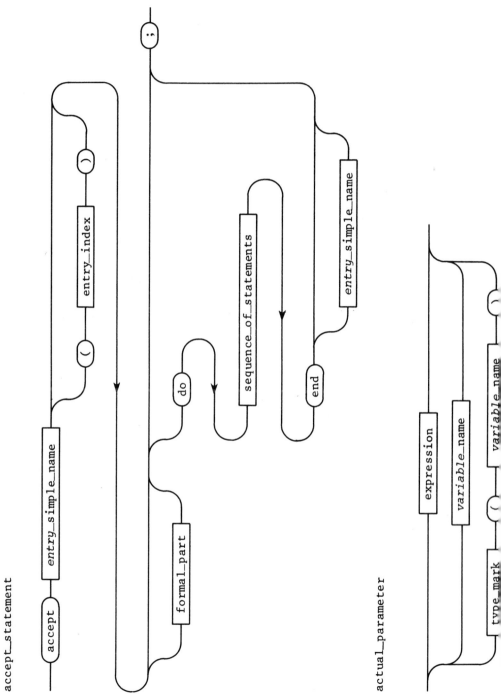

actual_parameter

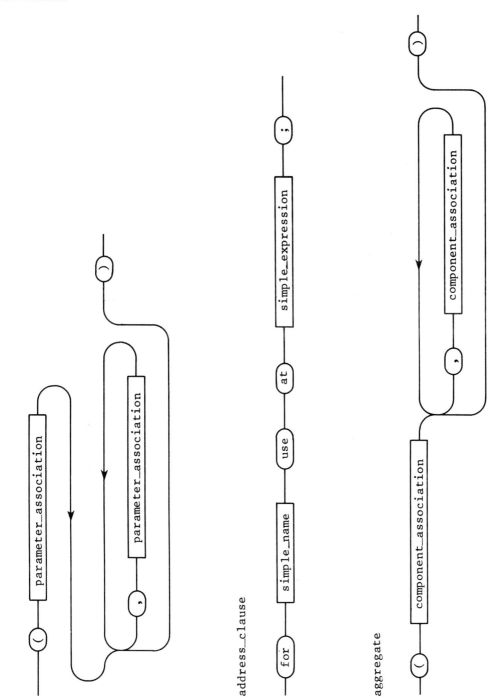

actual_parameter_part

address_clause

aggregate

alignment_clause

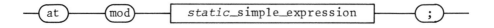

allocator

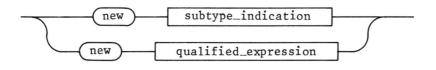

argument_association

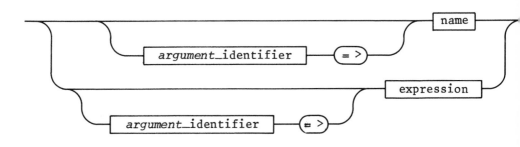

array_type_definition

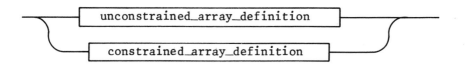

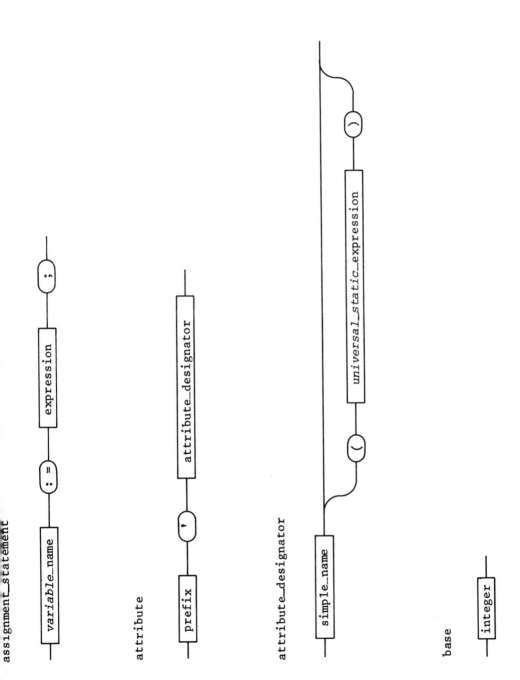

assignment_statement

attribute

attribute_designator

base

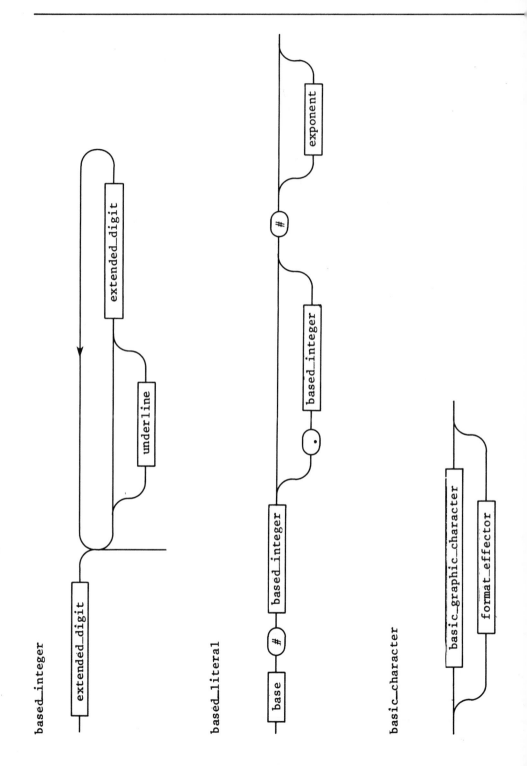

asic_declaration

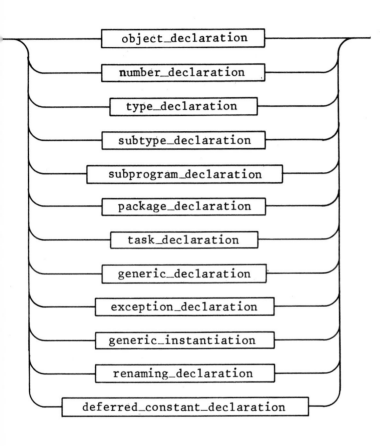

asic_declarative_item

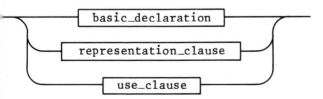

basic_graphic_character

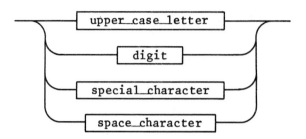

binary_adding_operator

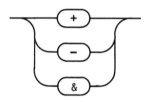

body

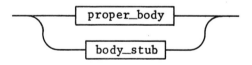

lock_statement

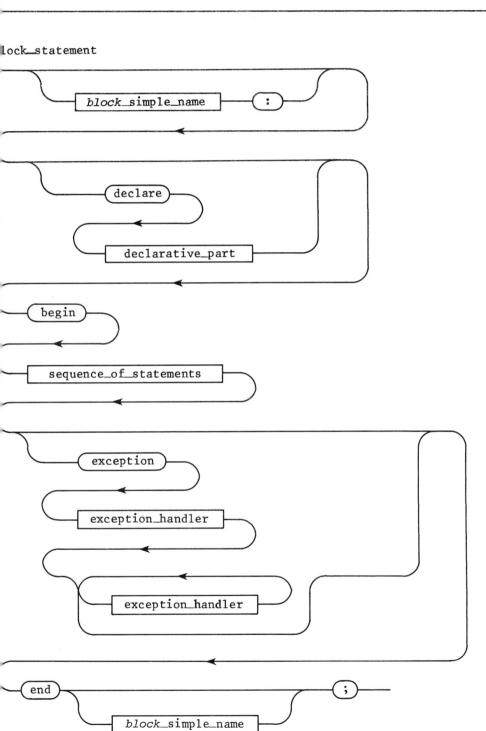

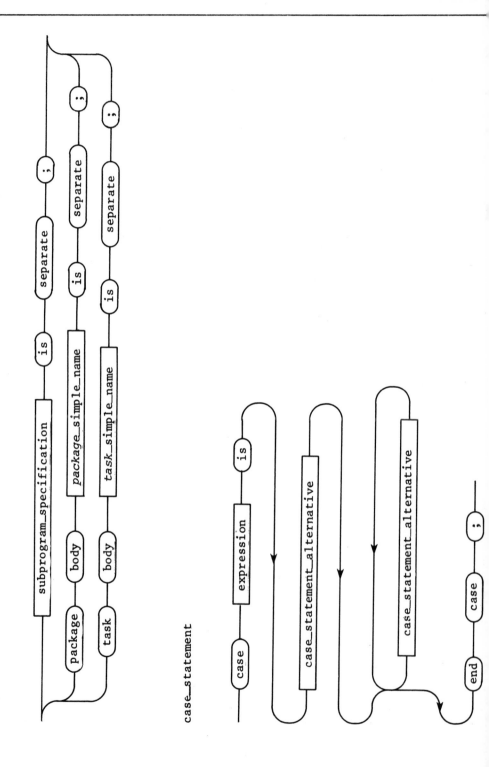

body_stub

case_statement

case_statement_alternative

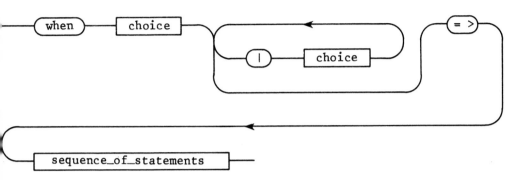

character_literal

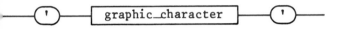

choice

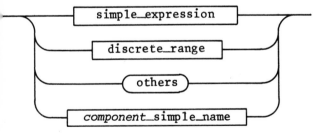

code_statement

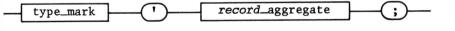

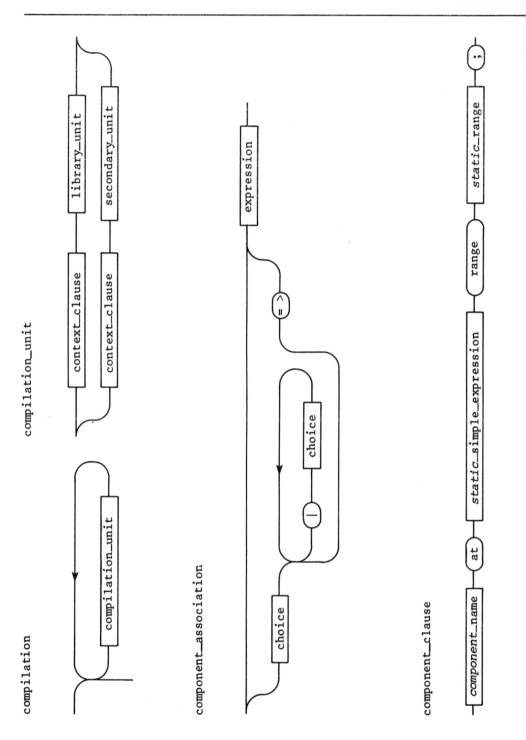

compilation_unit

compilation

component_association

component_clause

component_declaration

component_list

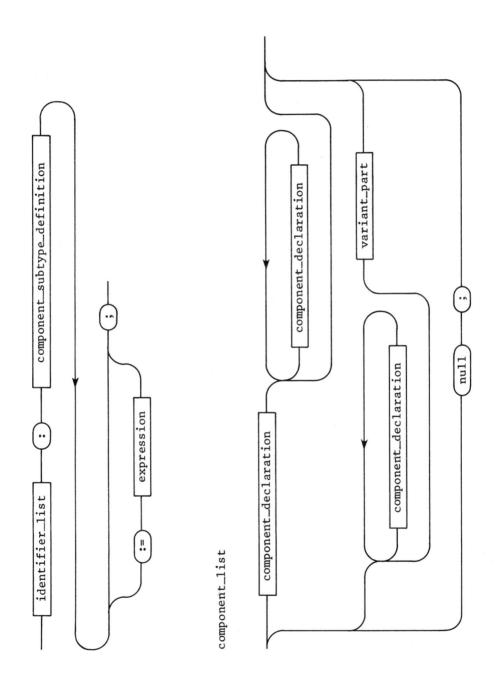

component_subtype_definition

compound_statement

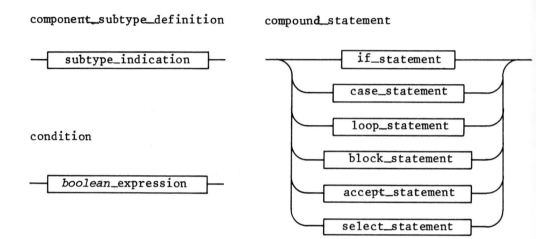

condition

*boolean*_expression

conditional_entry_call

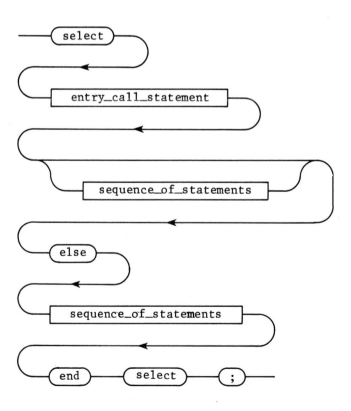

constrained_array_definition

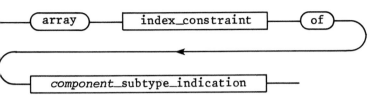

constraint

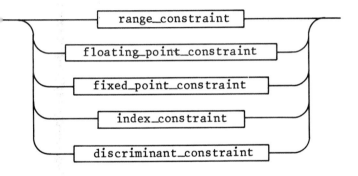

context_clause

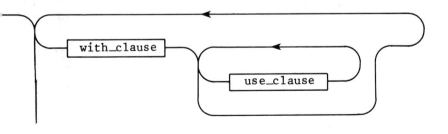

decimal_literal

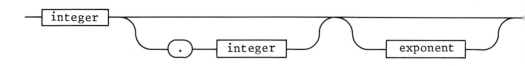

declarative_part

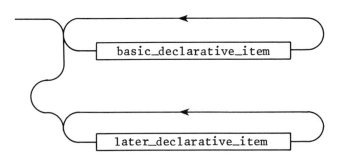

deferred_constant_declaration

delay_alternative

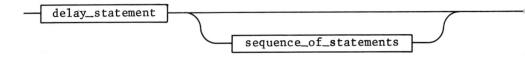

delay_statement

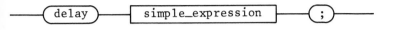

derived_type_definition

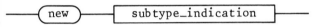

designator

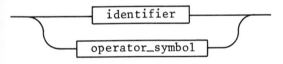

discrete_range

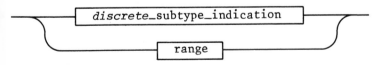

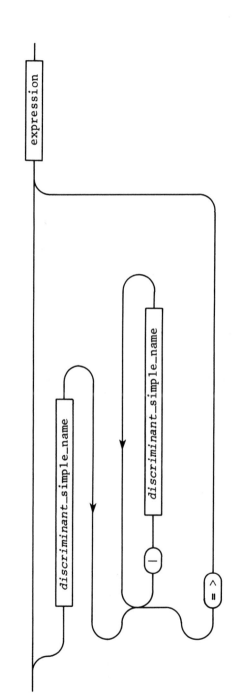

discriminant_association

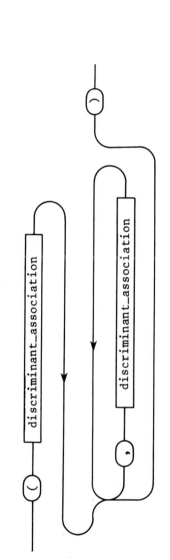

discriminant_constraint

discriminant_part

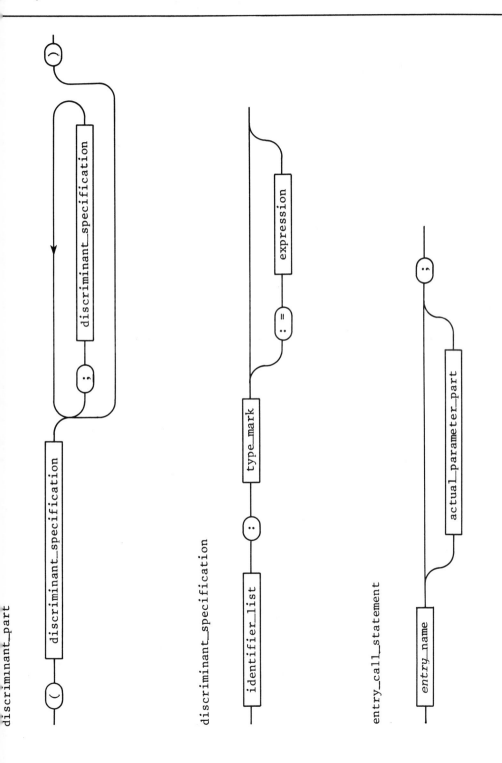

discriminant_specification

entry_call_statement

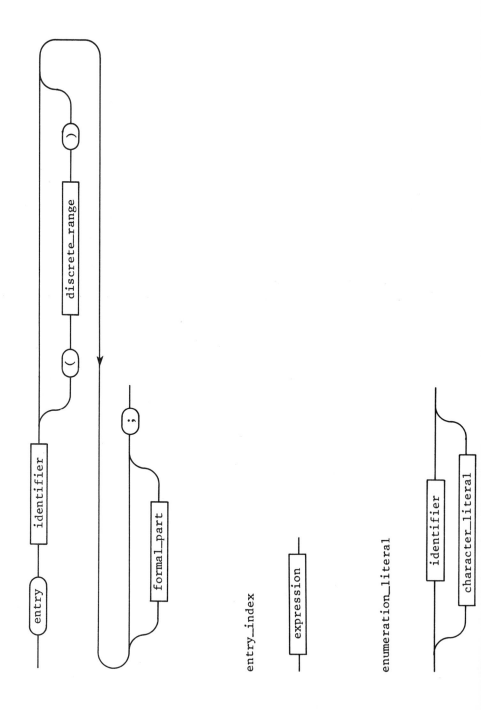

entry_declaration

entry_index

enumeration_literal

enumeration_literal_specification

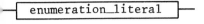

enumeration_representation_clause

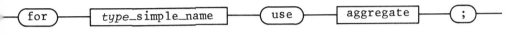

enumeration_type_definition

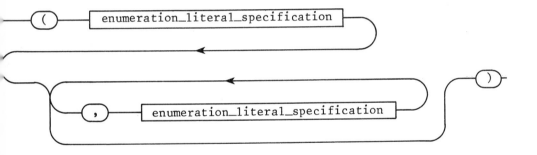

exception_choice

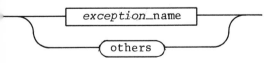

exception_declaration

exception_handler

exit_statement

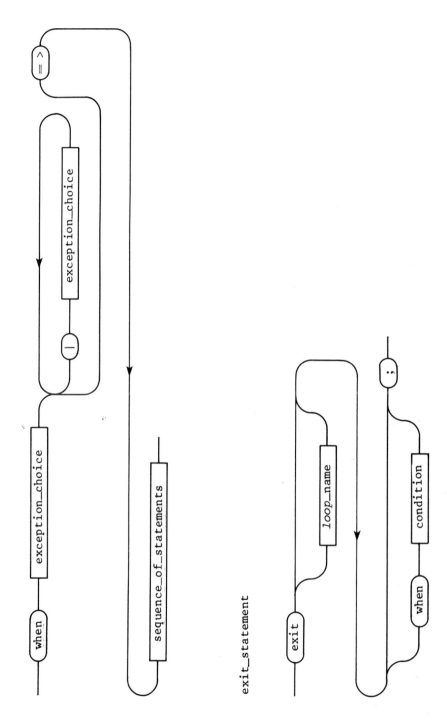

exponent

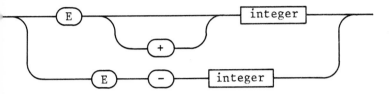

expression

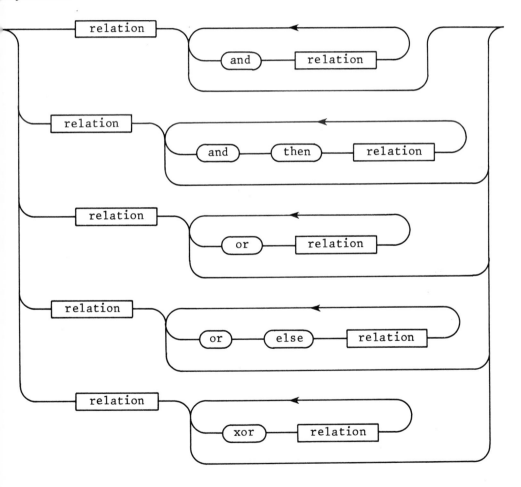

extended_digit

factor

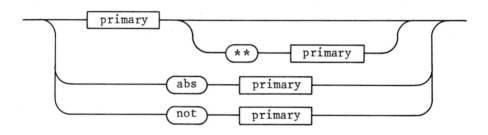

fixed_accuracy_definition

fixed_point_constraint

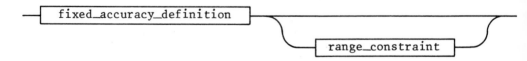

floating_accuracy_definition

floating_point_constraint

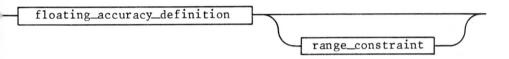

formal_parameter

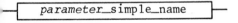

formal_part

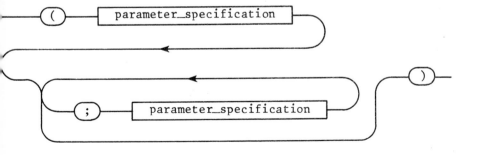

full_type_declaration

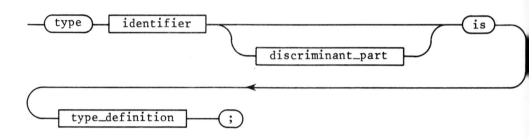

function_call

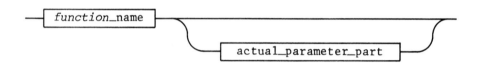

generic_actual_parameter

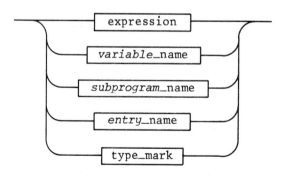

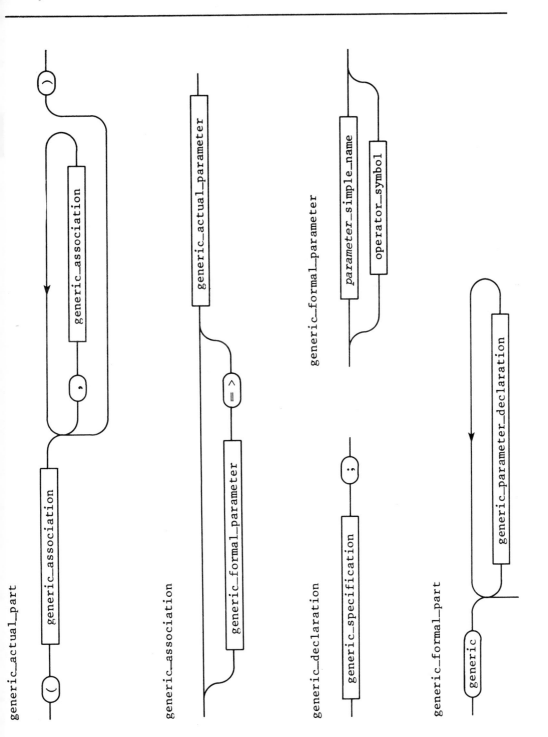

generic_actual_part

generic_association

generic_declaration

generic_formal_parameter

generic_formal_part

generic_instantiation

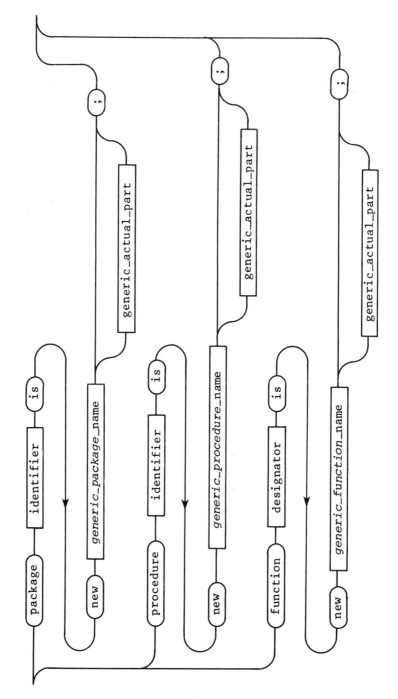

generic_parameter_declaration

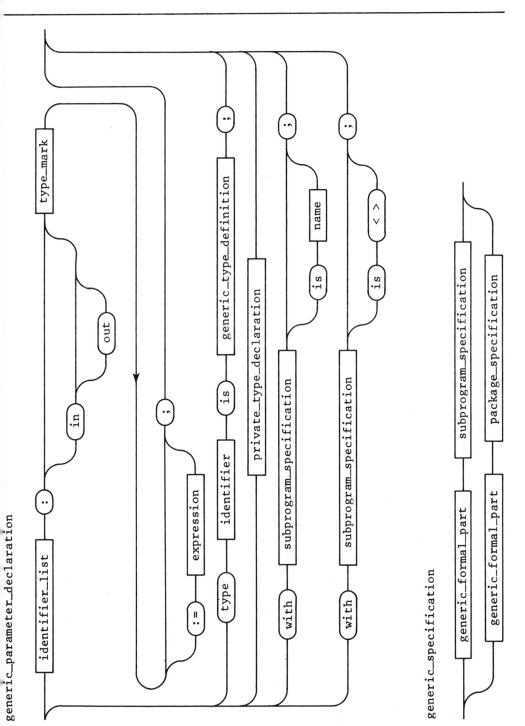

generic_specification

generic_type_definition

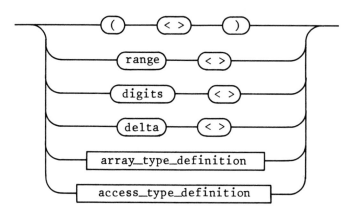

goto_statement

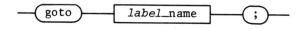

graphic_character

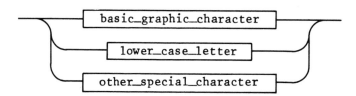

highest_precedence_operator

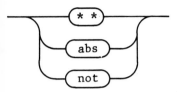

identifier

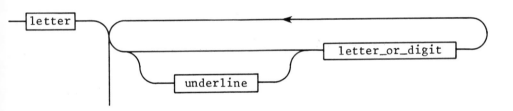

identifier_list

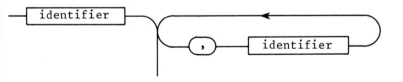

if_statement

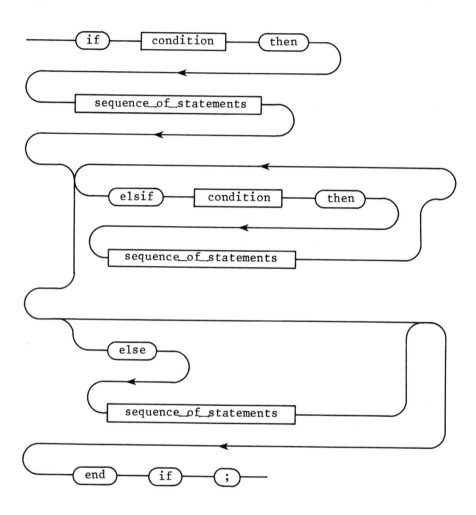

incomplete_type_declaration

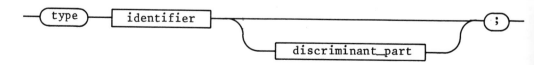

index_constraint

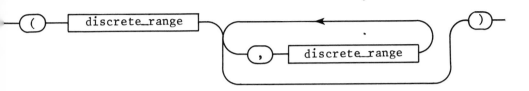

index_subtype_definition

indexed_component

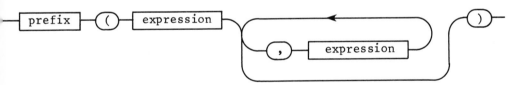

integer

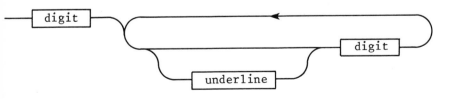

integer_type_definition

iteration_scheme

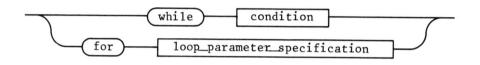

label

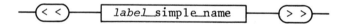

later_declarative_item

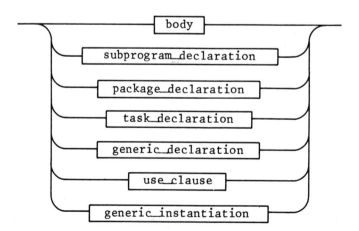

length_clause

letter

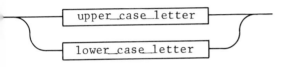

letter_or_digit

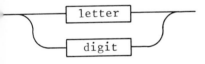

library_unit

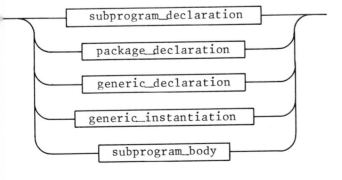

library_unit_body

logical_operator

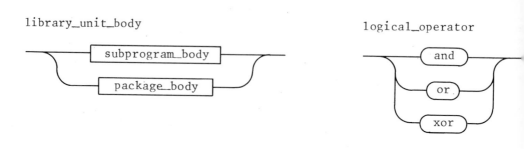

loop_parameter_specification

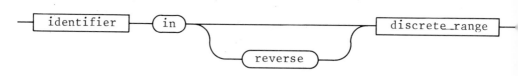

loop_statement

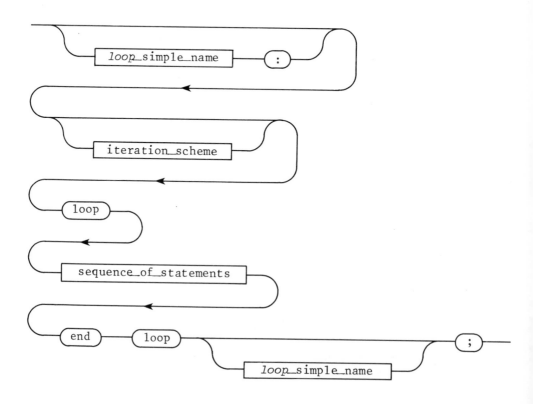

mode

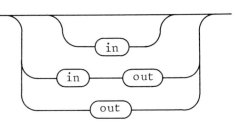

multiplying_operator

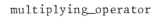

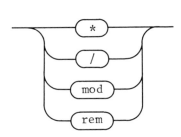

name

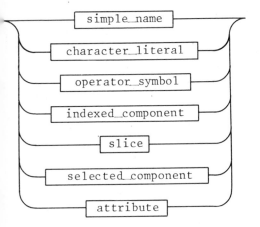

null_statement

number_declaration

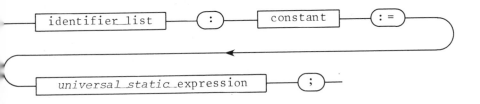

operator_symbol

numeric_literal

object_declaration

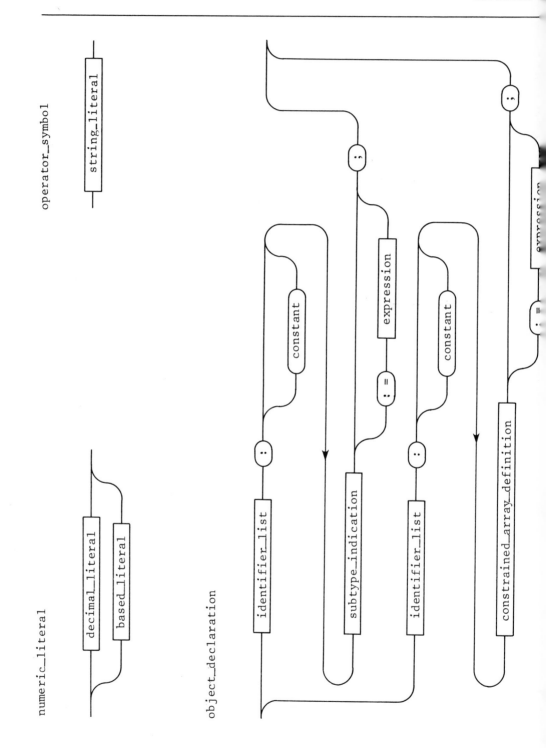

package_body

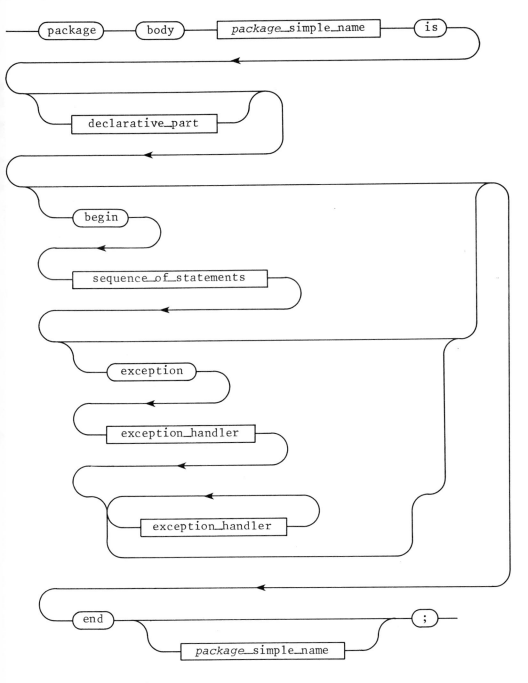

package_declaration

package_specification

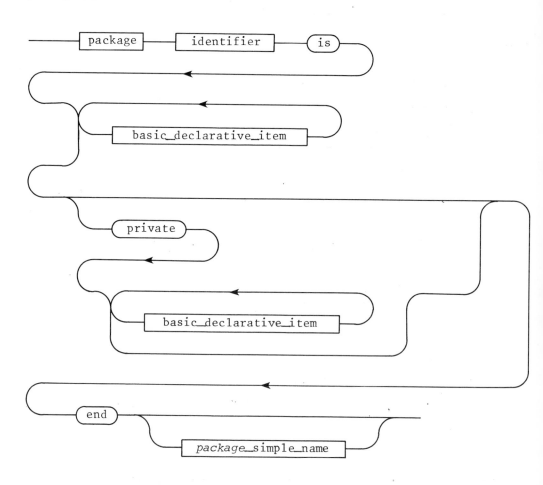

parameter_association

parameter_specification

pragma

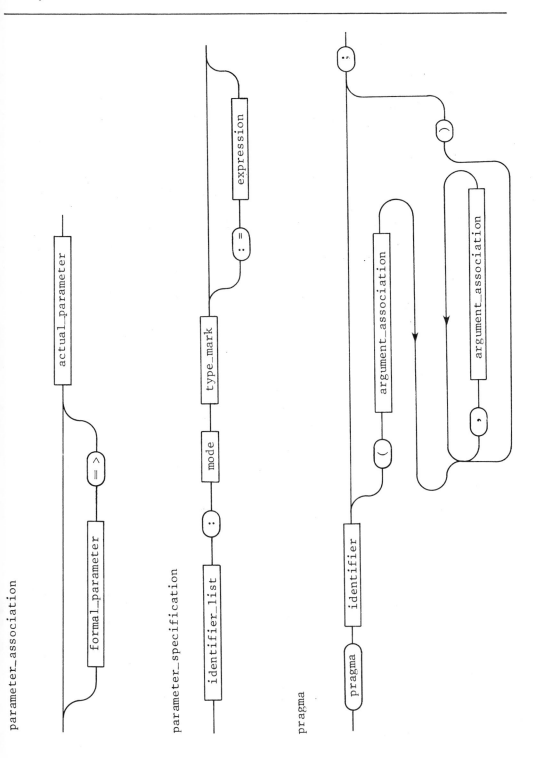

prefix

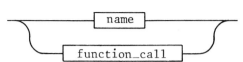

primary

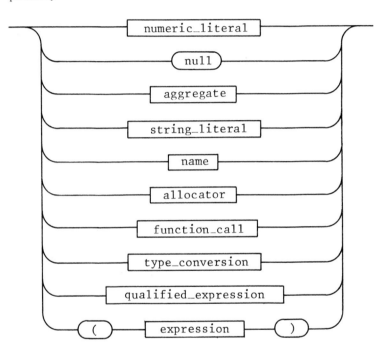

private_type_declaration

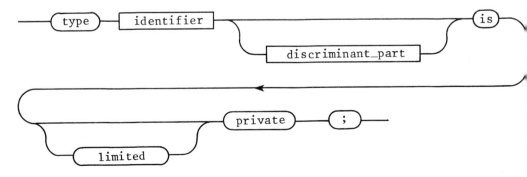

procedure_call_statement

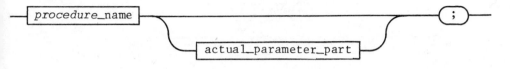

proper_body

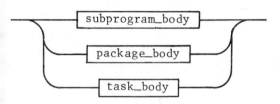

qualified_expression

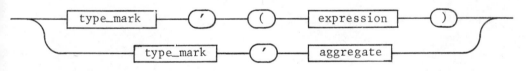

raise_statement

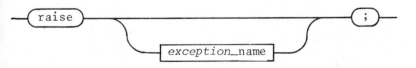

range

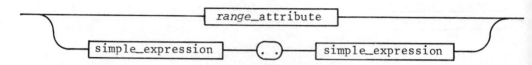

range_constraint

real_type_definition

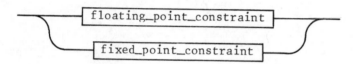

record_representation_clause

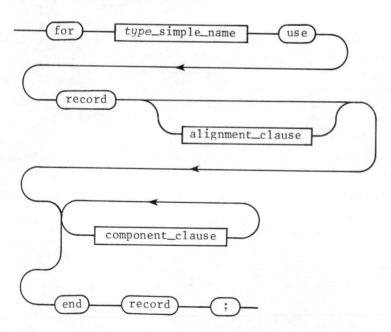

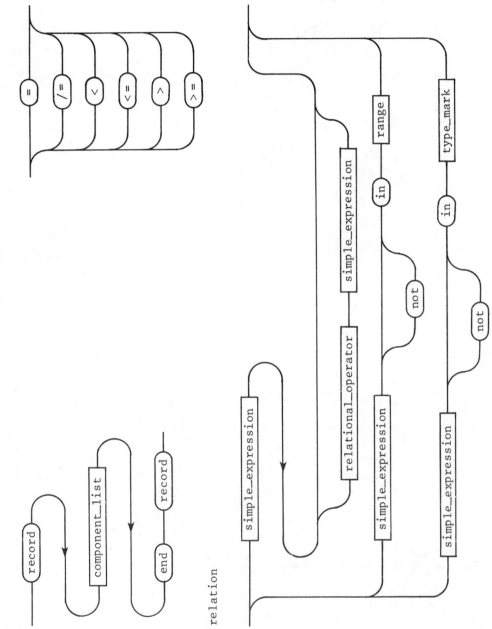

relational_operator

record_type_definition

relation

renaming_declaration

representation_clause

return_statement

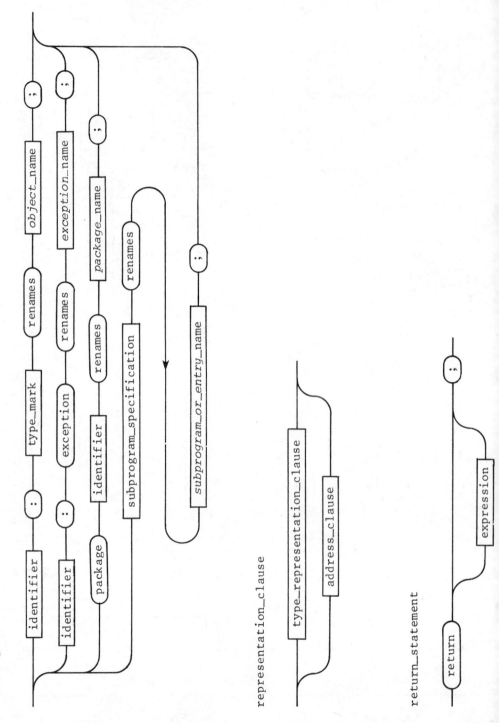

secondary_unit

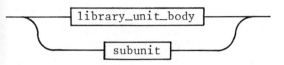

select_alternative

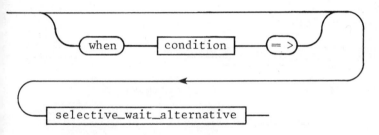

select_statement

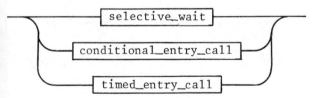

selected_component

selective_wait

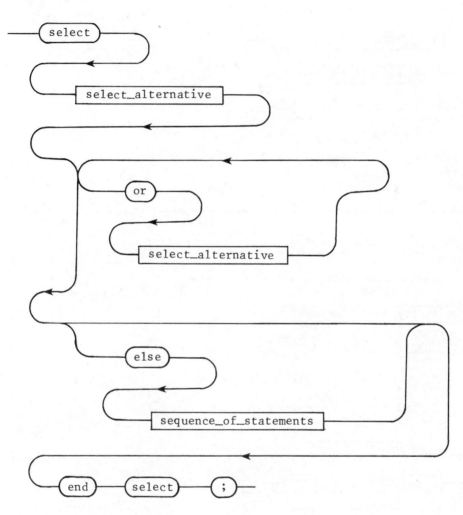

selective_wait_alternative

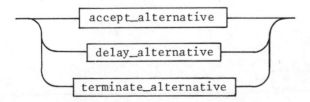

selector

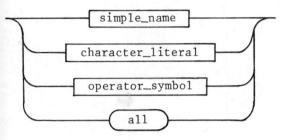

sequence_of_statements

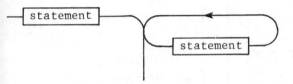

simple_expression

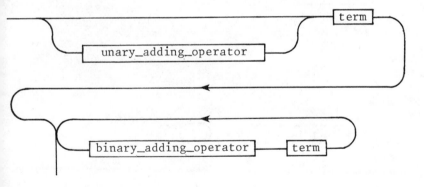

simple_name

—| identifier |—

simple_statement

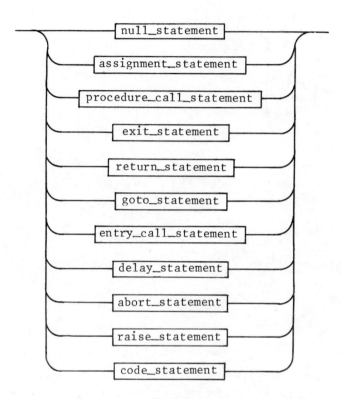

slice

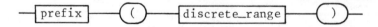

statement

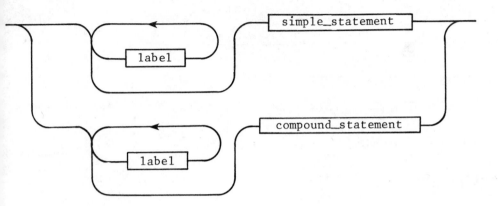

string_literal

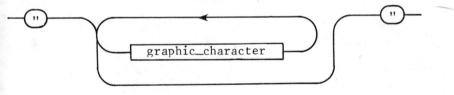

subprogram_body

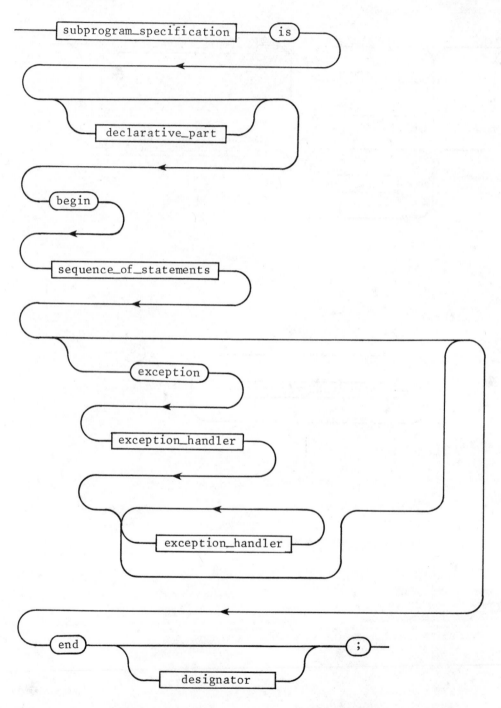

subprogram_declaration

subprogram_specification

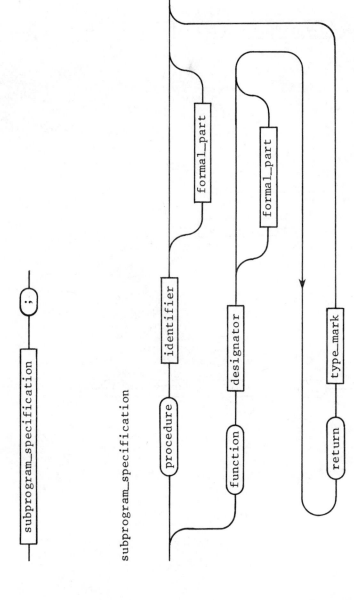

subtype_declaration

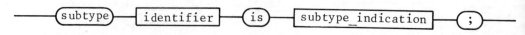

subtype_indication

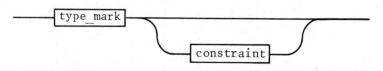

subunit

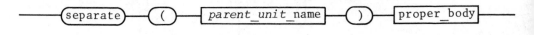

task_body

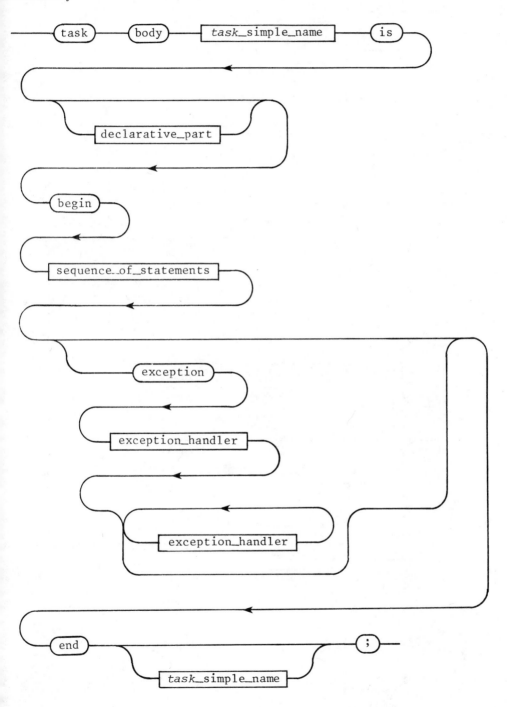

task_declaration

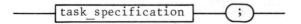

task_specification

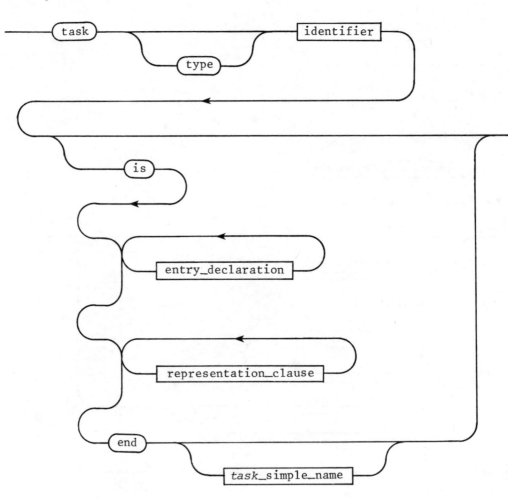

term

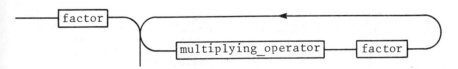

terminate_alternative

timed_entry_call

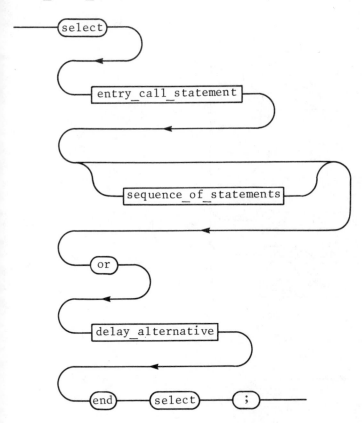

type_conversion

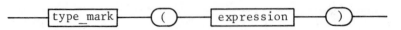

type_declaration

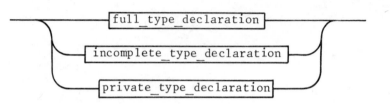

type_definition

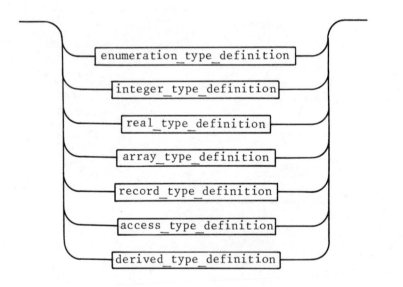

type_mark

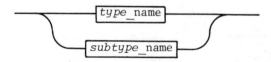

type_representation_clause

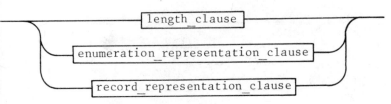

unary_adding_operator

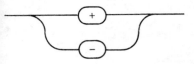

unconstrained_array_definition

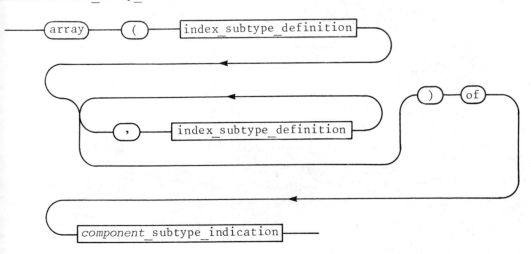

use_clause

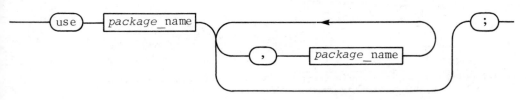

variant

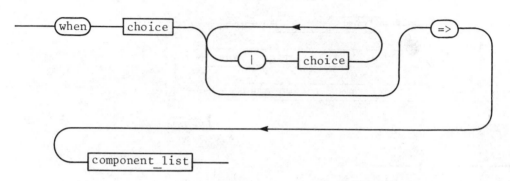

variant_part

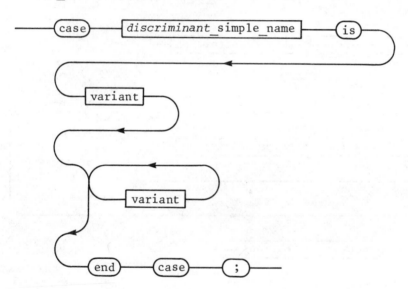

with_clause

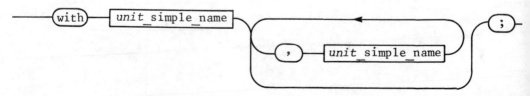

```
IN THE BYRON VAULT BELOW
   LIE THE REMAINS OF
      AUGUSTA ADA,
    ONLY DAUGHTER OF
   GEORGE GORDON NOEL,
     6TH LORD BYRON,
       AND WIFE OF
  WILLIAM EARL OF LOVELACE.

   BORN 10TH DEC  1815,
   DIED 27TH NOV  1852.

        R.I.P.
```

Inscription on a memorial tablet
in the parish church of Hucknall, England.
Courtesy of the rector, Canon D. Williams.